214

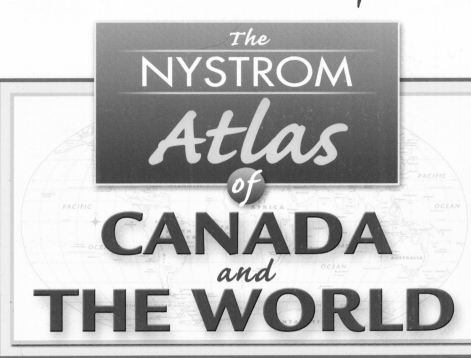

The NYSTROM Atlas of CANADA and THE WORLD

YEAR	L. C. S.	GR.
2014	Maxinne Masangcay	
2015	Linda Terceira	
2015	Shania Butt	
2017	Yemico Sarmiento	

YEAR	L. C. S.	GR.

YEAR	L. C. S.	GR.

D1530318

NYSTROM
HERFF JONES EDUCATION DIVISION

CONTENTS

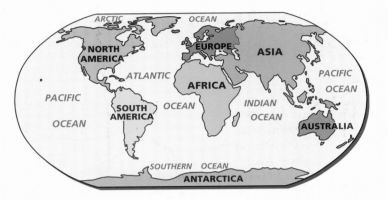

Copyright © 2009, 2003, 1995 by NYSTROM Herff Jones Education Division
4719 W. 62nd Street, Indianapolis, Indiana 46268

All rights reserved. No part of this book may be reproduced or transmitted in any form or by any means, electronic or mechanical, including photocopying, recording, or by any information storage and retrieval system, without permission in writing from the publisher.

Printed in U.S.A.

10 9 8 7 6 5 4 3 2 1   14 13 12 11 10 09 08

ISBN 13: 978-0-7825-1262-5   ISBN 10: 0-7825-1262-3

For information about ordering this atlas, 9ACW, call 800-621-8086.

Statistics and estimates are from government and United Nations sources: populations for the most recent available date, other data averaged over the three most recent available years.

Photo Credits

front cover left: © Keren Su/Corbis, right: © Sucheta Das/Reuters/Corbis; **back cover** top: © Pat O'Hara/Corbis, bottom: © Lester Lefkowitz/Corbis; **12** left: © Dietrich Rose/zefa/Corbis, right: © Craig Lovell/Corbis; **13** left: © Panorama Stock/First Light, right: © Herbert Spichtinger/zefa/Corbis; **14** © Crack Palinggi/Reuters/Corbis; **15** © Photo Researchers/First Light; **16** © Cousteau Society/Getty Images; **18** © Walter Geiersperger/Corbis; **19** © Adam Woolfitt/Corbis; **22** © Lester Lefkowitz/Corbis; **23** © Tom Stoddart/Getty Images; **24** left: © Royalty-Free/Corbis, right: © Andre Gallant/Getty Images; **25** left: © Keren Su/Corbis, top right: © Corbis, bottom right: Owen Franken/Corbis; **26** top: © David Hiser/Getty Images, bottom left: © WorldSat International, bottom right: © WorldSat International; **27** left: © NASA, right: © NASA; **29** © epa/Corbis; **30** © China Newsphoto/Reuters/Corbis;

How to Use This Atlas

To get the most out of *The Nystrom Atlas of Canada and the World*, follow these steps.

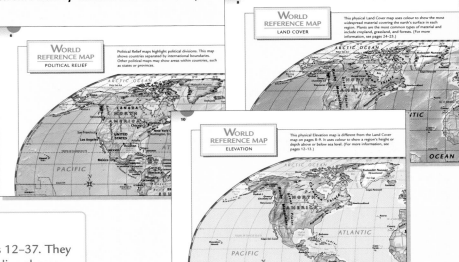

A

Get acquainted with the three styles of **REFERENCE MAPS** in this atlas. See the **Political Relief**, **Land Cover**, and **Elevation** maps of the world on pages 6–11. Their **detailed legends** are on page 5.

B

Check out **World Matters** on pages 12–37. They provide a foundation for understanding themes that are repeated throughout the atlas.

1. Look at the **title**, which tells you what the two-page spread is about.

2. Then read the **introduction** for an overview of the theme of the spread.

3. Look at the maps. Their **legends** explain what the map's colours and symbols mean. Always read the legend before examining a map.

4. Also look at the **graphs**, **photos**, and **diagrams**. Read their **captions** too—they help you understand the significance of each image.

5. Watch for **Geodes**, nuggets of geographic facts. Some define important terms; others provide helpful examples.

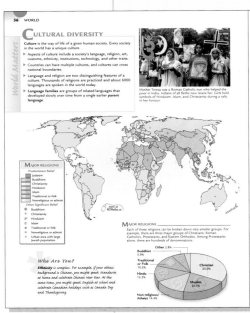

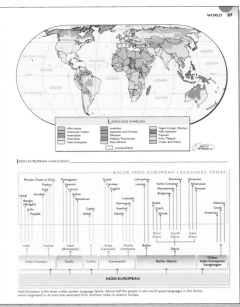

C

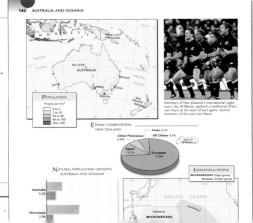

Then turn to the **continent sections**. First you'll find reference maps, followed by thematic maps, and then maps for regions on the continent.

Thematic maps focus on single topics or themes. Five recurring thematic maps appear throughout the atlas: Precipitation, Climate, Land Use, Energy Resources and Metals, and Population.

Graphs summarize facts in a visual way. Four recurring graphs appear throughout the atlas: Climographs, Balance of Trade, Natural Population Growth, and Ethnic Composition.

Continent sections . . .

Photos show people and places in a geographic context. They bring map categories and abstract ideas to life.

Regional maps offer close-up views of most populous areas of the world.

Diagrams illustrate concepts that are difficult to show in a map, photo, or graph.

Cross sections show slices of the earth. Their exaggerated height and depth make landscapes and features easy to see.

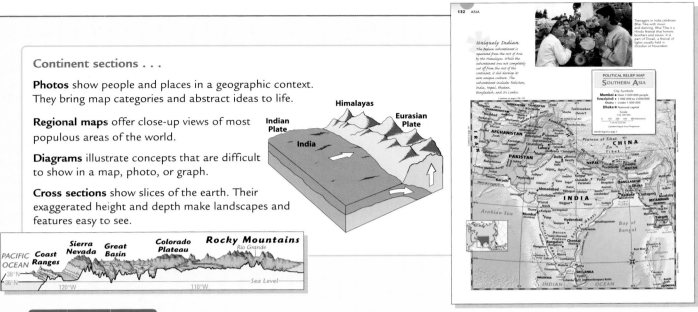

Detailed Legends

POLITICAL RELIEF MAPS
(For more information about Political Relief maps, see pages 6–7.)

Boundary Symbols
- Continental boundary
- International boundary
- Disputed or undefined boundary
- ▫ Small country
- Province, territory, or state boundary

Lettering Styles
- EUROPE — Continent
- *INDIAN OCEAN* — Ocean
- *Himalayas* — Land feature
- *Lake Victoria* — Water feature
- **CANADA** — Country
- **ALBERTA** — Province, territory, or state
- (U.S.) — National affiliation

City Symbols
- **Shanghai** ●
- **Vancouver** ●
- Cairns •

A city's population is shown by numbers in the legend and by the relative size of its symbol and lettering.

- **Dakar** ⊛ National capital
- **Halifax** ★ Province, territory, or state capital

Other Symbols
- Land beyond the subject area
- Polar sea ice
- Water and sea floor
- Lake and river
- Dry or seasonal lake and river
- Waterfall
- Canal
- Dam
- △ Mountain peak
- Trans-Canada Highway
- (80) U.S. Interstate highway
- (101) Other highway

LAND COVER MAPS
(For more information about Land Cover maps see pages 8–9 and 24–25.)

Boundary Symbols
- Continental boundary
- International boundary
- Disputed or undefined boundary
- ▫ Small country
- Province, territory, or state boundary

Lettering Styles
- EUROPE — Continent
- *INDIAN OCEAN* — Ocean
- *Himalayas* — Land feature
- *Lake Victoria* — Water feature
- CANADA — Country
- ALBERTA — Province, territory, or state
- (U.S.) — National affiliation

City Symbols
- **Shanghai** ●
- **Vancouver** ●
- Cairns •

A city's population is shown by the relative size of its symbol and lettering.

- **Dakar** ⊛ National capital
- **Halifax** ★ Province, territory, or state capital

Other Symbols
- Land beyond the subject area
- Polar sea ice
- Water and sea floor
- Lake and river
- Dry or seasonal lake and river
- Waterfall
- Canal
- Dam
- ▲ Mountain peak
- Wetland
- Sand dunes

ELEVATION MAPS
(For more information about Elevation maps, see pages 10–11 and 12–13.)

Boundary Symbols
- Continental boundary
- International boundary
- Disputed or undefined boundary
- ▫ Small country
- Province, territory, or state boundary

Lettering Styles
- EUROPE — Continent
- *INDIAN OCEAN* — Ocean
- *Himalayas* — Land feature
- *Lake Victoria* — Water feature
- CANADA — Country
- ALBERTA — Province, territory, or state
- (U.S.) — National affiliation

City Symbols
- **Shanghai** ●
- **Vancouver** ●
- Cairns •

A city's population is shown by the relative size of its symbol and lettering.

- **Dakar** ⊛ National capital
- **Halifax** ★ Province, territory, or state capital

Other Symbols
- Land beyond the subject area
- Ice covered land
- Water
- Lake and river
- Dry or seasonal lake
- Waterfall
- Canal
- Dam
- ▲ Mountain peak

WORLD REFERENCE MAP
POLITICAL RELIEF

Political Relief maps highlight political divisions. This map shows countries separated by international boundaries. Other political maps may show areas within countries, such as provinces or states.

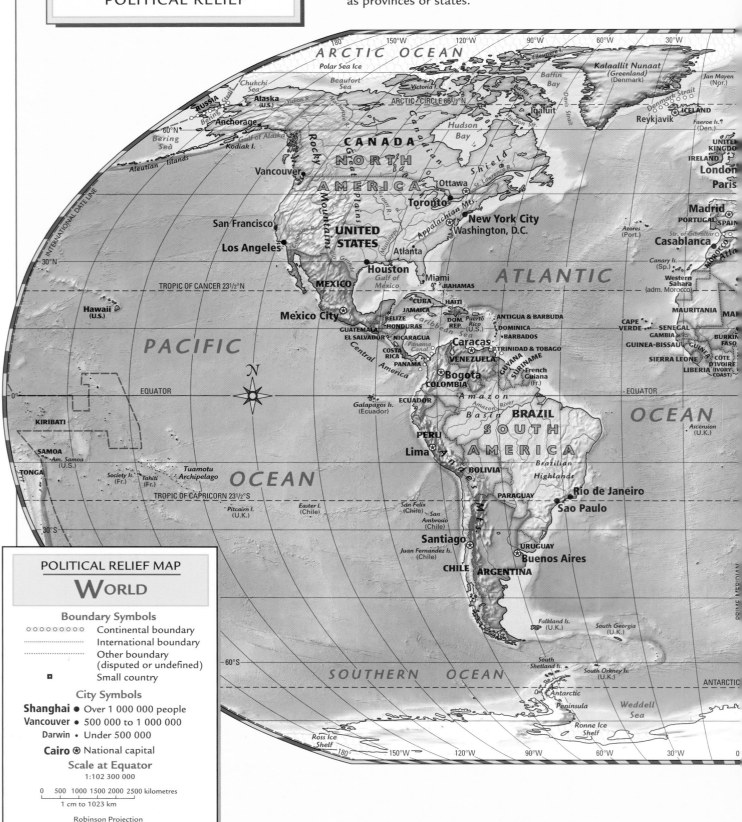

POLITICAL RELIEF MAP
WORLD

Boundary Symbols

○○○○○○○○○ Continental boundary

.... International boundary

.... Other boundary (disputed or undefined)

▣ Small country

City Symbols

Shanghai ● Over 1 000 000 people

Vancouver ● 500 000 to 1 000 000

Darwin • Under 500 000

Cairo ⊕ National capital

Scale at Equator

1:102 300 000

0   500 1000 1500 2000 2500 kilometres

1 cm to 1023 km

Robinson Projection

Detailed legend on page 5

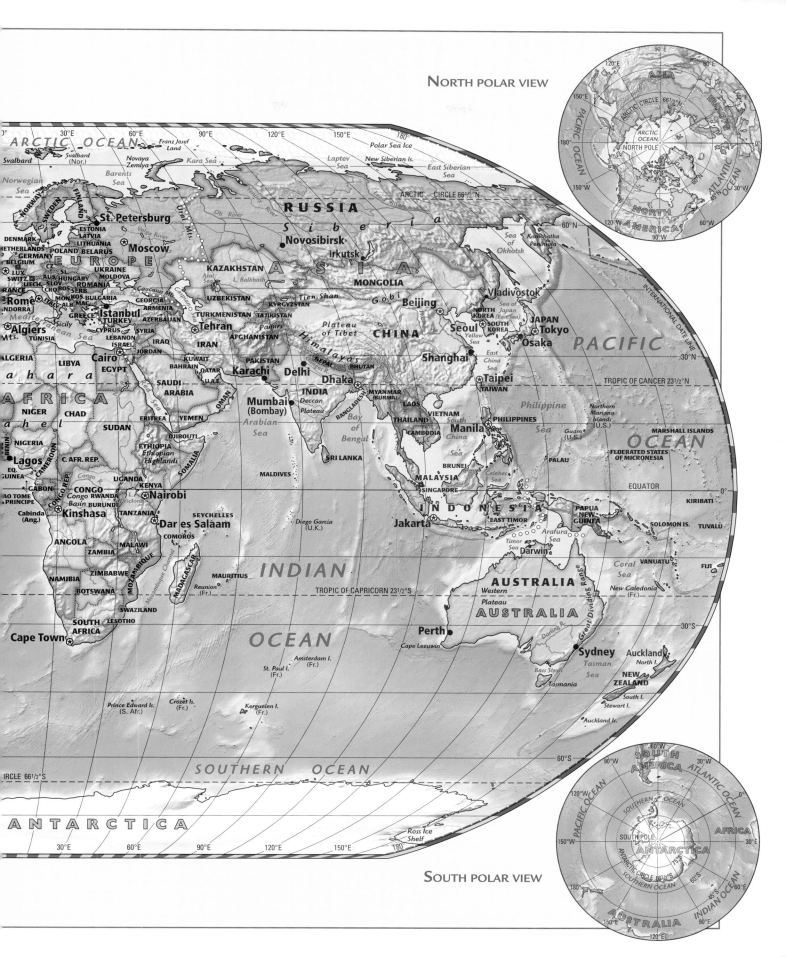

NORTH POLAR VIEW

ASIA
EUROPE
90°E
120°E
60°E
150°E
30°E
ARCTIC CIRCLE 66½°N
PACIFIC OCEAN
ARCTIC OCEAN
180°
ATLANTIC OCEAN
NORTH POLE
150°W
30°W
120°W
60°W
90°W
NORTH AMERICA

ARCTIC OCEAN
30°E
60°E
90°E
120°E
150°E
180°
Polar Sea Ice
Svalbard
Svalbard (Nor.)
Franz Josef Land
Novaya Zemlya
Kara Sea
Laptev Sea
New Siberian Is.
East Siberian Sea
Norwegian Sea
Barents Sea
NORWAY
SWEDEN
FINLAND
Ob River
Yenisey River
ARCTIC CIRCLE 66½°N
St. Petersburg
ESTONIA
LATVIA
LITHUANIA
Ural Mts.
RUSSIA
Siberia
60°N
DENMARK
Volga River
Moscow
Novosibirsk
Irkutsk
Amur River
Sea of Okhotsk
Kamchatka Peninsula
NETHERLANDS
POLAND
BELARUS
GERMANY
BELGIUM
EUROPE
KAZAKHSTAN
A S I A
LUX
SWITZ
SL
HUNGARY
UKRAINE
Aral Sea
L. Balkhash
Caspian Sea
MOLDOVA
ROMANIA
MONGOLIA
Vladivostok
LIECH
FRANCE
AUS
SLOV
CRO
BOS-SERB
Black Sea
Caucasus Mts.
Tien Shan
Gobi
Sea of Japan (East Sea)
JAPAN
MON
KOS
ALB MAC
GEORGIA
Beijing
NORTH KOREA
Rome
ITALY
BULGARIA
ARMENIA
AZERBAIJAN
UZBEKISTAN
KYRGYZSTAN
Tokyo
ANDORRA
GREECE
Istanbul
TURKMENISTAN
TAJIKISTAN
Plateau of Tibet
CHINA
Seoul
SOUTH KOREA
Osaka
Mediterranean Sea
Sicily
CYPRUS
TURKEY
Tehran
Pamirs
Yellow Sea
Shanghai
East China Sea
PACIFIC
Algiers
SYRIA
LEBANON
ISRAEL
AFGHANISTAN
Himalayas
30°N
TUNISIA
IRAQ
JORDAN
IRAN
NEPAL
BHUTAN
Taipei
TROPIC OF CANCER 23½°N
ALGERIA
Cairo
KUWAIT
BAHRAIN
QATAR
PAKISTAN
Delhi
Dhaka
TAIWAN
Sahara
LIBYA
EGYPT
SAUDI ARABIA
U.A.E.
Karachi
INDIA
BANGLADESH
MYANMAR (BURMA)
LAOS
Philippine Sea
Northern Mariana Islands (U.S.)
OCEAN
AFRICA
Red Sea
OMAN
Mumbai (Bombay)
Deccan Plateau
VIETNAM
THAILAND
South China Sea
Manila
PHILIPPINES
Guam (U.S.)
MARSHALL ISLANDS
NIGER
CHAD
SUDAN
ERITREA
YEMEN
Arabian Sea
CAMBODIA
FEDERATED STATES OF MICRONESIA
Sahel
DJIBOUTI
SRI LANKA
NIGERIA
ETHIOPIA
Ethiopian Highlands
SOMALIA
MALDIVES
MALAYSIA
BRUNEI
PALAU
BENIN
Lagos
C. AFR. REP.
UGANDA
KENYA
SINGAPORE
Celebes Sea
EQUATOR
0°
EQ. GUINEA
CAMEROON
Congo R.
RWANDA
L. Victoria
Nairobi
KIRIBATI
GABON
CONGO REP.
CONGO
Congo Basin
BURUNDI
I N D O N E S I A
EAST TIMOR
PAPUA NEW GUINEA
SAO TOME & PRINCIPE
Cabinda (Ang.)
Kinshasa
TANZANIA
SEYCHELLES
Jakarta
Arafura Sea
SOLOMON IS.
TUVALU
Dar es Salaam
COMOROS
Diego Garcia (U.K.)
Timor Sea
Darwin
VANUATU
ANGOLA
ZAMBIA
MALAWI
MADAGASCAR
Mozambique Channel
MOZAMBIQUE
INDIAN
MAURITIUS
Coral Sea
FIJI
New Caledonia (Fr.)
NAMIBIA
ZIMBABWE
BOTSWANA
Reunion (Fr.)
TROPIC OF CAPRICORN 23½°S
AUSTRALIA
Western Plateau
SWAZILAND
SOUTH AFRICA
LESOTHO
OCEAN
AUSTRALIA
30°S
Cape Town
Perth
Cape Leeuwin
Darling R.
Great Dividing Range
Amsterdam I. (Fr.)
St. Paul I. (Fr.)
Sydney
Auckland
North I.
Bass Strait
Tasman Sea
NEW ZEALAND
Prince Edward Is. (S. Afr.)
Crozet Is. (Fr.)
Kerguelen I. (Fr.)
Tasmania
South I.
Stewart I.
Auckland Is.
60°S
CIRCLE 66½°S
SOUTHERN OCEAN
A N T A R C T I C A
Ross Ice Shelf
30°E
60°E
90°E
120°E
150°E
180°

SOUTH POLAR VIEW

SOUTH AMERICA
60°W
30°W
ATLANTIC OCEAN
90°W
120°W
PACIFIC OCEAN
SOUTHERN OCEAN
AFRICA
SOUTH POLE
ANTARCTICA
ANTARCTIC CIRCLE 66½°S
150°W
60°S
30°E
180°
AUSTRALIA
INDIAN OCEAN
150°E
90°E
120°E

INTERNATIONAL DATE LINE

WORLD REFERENCE MAP
LAND COVER

This physical Land Cover map uses colour to show the most widespread material covering the earth's surface in each region. Plants are the most common types of material and include cropland, grassland, and forests. (For more information, see pages 24–25.)

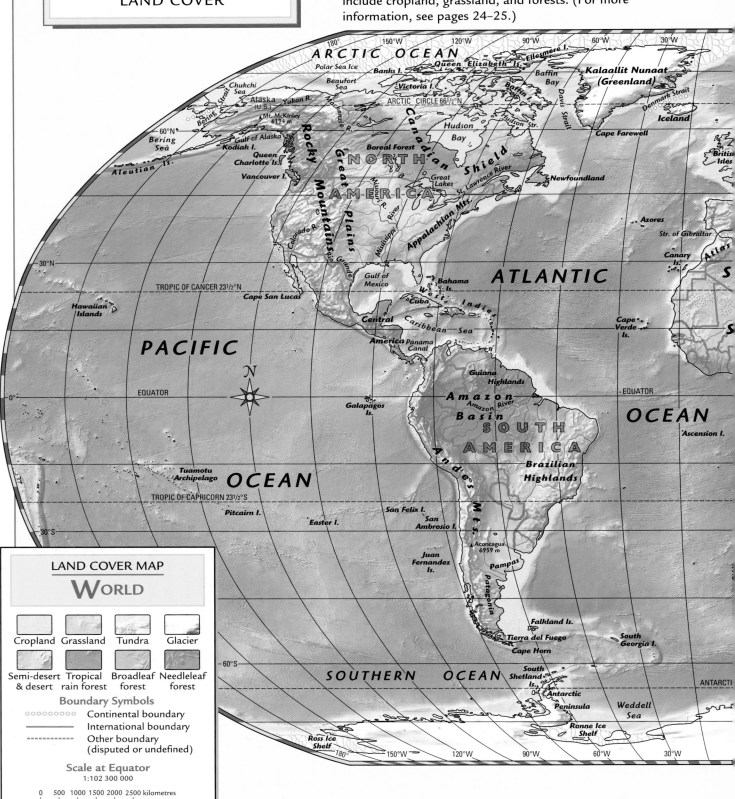

LAND COVER MAP
WORLD

Cropland Grassland Tundra Glacier

Semi-desert Tropical Broadleaf Needleleaf
& desert rain forest forest forest

Boundary Symbols

∘∘∘∘∘∘∘∘∘∘ Continental boundary
—————— International boundary
- - - - - - - Other boundary
(disputed or undefined)

Scale at Equator
1:102 300 000

0 500 1000 1500 2000 2500 kilometres
1 cm to 1023 km

Robinson Projection

Detailed legend on page 5

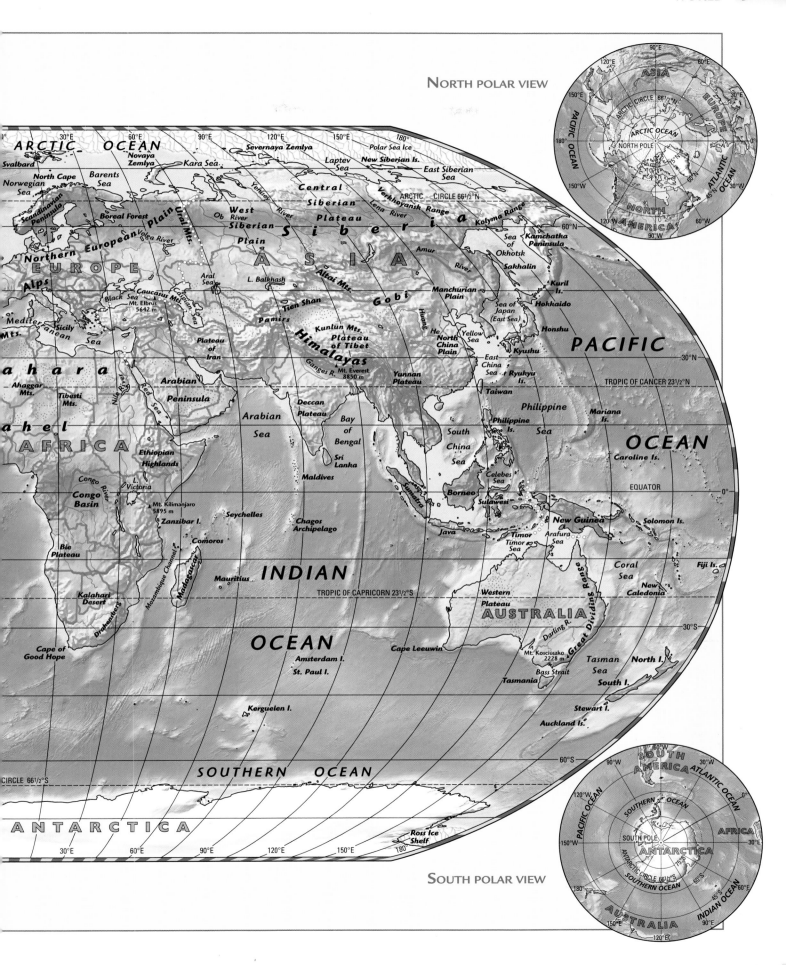

NORTH POLAR VIEW

ARCTIC OCEAN
ARCTIC CIRCLE 66½°N
ARCTIC OCEAN
NORTH POLE
PACIFIC OCEAN
ASIA
EUROPE
ATLANTIC OCEAN
NORTH AMERICA

ARCTIC OCEAN
Svalbard
Norwegian Sea
North Cape
Scandinavian Peninsula
Novaya Zemlya
Barents Sea
Kara Sea
Severnaya Zemlya
Laptev Sea
Polar Sea Ice
New Siberian Is.
East Siberian Sea
Boreal Forest
Northern European Plain
Ural Mts.
Volga River
Ob River
West Siberian Plain
Yenisey River
Central Siberian Plateau
Siberia
Verkhoyansk Range
Lena River
ARCTIC CIRCLE 66½°N
Kolyma Range
EUROPE
Alps
Black Sea
Caucasus Mts.
Mt. Elbrus 5642 m
Caspian Sea
Aral Sea
L. Balkhash
Altai Mts.
Tien Shan
Pamirs
Gobi
Amur River
Sea of Okhotsk
Kamchatka Peninsula
Sakhalin
60°N
Kuril Is.
Manchurian Plain
Sea of Japan (East Sea)
Hokkaido
Mediterranean Sea
Sicily
ASIA
Kunlun Mts.
Plateau of Tibet
Himalayas
Huang He
North China Plain
Yellow Sea
Honshu
Kyushu
PACIFIC
Plateau of Iran
Ganges R.
Mt. Everest 8850 m
Yunnan Plateau
East China Sea
Ryukyu Is.
30°N
Sahara
Ahaggar Mts.
Tibesti Mts.
Nile River
Red Sea
Arabian Peninsula
Deccan Plateau
Bay of Bengal
Taiwan
Philippine
Mariana Is.
TROPIC OF CANCER 23½°N
Sahel
AFRICA
Arabian Sea
Sri Lanka
South China Sea
Philippine Is.
Philippine Sea
OCEAN
Ethiopian Highlands
Maldives
Caroline Is.
Congo River
Congo Basin
L. Victoria
Mt. Kilimanjaro 5895 m
Zanzibar I.
Seychelles
Chagos Archipelago
Celebes Sea
Borneo
Sulawesi
EQUATOR
0°
Bie Plateau
Comoros
Sumatra
Java
New Guinea
Timor
Timor Sea
Arafura Sea
Solomon Is.
INDIAN
Mauritius
Mozambique Channel
Madagascar
Western Plateau
Great Dividing Range
Coral Sea
New Caledonia
Fiji Is.
Kalahari Desert
Drakensberg
TROPIC OF CAPRICORN 23½°S
AUSTRALIA
Darling R.
Cape of Good Hope
OCEAN
Amsterdam I.
St. Paul I.
Cape Leeuwin
Mt. Kosciusko 2228 m
Bass Strait
Tasmania
Tasman Sea
North I.
South I.
30°S
Kerguelen I.
Stewart I.
Auckland Is.
CIRCLE 66½°S
SOUTHERN OCEAN
60°S
ANTARCTICA
Ross Ice Shelf
30°E 60°E 90°E 120°E 150°E 180°

SOUTH POLAR VIEW

SOUTH AMERICA
ATLANTIC OCEAN
PACIFIC OCEAN
SOUTHERN OCEAN
SOUTH POLE
ANTARCTICA
ANTARCTIC CIRCLE 66½°S
SOUTHERN OCEAN
AFRICA
AUSTRALIA
INDIAN OCEAN

WORLD REFERENCE MAP
ELEVATION

This physical Elevation map is different from the Land Cover map on pages 8–9. It uses colour to show a region's height above or depth below sea level. (For more information, see pages 12–13.)

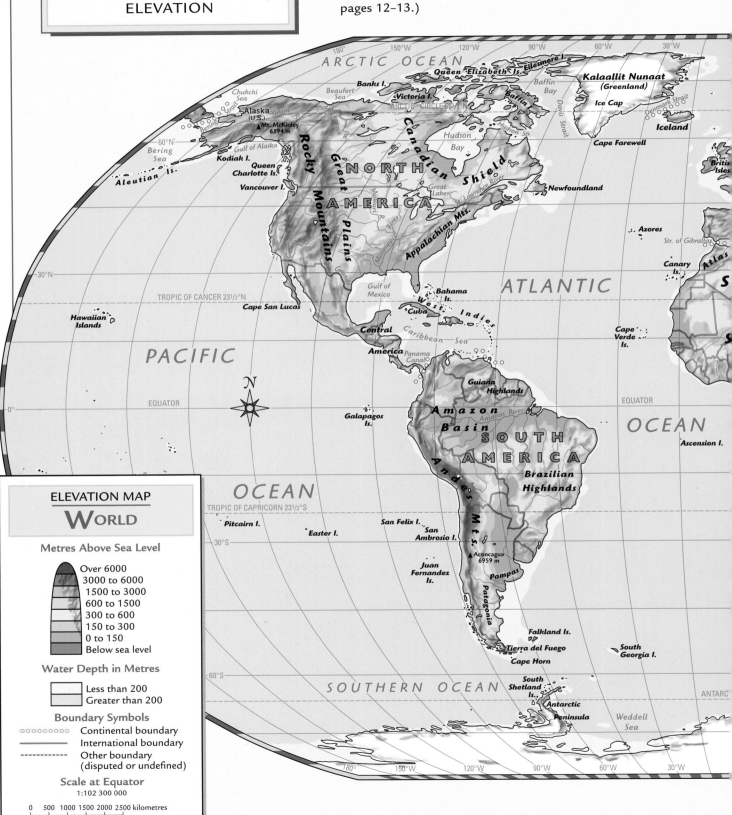

ARCTIC OCEAN

Chukchi Sea
Beaufort Sea
Banks I.
Queen Elizabeth Is.
Ellesmere I.
Victoria I.
Baffin Bay
Baffin
ARCTIC CIRCLE 66½°N
Kalaallit Nunaat (Greenland)
Ice Cap
Iceland
Denmark Strait
Alaska (U.S.)
Mt. McKinley 6194 m
Bering Strait
Hudson Str.
Davis Strait
Hudson Bay
Cape Farewell
60°N
Bering Sea
Gulf of Alaska
Kodiak I.
Queen Charlotte Is.
Vancouver I.
Aleutian Is.
Rocky Mountains
Great Plains
NORTH AMERICA
Canadian Shield
St. Lawrence River
Great Lakes
Newfoundland
British Isles
Missouri R.
Mississippi R.
Appalachian Mts.
Azores
Str. of Gibraltar
30°N
Rio Grande
Gulf of Mexico
ATLANTIC
Canary Is.
Atlas
TROPIC OF CANCER 23½°N
Cape San Lucas
Bahama Is.
West Indies
Cape Verde Is.
Hawaiian Islands
Cuba
Caribbean Sea
Central America
Panama Canal
PACIFIC
Galapagos Is.
Guiana Highlands
Amazon River
Amazon Basin
SOUTH AMERICA
EQUATOR
OCEAN
Ascension I.
0°
Andes Mts.
Brazilian Highlands
OCEAN
TROPIC OF CAPRICORN 23½°S
Pitcairn I.
San Felix I.
San Ambrosio I.
Easter I.
30°S
Juan Fernandez Is.
Aconcagua 6959 m
Pampas
Patagonia
Falkland Is.
South Georgia I.
Tierra del Fuego
Cape Horn
60°S
South Shetland Is.
Antarctic Peninsula
Weddell Sea
SOUTHERN OCEAN
ANTARC

ELEVATION MAP
WORLD

Metres Above Sea Level

Over 6000
3000 to 6000
1500 to 3000
600 to 1500
300 to 600
150 to 300
0 to 150
Below sea level

Water Depth in Metres

Less than 200
Greater than 200

Boundary Symbols

○○○○○○○○○ Continental boundary
——————— International boundary
- - - - - - - Other boundary (disputed or undefined)

Scale at Equator

1:102 300 000

0 500 1000 1500 2000 2500 kilometres

1 cm to 1023 km

Robinson Projection

Detailed legend on page 5

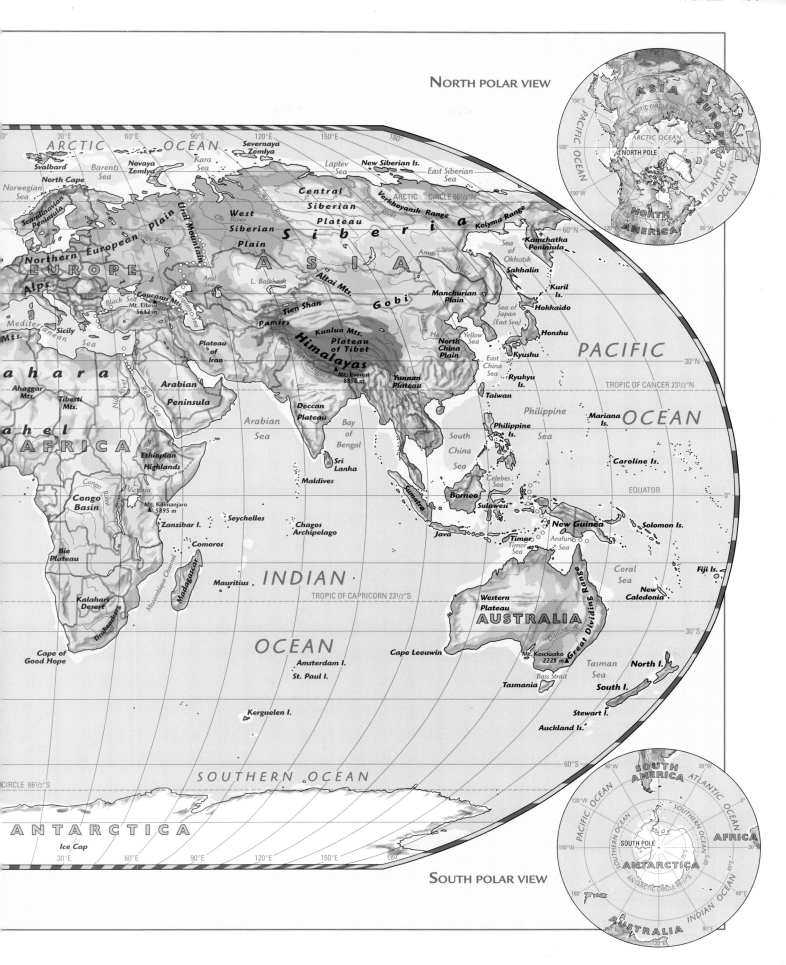

NORTH POLAR VIEW

ARCTIC OCEAN

Svalbard
North Cape
Norwegian Sea
Scandinavian Peninsula
Barents Sea
Novaya Zemlya
Kara Sea
Severnaya Zemlya
Laptev Sea
New Siberian Is.
East Siberian Sea
Central Siberian Plateau
Verkhoyansk Range
Kolyma Range
Kamchatka Peninsula

EUROPE
Northern European Plain
Alps
Black Sea
Caucasus Mts.
Mt. Elbrus 5642 m
Mediterranean Sea
Sicily
Mts.
Ural Mountains
Volga River
Caspian Sea
Aral Sea
L. Balkhash
Ob River
Yenisey River
Lena River
West Siberian Plain
Amur River
S I B E R I A
A S I A
Altai Mts.
Tien Shan
Pamirs
Gobi
Kunlun Mts.
Plateau of Tibet
Himalayas
Mt. Everest 8850 m
Ganges R.
Deccan Plateau
Plateau of Iran
Arabian Peninsula
Yunnan Plateau
Manchurian Plain
Huang He
North China Plain
Yellow Sea
East China Sea
Sea of Okhotsk
Sakhalin
Kuril Is.
Hokkaido
Sea of Japan (East Sea)
Honshu
Kyushu
Ryukyu Is.
Taiwan
PACIFIC
OCEAN
TROPIC OF CANCER 23½°N

a h a r a
Ahaggar Mts.
Tibesti Mts.
a h e l
AFRICA
Nile River
Red Sea
Ethiopian Highlands
L. Victoria
Mt. Kilimanjaro 5895 m
Zanzibar I.
Congo River
Congo Basin
Bie Plateau
Kalahari Desert
Drakensberg
Cape of Good Hope
Comoros
Madagascar
Mozambique Channel
Seychelles
Mauritius
Arabian Sea
Bay of Bengal
Sri Lanka
Maldives
Chagos Archipelago
Sumatra
Java
Borneo
Sulawesi
Celebes Sea
Philippine Is.
South China Sea
Philippine Sea
Caroline Is.
Mariana Is.
OCEAN
EQUATOR
New Guinea
Timor
Timor Sea
Arafura Sea
Solomon Is.
Coral Sea
Fiji Is.
New Caledonia

INDIAN
TROPIC OF CAPRICORN 23½°S
OCEAN
Amsterdam I.
St. Paul I.
Kerguelen I.
Western Plateau
AUSTRALIA
Great Dividing Range
Darling
Mt. Kosciuszko 2228 m
Cape Leeuwin
Bass Strait
Tasmania
Tasman Sea
North I.
South I.
Stewart I.
Auckland Is.

SOUTHERN OCEAN
CIRCLE 66½°S

A N T A R C T I C A
Ice Cap

SOUTH POLAR VIEW

SOUTH AMERICA
ATLANTIC OCEAN
PACIFIC OCEAN
SOUTHERN OCEAN
SOUTH POLE
ANTARCTICA
AFRICA
ANTARCTIC CIRCLE 66½°S
AUSTRALIA
INDIAN OCEAN

ELEVATION AND LANDFORMS

Elevation is the measure of land's height above or depth below sea level. **Landforms** are the physical features of the landscape. Most extensive landforms have patterns of high, low, or changing elevation.

▶ Most vast, level landforms are sections of the relatively flat tectonic plates that make up the continents.

▶ High landforms are produced when plates collide and push up the earth's crust or the magma below.

▶ Other landforms are carved or deposited by wind, water, and living beings.

▶ **Relief** is the difference between the highest and lowest elevation of a feature or region. Shading on a map shows landforms with rugged relief, such as mountains and hills.

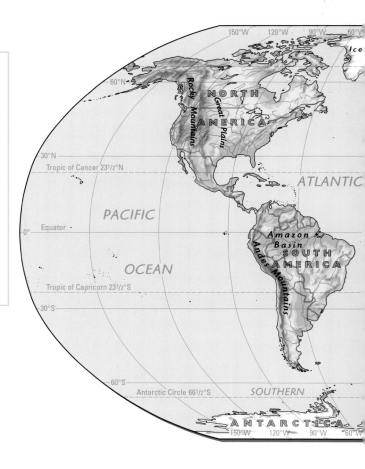

Every Breath You Take

The higher you travel above sea level, the thinner the air is and the less oxygen you get with each breath. That is why climbers aiming for the world's highest peaks must first acclimatize or get accustomed to the oxygen level at one elevation range before attempting the next.

A **Mountains** can be single peaks or part of a range. The summit of Lhotse Mountain in Nepal lies at 8516 metres. Lhotse is part of the Himalayas, the highest mountain range in the world. (For more information, see page 125.)

B **Plateaus** are vast areas of relatively flat land at high elevation. The Plateau of Tibet, located in China, is the world's highest plateau. It has an average elevation of more than 4500 metres.

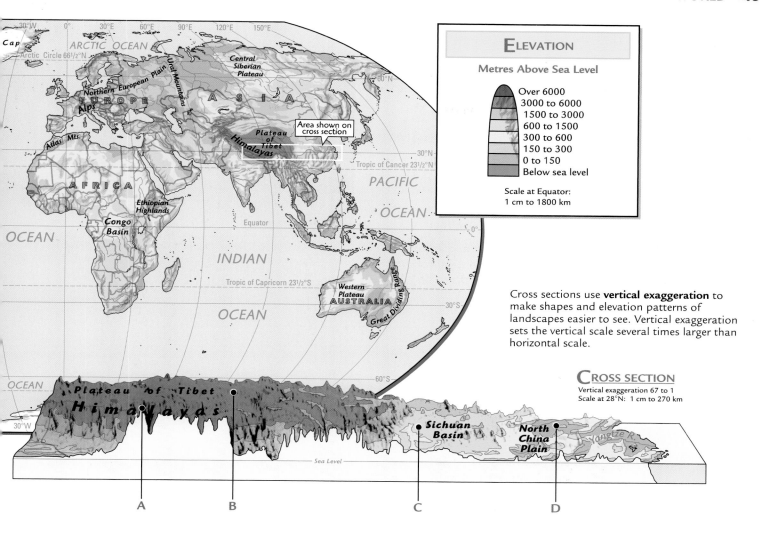

ELEVATION

Metres Above Sea Level

Over 6000
3000 to 6000
1500 to 3000
600 to 1500
300 to 600
150 to 300
0 to 150
Below sea level

Scale at Equator:
1 cm to 1800 km

Cross sections use **vertical exaggeration** to make shapes and elevation patterns of landscapes easier to see. Vertical exaggeration sets the vertical scale several times larger than horizontal scale.

CROSS SECTION
Vertical exaggeration 67 to 1
Scale at 28°N: 1 cm to 270 km

C **Basins** are low areas surrounded by higher ground. The Sichuan Basin, along the Yangtze River in southern China, is surrounded by rugged mountains. It has an elevation range between 200 and 750 metres.

D **Plains** are broad stretches of nearly level land, usually found at low elevations. The fertile lowlands of the North China Plain have the best farmland in China. The elevation of the North China Plain ranges from 0 to 150 metres above sea level.

World Matters

THE MOVING EARTH

The land and water features of the earth appear stable, but actually they move between 2.5 to 15 centimetres each year.

▶ The earth's crust is made up of about 30 **plates** that float above the molten interior of the planet. Lighter, thicker areas of the plates form the continents. Denser, thinner areas form the ocean floors.

▶ Plates slide along, bump into, and move away from each other.

▶ **Earthquakes** and **volcanoes** are common near the boundaries between plates. When an earthquake takes place beneath the ocean, a massive, destructive wave called a **tsunami** may result.

In 2005 an earthquake shook towns on western Java in Indonesia. With a magnitude of 8.7, it destroyed homes and offices and wrecked power lines and sewage systems. Over 900 people died in this quake.

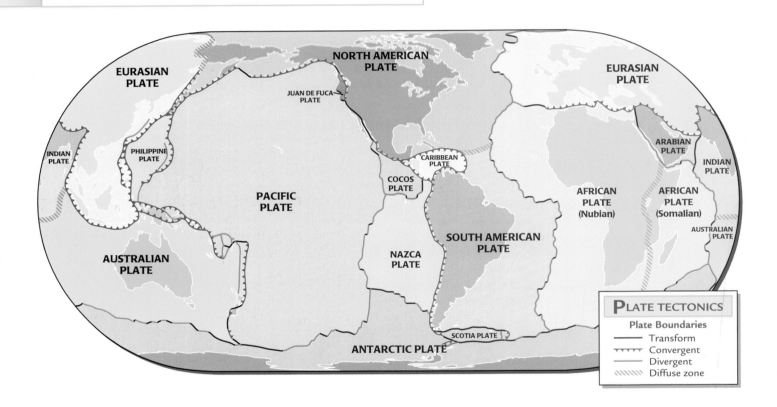

PLATE TECTONICS

Plate Boundaries
— Transform
ᴛᴛᴛᴛ Convergent
— Divergent
▨ Diffuse zone

TRANSFORM PLATE BOUNDARIES

These plates move side-by-side—sometimes in opposite directions, sometimes in the same direction. This type of plate movement can cause earthquakes.

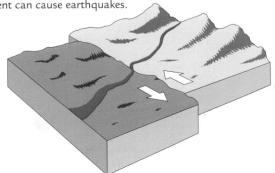

CONVERGENT PLATE BOUNDARIES

When one plate moves under another plate—**subduction**—earthquakes and volcanoes can occur. In the long run, the subducted plate will disappear. Convergent plates can be found near South America and the coasts of Asia, and in the western Pacific.

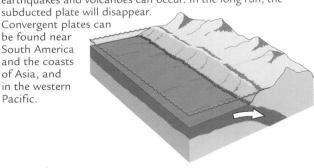

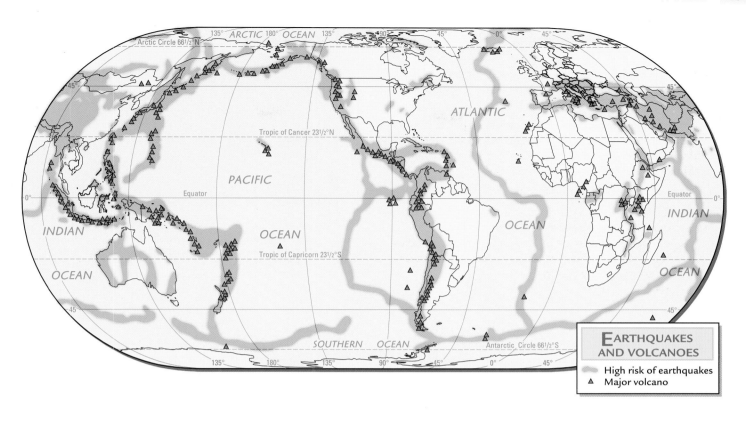

EARTHQUAKES
AND VOLCANOES

High risk of earthquakes
▲ Major volcano

Location, Location

Why does one earthquake with a magnitude of 9.0 cause over 283 000 deaths, while another quake of the same magnitude results in none? It's all in the location. When a quake strikes near a populous area without earthquake-resistant buildings, death rates are high. Depth of the quake and stability of the overlying rock also can affect the death rate.

DIVERGENT PLATE BOUNDARIES

These plates move in opposite directions, pulling away from each other. The Mid-Atlantic Ridge is on a divergent plate boundary. This movement causes the Atlantic Ocean to widen by about 2.5 kilometres every 100 000 years.

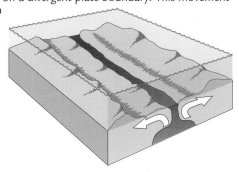

The volcano at Soufriere Hills on the West Indian island of Montserrat buried villages and destroyed the capital city of Plymouth.

World Matters

OCEANS

Ocean waters cover about 71 percent of the earth's surface. There is only one world ocean, but the continents divide the ocean into five distinct parts—the five oceans named on the map.

▶ A **continental shelf** is shallow, submerged land found just beyond the coastlines of the continents. A shelf may extend 30 to 300 kilometres from shore.

▶ **Abyssal plains** are the vast, flat stretches of ocean floor, usually found in undersea **basins**.

▶ The deepest parts of the ocean are **trenches**, which often lie 3.2 to 4.0 kilometres below the plains.

▶ The vast majority of sea exploitation—including fishing and gas and oil drilling—occurs on the continental shelf. Coastal areas are in the greatest danger of pollution.

Divers off the coast of Indonesia explore the ocean depths. The deep ocean remains the most mysterious and least-explored habitat on Earth. The deepest known spot is in the Mariana Trench east of the island of Guam. It plummets almost 11 kilometres below sea level.

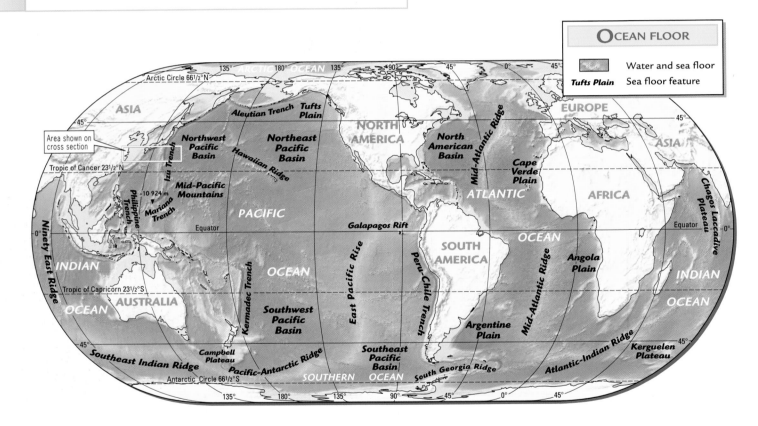

OCEAN FLOOR

	Water and sea floor
Tufts Plain	Sea floor feature

CROSS SECTION

Vertical exaggeration 14 to 1
Scale at 28°N: 1 cm to 158 km

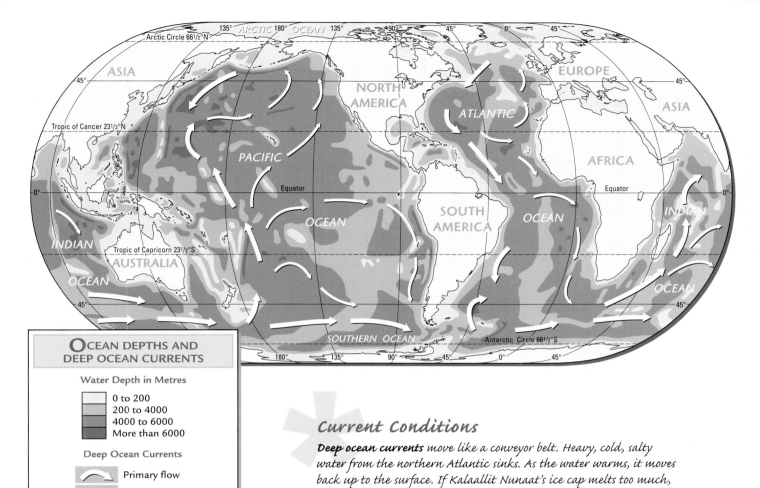

OCEAN DEPTHS AND DEEP OCEAN CURRENTS

Water Depth in Metres

- 0 to 200
- 200 to 4000
- 4000 to 6000
- More than 6000

Deep Ocean Currents

- Primary flow
- Secondary flow

Current Conditions

Deep ocean currents move like a conveyor belt. Heavy, cold, salty water from the northern Atlantic sinks. As the water warms, it moves back up to the surface. If Kalaallit Nunaat's ice cap melts too much, it could cause the conveyor belt to shut down.

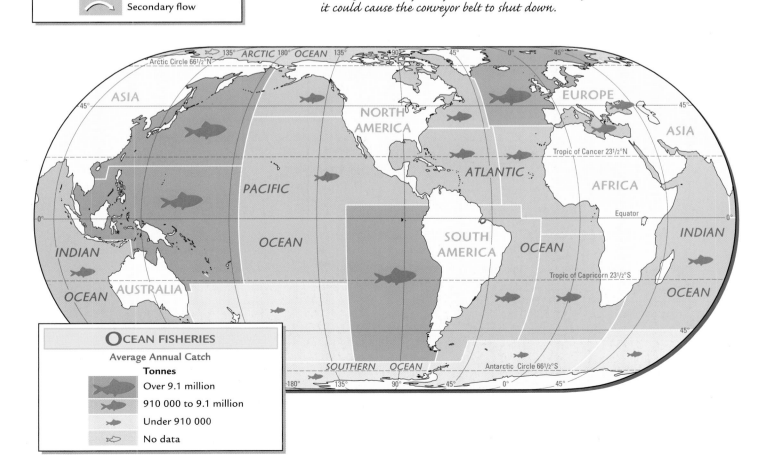

OCEAN FISHERIES

Average Annual Catch

Tonnes

- Over 9.1 million
- 910 000 to 9.1 million
- Under 910 000
- No data

World Matters

WEATHER PATTERNS

Weather is the condition of the atmosphere at a given time and place. Weather involves temperature, precipitation, humidity, wind, and other factors.

▶ **Temperature** is a measure of how hot or cold the air is near the earth's surface.

▶ **Precipitation** includes rain, snow, sleet, and hail. Although, on average, 10 centimetres of snow equals about 1 centimetre of rain, the actual ratio varies. Dry, powdery snow equals less rain than wet, heavy snow.

▶ **Humidity** is the amount of water vapor in the air, affecting the level of comfort and chance that clouds will form.

▶ **Seasonal winds** affect weather patterns by moving warm, cold, moist, or dry air to a region. (See the monsoon maps on page 126.)

Salzburg, Austria, is located in the Alps of Central Europe. Its summers are warm, with an average temperature in July of 18°C. In summer the city experiences *Schnürlregen*, a heavy downpour that suddenly appears and then disappears.

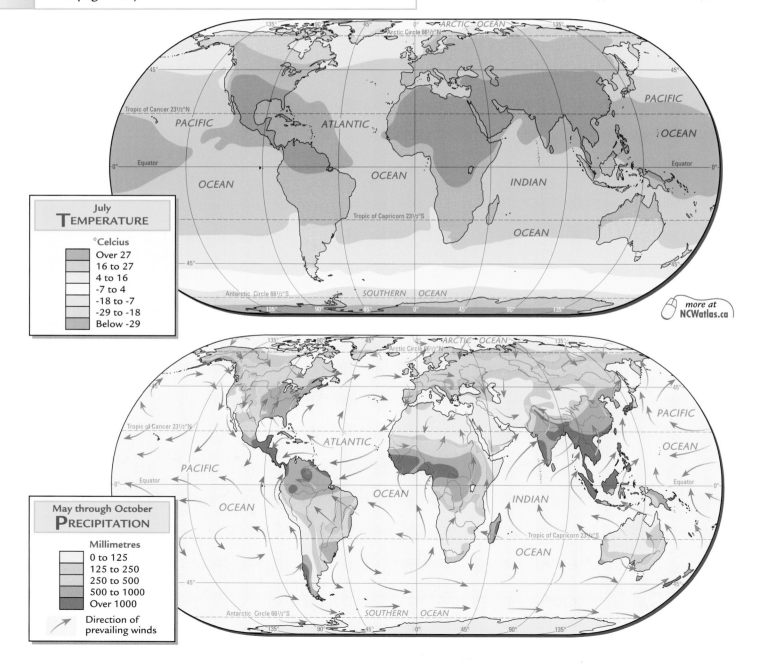

July TEMPERATURE

°Celcius
- Over 27
- 16 to 27
- 4 to 16
- -7 to 4
- -18 to -7
- -29 to -18
- Below -29

more at NCWatlas.ca

May through October PRECIPITATION

Millimetres
- 0 to 125
- 125 to 250
- 250 to 500
- 500 to 1000
- Over 1000

➚ Direction of prevailing winds

Sun and seasons

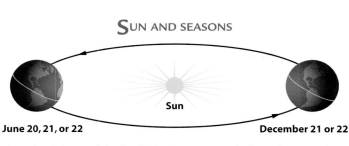

June 20, 21, or 22   **Sun**   **December 21 or 22**

The axis of the earth is tilted 23½°. From March through September, the Northern Hemisphere is tilted toward the sun and temperatures rise. The Southern Hemisphere gets warmer from September through March, when it is tilted toward the sun.

Winters in Salzburg are cold with an average temperature in January of -2°C. Winters there are snowy and drier than its summers.

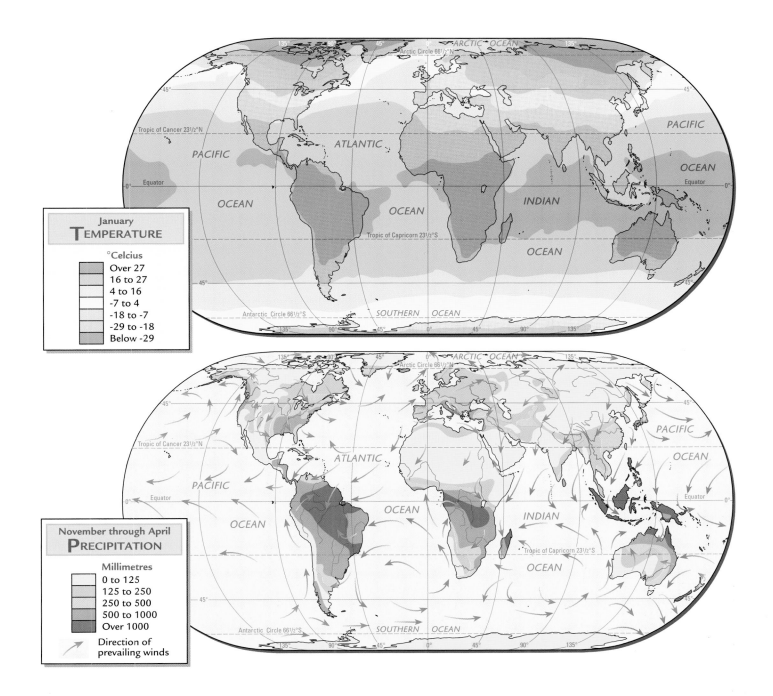

January
TEMPERATURE

°Celcius
- Over 27
- 16 to 27
- 4 to 16
- -7 to 4
- -18 to -7
- -29 to -18
- Below -29

November through April
PRECIPITATION

Millimetres
- 0 to 125
- 125 to 250
- 250 to 500
- 500 to 1000
- Over 1000

→ Direction of prevailing winds

World Matters

CLIMATE

While **weather** describes an area's atmosphere at a *specific* time, **climate** describes the usual weather pattern of a region over a *period* of time. Elevation, latitude, distance from oceans, and surface currents help determine a region's climate.

▶ Temperature and moisture decrease with **elevation**.

▶ **Latitude** affects temperature. Regions within the **Tropics of Cancer** and **Capricorn** receive direct sunlight and are warmer than polar areas within the **Arctic** and **Antarctic Circles**.

▶ Earth's rotation and the coasts of the continents drive most **surface currents** in a circular pattern, transferring warm ocean water near the Equator to higher northern and southern latitudes.

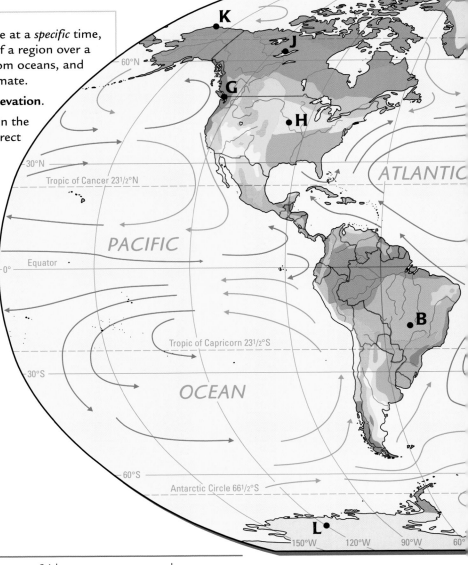

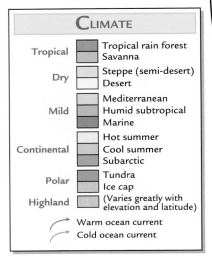

CLIMOGRAPHS

The **climographs** below show location, elevation, average 24-hour temperatures, and average monthly rainfall for several places. Letters refer to locations on the map. Colours indicate climate type. Curved lines show temperatures, while bars represent rainfall.

more at NCWatlas.ca

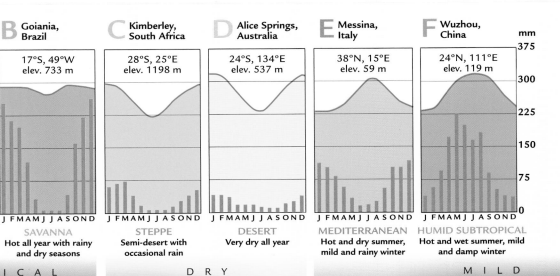

30°W 0° 30°E 60°E 90°E 120°E 150°E

ARCTIC OCEAN

Arctic Circle 66½°N

•I

E•

•F

PACIFIC

Tropic of Cancer 23½°N

A•

INDIAN

OCEAN

Equator 0°

•D

OCEAN

Tropic of Capricorn 23½°S

OCEAN

30°S

C•

SOUTHERN OCEAN

60°S

Antarctic Circle 66½°S

30°W 0° 30°E 60°E 90°E 120°E 150°E

Unseasonably Warm

The El Niño phenomenon occcurs when the usual east-to-west equatorial current in the tropical Pacific weakens or reverses, pushing warm waters to the west coast of South America. El Niño events can influence world climate, but they mainly affect regions near the Pacific.

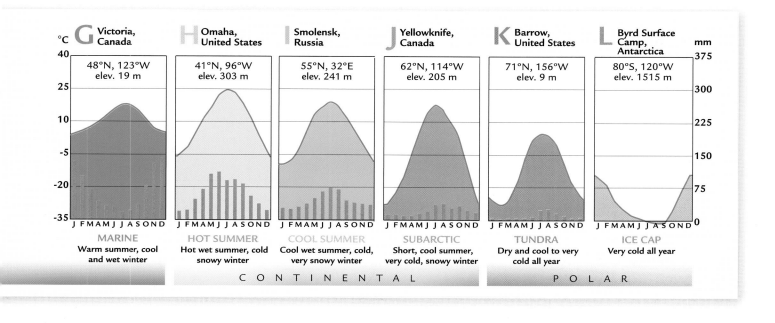

	G Victoria, Canada	H Omaha, United States	I Smolensk, Russia	J Yellowknife, Canada	K Barrow, United States	L Byrd Surface Camp, Antarctica
	48°N, 123°W elev. 19 m	41°N, 96°W elev. 303 m	55°N, 32°E elev. 241 m	62°N, 114°W elev. 205 m	71°N, 156°W elev. 9 m	80°S, 120°W elev. 1515 m
	MARINE	HOT SUMMER	COOL SUMMER	SUBARCTIC	TUNDRA	ICE CAP
	Warm summer, cool and wet winter	Hot wet summer, cold snowy winter	Cool wet summer, cold, very snowy winter	Short, cool summer, very cold, snowy winter	Dry and cool to very cold all year	Very cold all year

CONTINENTAL   POLAR

World Matters

ENERGY AND METALS

Earth's **natural resources** are vital to our daily lives. Coal, oil (petroleum), uranium, and natural gas fill most of the world's **energy** requirements. **Metals** are natural resources whose properties include strength, hardness, and conductivity.

▶ **Fossil fuels**—coal, natural gas, and oil—are used to heat homes and power transportation. However, these fuel deposits are **consumable** and their use damages the environment.

▶ **Metals** are mined in metal-bearing rocks called **ore**. The ore is **processed** into usable metals. Precious metals, like gold, are used for expensive jewelry. Other metals, such as iron, are used for construction and manufacturing.

▶ **Renewable energy resources** are an important alternative to consumable ones. Hydroelectricity, biomass, and solar and wind energy are all renewable.

This solar power plant is in California. It provides electricity 24 hours a day by capturing energy from the sun during the day and converting it into electrical power.

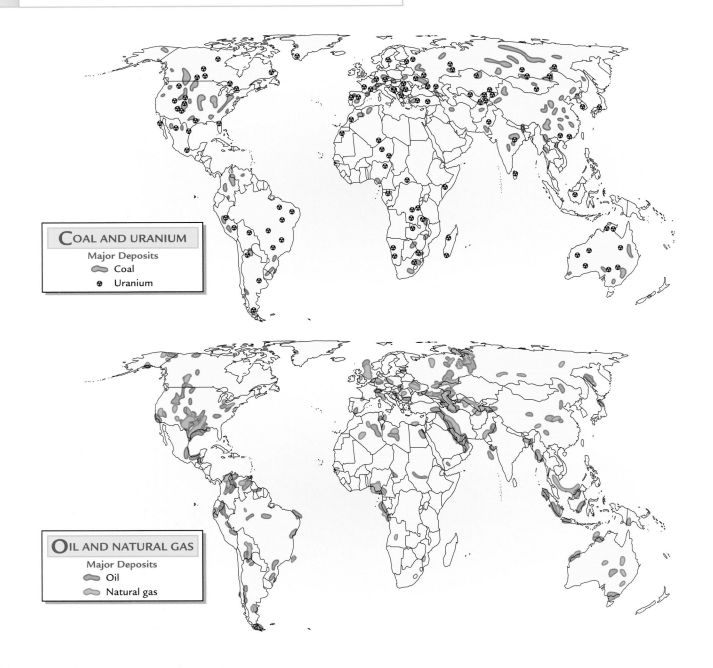

COAL AND URANIUM

Major Deposits

- Coal
- ⊗ Uranium

OIL AND NATURAL GAS

Major Deposits

- Oil
- Natural gas

Sources of World Energy

Oil is the most-used energy source in the world today. Hydroelectricity is the only major energy source that is renewable. (For more information, see pages 49, 56, 63, 67, 114, and 128–129.)

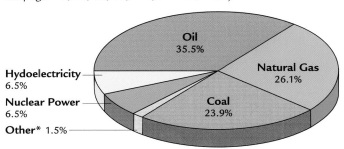

Oil 35.5%

Natural Gas 26.1%

Coal 23.9%

Hydoelectricity 6.5%

Nuclear Power 6.5%

Other* 1.5%

*Other includes: geothermal, ocean thermal, solar, wind, and biomass (wood, ethanol from corn or sugar, biodiesel from vegetable oils, methane made from waste)

Gold mining is an intricate, but rewarding, process. One ounce of gold is worth an average of C$ 511. Here, a refinery worker pours gold at a mine in South Africa.

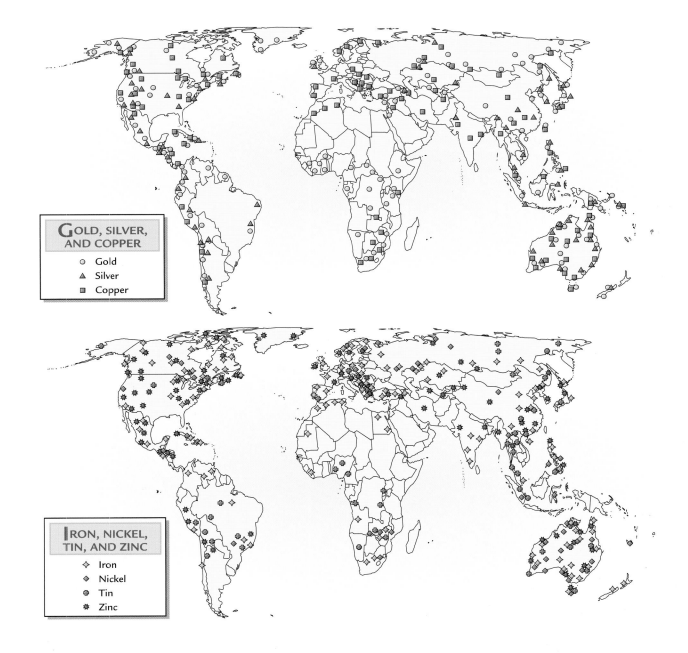

GOLD, SILVER, AND COPPER

- ○ Gold
- ▲ Silver
- ▪ Copper

IRON, NICKEL, TIN, AND ZINC

- ◇ Iron
- ◆ Nickel
- ✚ Tin
- ✳ Zinc

World Matters

USING THE LAND

Land cover, such as desert or cropland, is the most common ground cover found in a given area, though most areas also may contain other types of land cover. **Land use**, such as farming or herding, is the most economically valuable human use of land in a given area, though the area often has other uses as well.

▶ Land cover often affects the way an area's land can be used.

▶ At nearly a third of the world's total land cover, **forests** are the most prevalent land cover on Earth.

▶ **Urban areas** are cities and their surrounding suburbs. Although urban areas are home to about half the world's population, they are the least widespread use of land on Earth.

Tundra

No widespread use

B **Tundra** is used for **nomadic herding** or has **no widespread use** at all. In spring and summer, the frozen soil thaws 0.3 to 3 metres below the surface, allowing only small plants and low shrubs to grow. This tundra is in far northern Canada.

Needleleaf forest

Forestry

A **Needleleaf forests**, as well as **tropical rain forests** and **broadleaf forests**, are used for **forestry**. Only half of the world's original forests remain standing. Canada is home to one-tenth of them.

Cartography 101

How do you map land cover? With a combination of high-tech sources and cartographic techniques. Satellite imagery and scientific analysis provide a detailed picture of the land. Then map makers adjust colors and add shading.

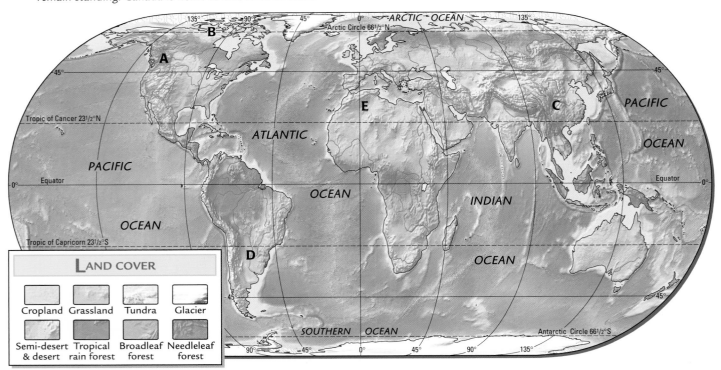

LAND COVER

Cropland   Grassland   Tundra   Glacier

Semi-desert & desert   Tropical rain forest   Broadleaf forest   Needleleaf forest

Grassland

Ranching or herding

D **Grasslands** are primarily used for **ranching or herding**. Ranching often takes place on land too dry to farm. This gaucho is herding cattle on the plains of northern Argentina.

Semi-desert & desert

Nomadic herding

Cropland

Commercial farming

C **Cropland** is used for **subsistence farming** or **commercial farming**. Subsistence farmers only are able to raise enough food for their families. Commercial farms raise enough food to sell. These terraced commercial rice fields in China maximize the use of hilly land.

E **Desert** and **semi-desert** are typically used for **nomadic herding** or have **no widespread use**. Nomadic herders seasonally move their animals to fresh grazing areas and water. This herder leads camels across the Sahara in Algeria.

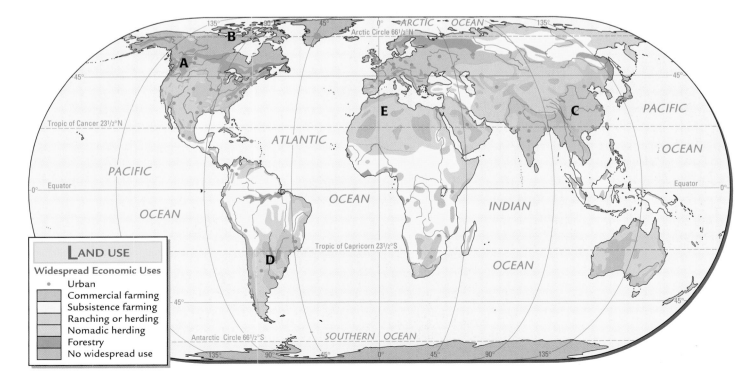

LAND USE

Widespread Economic Uses
- Urban
  - Commercial farming
  - Subsistence farming
  - Ranching or herding
  - Nomadic herding
  - Forestry
  - No widespread use

World Matters

ENVIRONMENTAL ISSUES

The **environment**, the natural world that we inhabit with all other living things, is affected and often harmed by human activities.

▶ **Unsustainable development** occurs when the environment is depleted by human use to the point that it is no longer capable of replenishing itself.

▶ **Tropical rain forests** are shrinking at an alarming rate due to logging, mining, and clearing land for agriculture.

▶ **Acid rain** is precipitation that contains sulfuric, nitric, or other acids. This precipitation, caused by the burning of fossil fuels, can kill plants and make lakes too acidic for fish.

▶ **Global warming** is the increase in the temperature of the earth's atmosphere, caused by such human activities as burning fossil fuels and clearing forests.

These Guatemalan farmers slash-and-burn rain forests to grow crops. The soil loses its fertility in a few years, and then farmers move on to deforest more land.

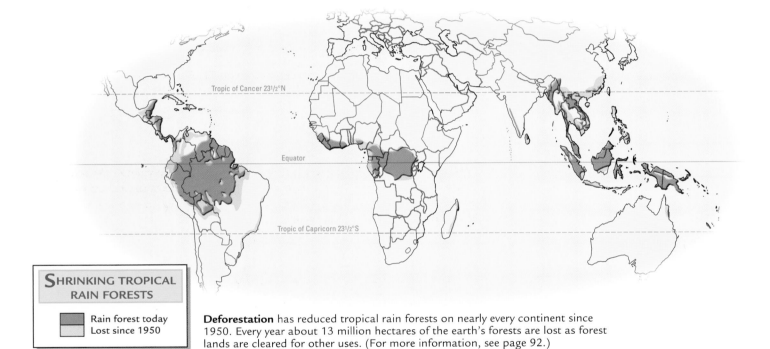

Tropic of Cancer 23½°N

Equator

Tropic of Capricorn 23½°S

SHRINKING TROPICAL RAIN FORESTS

■ Rain forest today
□ Lost since 1950

Deforestation has reduced tropical rain forests on nearly every continent since 1950. Every year about 13 million hectares of the earth's forests are lost as forest lands are cleared for other uses. (For more information, see page 92.)

ARAL SEA

The Aral Sea in Central Asia is an example of unsustainable development. The Amu Darya flows northward into the Aral Sea. Beginning in 1956, water from this river was diverted to irrigate cotton fields in the desert of what is now Turkmenistan. Today the Aral Sea is a fourth of its former size. The seaside town of Muynak (M) is now 150 kilometres from the shores of the Aral Sea. Without a change in water use, the sea will soon disappear.

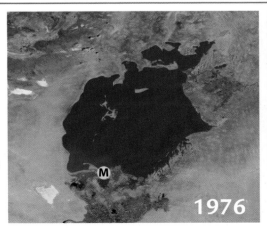

1976

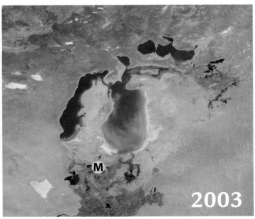

2003

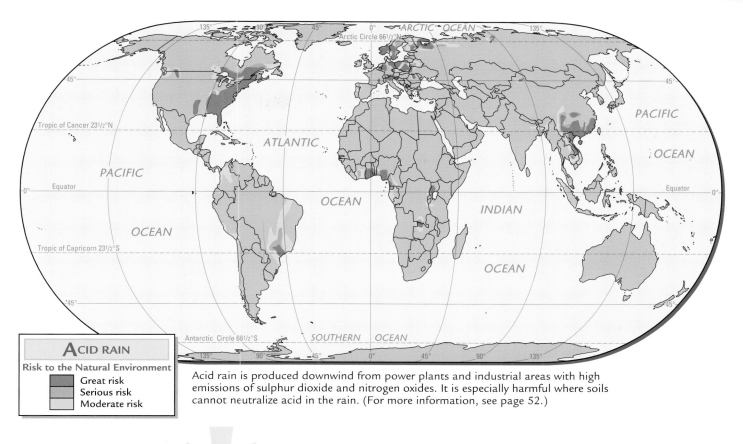

more at NCWatlas.ca

ACID RAIN

Risk to the Natural Environment

- Great risk
- Serious risk
- Moderate risk

Acid rain is produced downwind from power plants and industrial areas with high emissions of sulphur dioxide and nitrogen oxides. It is especially harmful where soils cannot neutralize acid in the rain. (For more information, see page 52.)

Rising Costs

Tuvalu is a small island country in the western Pacific Ocean near the Equator. As the oceans rise due to global warming, Tuvalu may soon be underwater, forcing its inhabitants to evacuate. By the year 2050, several island countries will spend more than 10 percent of their gross domestic product each year to combat the earth's rising water levels.

GLOBAL WARMING AND SEA ICE

The polar ice cap expands and contracts every year, melting to its smallest size in September, before freezing weather returns. Compare the ice cap in 1979 and 2005. More ice melts now because polar summers are warmer and longer. Melting sea ice does not raise sea level, but melting glaciers do.

September 1979

September 2005

World Matters

GROWING POPULATION

Earth is home to more than 6.5 billion people. Its population continues to grow by about 80 million people per year.

▶ **Population density** is the average number of people living in a square kilometre of a region. The world's population density is about 44 people per square kilometre.

▶ **Overpopulation** occurs when a population has outgrown an area's resources, such as land and water. Large parts of India, China, and Nigeria are overpopulated.

▶ **Natural population growth** is calculated by subtracting the total deaths from the total births in a area. It does not include migration to or from the area. The world has a growth rate of 1.1 percent.

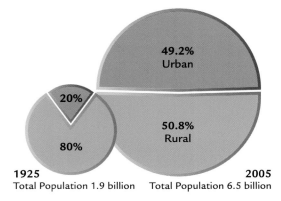

1925
Total Population 1.9 billion

2005
Total Population 6.5 billion

URBANIZATION

The world's urban population has more than quadrupled in the past 50 years. As farming becomes more efficient, people move to cities in search of jobs. Nearly half of the world's population now lives in urban areas.

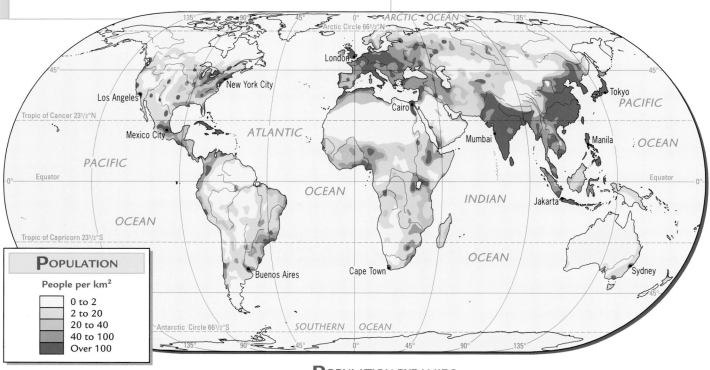

POPULATION

People per km²

- 0 to 2
- 2 to 20
- 20 to 40
- 40 to 100
- Over 100

Ups and Downs

There is an inverse relationship between prosperity and population. When people have access to quality health care and proper nutrition, they live longer. When women are educated, employed, and can expect that their children will survive childhood, they tend to have fewer children.

more at **NCWatlas.ca**

POPULATION PYRAMIDS

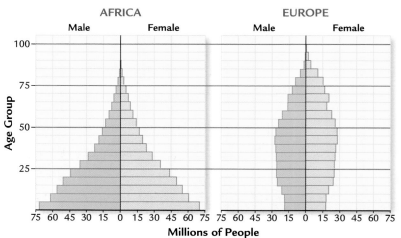

Most of Africa's population is young. This is in stark contrast to the population of Europe, which has nearly four times as many people over the age of 64 as Africa.

more at **NCWatlas.ca**

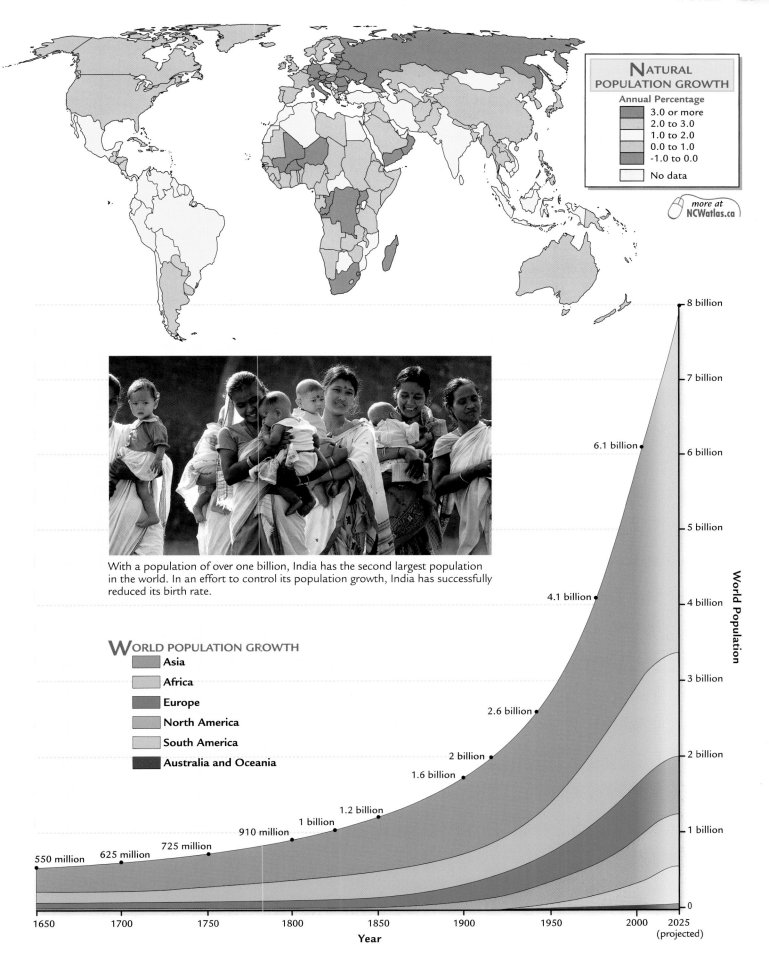

NATURAL
POPULATION GROWTH

Annual Percentage

3.0 or more
2.0 to 3.0
1.0 to 2.0
0.0 to 1.0
-1.0 to 0.0

No data

more at
NCWatlas.ca

With a population of over one billion, India has the second largest population
in the world. In an effort to control its population growth, India has successfully
reduced its birth rate.

WORLD POPULATION GROWTH

Asia
Africa
Europe
North America
South America
Australia and Oceania

World Population

8 billion
7 billion
6.1 billion • 6 billion
5 billion
4.1 billion • 4 billion
3 billion
2.6 billion •
2 billion • 2 billion
1.6 billion •
1.2 billion
1 billion • 1 billion
910 million •
725 million
625 million
550 million

0

1650   1700   1750   1800   1850   1900   1950   2000   2025
Year   (projected)

World Matters

HEALTH CONCERNS

Better access to clean water and health care increases life expectancy. However, more than one billion people lack safe drinking water, and one-third of the world's population has no access to needed medicine.

▶ **Life expectancy** is the average number of years a person is expected to live. It is based on the death rates of specific age groups in a given population.

▶ In the developing world, rural water sources are more polluted than urban water sources. Eighty percent of all sickness in the developing world is attributed to water–related illnesses.

▶ Prevention controls disease. For example, smallpox killed approximately 300 million people in the twentieth century, but the disease was eradicated by 1979 through a global vaccination program.

Immunization programs have drastically reduced the spread of infectious diseases, such as diphtheria and polio, worldwide. In China, a meningitis outbreak led this child to a local vaccination center.

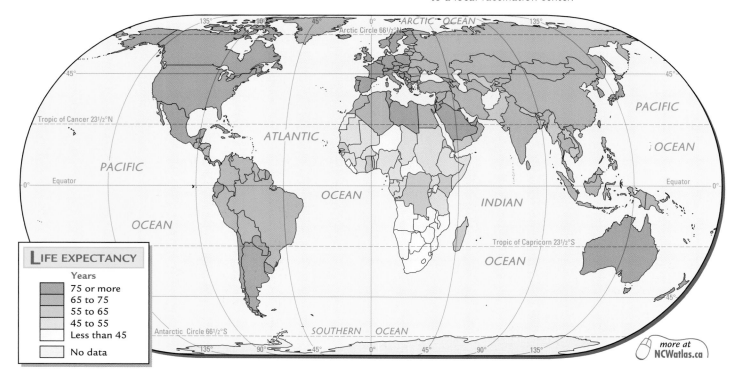

LIFE EXPECTANCY

Years
- 75 or more
- 65 to 75
- 55 to 65
- 45 to 55
- Less than 45
- No data

more at NCWatlas.ca

LEADING CAUSES OF DEATH

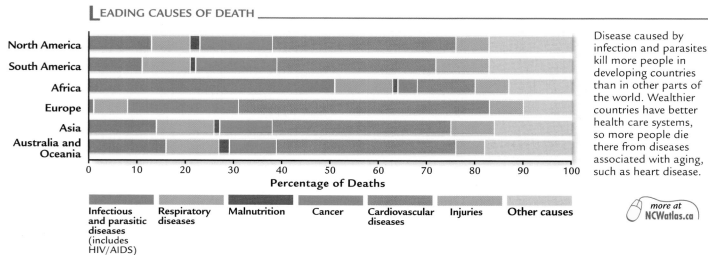

North America
South America
Africa
Europe
Asia
Australia and Oceania

Percentage of Deaths

Infectious and parasitic diseases (includes HIV/AIDS) | Respiratory diseases | Malnutrition | Cancer | Cardiovascular diseases | Injuries | Other causes

Disease caused by infection and parasites kill more people in developing countries than in other parts of the world. Wealthier countries have better health care systems, so more people die there from diseases associated with aging, such as heart disease.

more at NCWatlas.ca

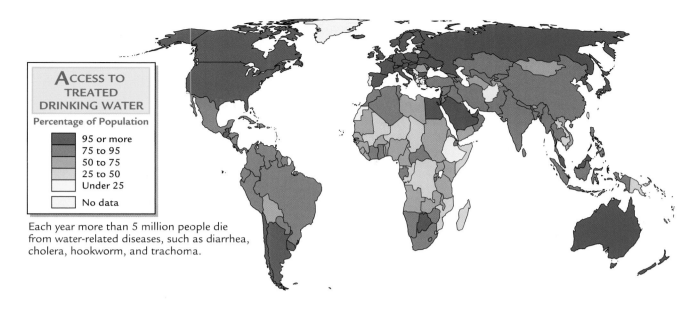

ACCESS TO TREATED DRINKING WATER

Percentage of Population

- 95 or more
- 75 to 95
- 50 to 75
- 25 to 50
- Under 25
- No data

Each year more than 5 million people die from water-related diseases, such as diarrhea, cholera, hookworm, and trachoma.

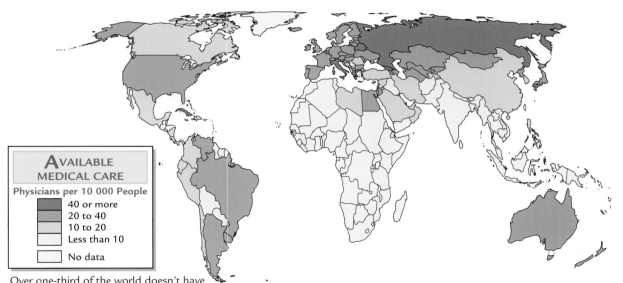

AVAILABLE MEDICAL CARE

Physicians per 10 000 People

- 40 or more
- 20 to 40
- 10 to 20
- Less than 10
- No data

Over one-third of the world doesn't have access to essential drugs. Millions die from diseases which easily could have been treated.

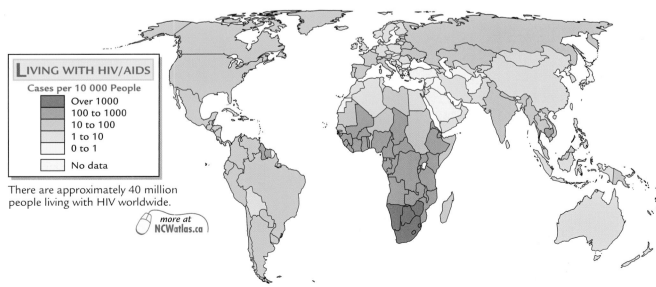

LIVING WITH HIV/AIDS

Cases per 10 000 People

- Over 1000
- 100 to 1000
- 10 to 100
- 1 to 10
- 0 to 1
- No data

There are approximately 40 million people living with HIV worldwide.

more at NCWatlas.ca

World Matters

RICH AND POOR

When people cannot afford basic human needs, such as food and housing, they are living in **poverty**. Poverty has different meanings in different parts of the world.

▶ **Absolute poverty** is poverty that threatens a person's life. In global terms, this is a household earning less than the equivalent of C$ 1.15 a day. Disease, hunger, and child labour plague people living in absolute poverty.

▶ **Relative poverty** is having fewer resources than others in a community or country. Countries define their national poverty lines differently.

▶ Depending on the community, a Canadian earning less than $14 303 to $20 778 a year, or $39 to $57 a day, is living in poverty. According to the Canadian Council on Social Development, about 5 million Canadians are living in poverty.

In Buenos Aires, Argentina, this shanty-town is home to 20 000 poverty-stricken residents. It is separated by railroad tracks from the city's wealthiest neighborhood, visible in the background.

CONCENTRATION OF WEALTH

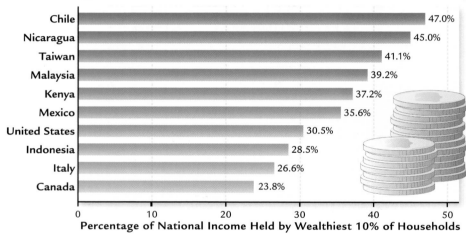

Country	Percentage
Chile	47.0%
Nicaragua	45.0%
Taiwan	41.1%
Malaysia	39.2%
Kenya	37.2%
Mexico	35.6%
United States	30.5%
Indonesia	28.5%
Italy	26.6%
Canada	23.8%

Percentage of National Income Held by Wealthiest 10% of Households

In many countries the largest portion of wealth is controlled by a small portion of the population. This **disparity of income** can lead to social unrest.

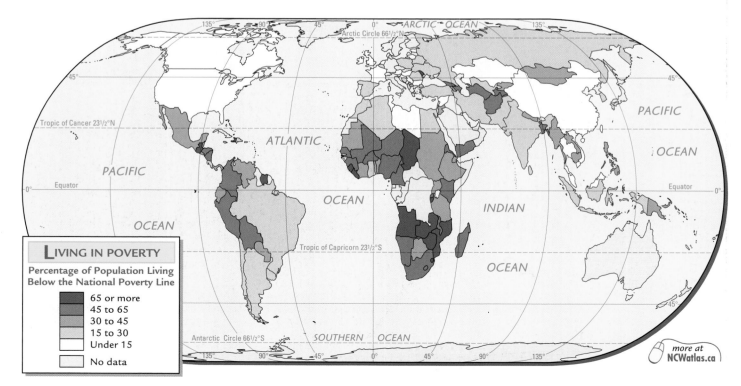

LIVING IN POVERTY

Percentage of Population Living Below the National Poverty Line

- 65 or more
- 45 to 65
- 30 to 45
- 15 to 30
- Under 15
- No data

more at NCWatlas.ca

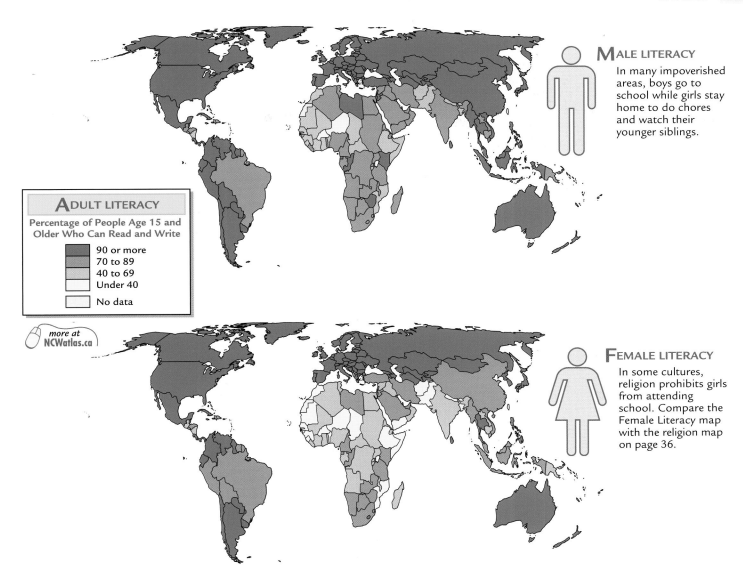

ADULT LITERACY

Percentage of People Age 15 and Older Who Can Read and Write

- 90 or more
- 70 to 89
- 40 to 69
- Under 40
- No data

more at NCWatlas.ca

MALE LITERACY

In many impoverished areas, boys go to school while girls stay home to do chores and watch their younger siblings.

FEMALE LITERACY

In some cultures, religion prohibits girls from attending school. Compare the Female Literacy map with the religion map on page 36.

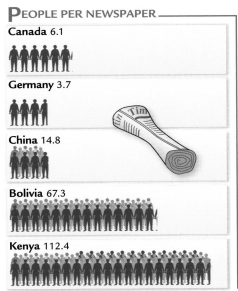

PEOPLE PER NEWSPAPER

Canada 6.1

Germany 3.7

China 14.8

Bolivia 67.3

Kenya 112.4

The proportion of newspapers to people is more an indicator of literacy than of wealth. However, a population's level of education can affect its wealth.

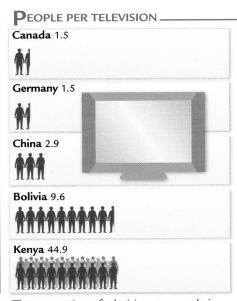

PEOPLE PER TELEVISION

Canada 1.5

Germany 1.5

China 2.9

Bolivia 9.6

Kenya 44.9

The proportion of televisions to people is a strong indicator of wealth. While many homes in Canada have a television in nearly every room, in some countries most communities have no televisions at all.

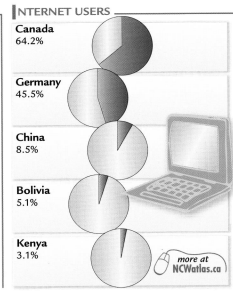

INTERNET USERS

Canada 64.2%

Germany 45.5%

China 8.5%

Bolivia 5.1%

Kenya 3.1%

more at NCWatlas.ca

As our world continues to become more technologically sophisticated, access to information is increasingly vital to economic prosperity.

World Matters

GLOBAL ECONOMY

As products, services, and money circulate around the world at a rapid rate, most countries have become economically interdependent, forming a **global economy**.

▶ **Gross Domestic Product**, or GDP, is the value of all goods and services produced within a country in a year. The United States alone accounts for one-fifth of the world's GDP.

▶ A **trade deficit** occurs when a country's imports exceed its exports. A **trade surplus** occurs when a country's exports exceed its imports.

▶ **Free trade** allows people to buy and sell goods across international borders without restrictions. It provides consumers with the cheapest possible goods, but cheaper imports may threaten domestic jobs.

BALANCE OF TRADE
CANADA

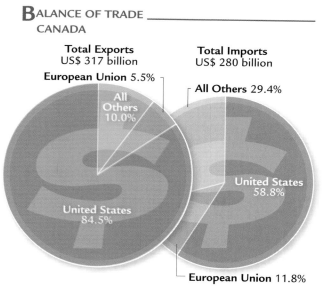

Total Exports
US$ 317 billion

European Union 5.5%
All Others 10.0%
United States 84.5%

Total Imports
US$ 280 billion

All Others 29.4%
United States 58.8%
European Union 11.8%

Balance of trade is the value of a country's exports minus the value of its imports. Canada has the seventh highest trade surplus in the world.

more at NCWatlas.ca

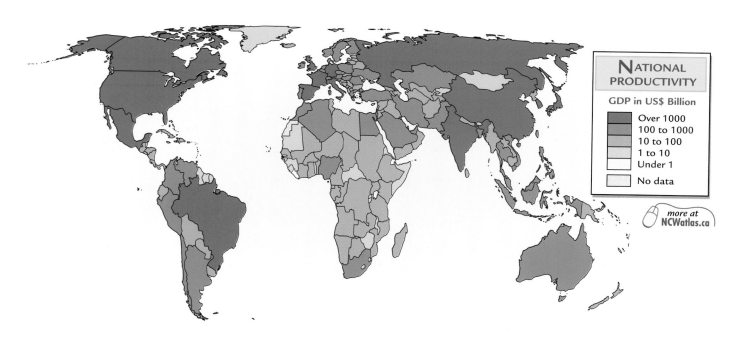

NATIONAL PRODUCTIVITY

GDP in US$ Billion

- Over 1000
- 100 to 1000
- 10 to 100
- 1 to 10
- Under 1
- No data

more at NCWatlas.ca

SINGLE-COMMODITY ECONOMIES

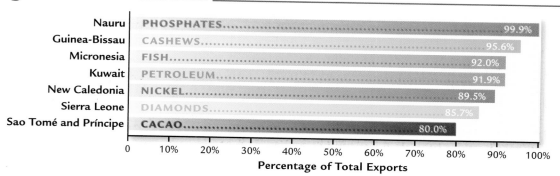

Country	Commodity	Percentage
Nauru	PHOSPHATES	99.9%
Guinea-Bissau	CASHEWS	95.6%
Micronesia	FISH	92.0%
Kuwait	PETROLEUM	91.9%
New Caledonia	NICKEL	89.5%
Sierra Leone	DIAMONDS	85.7%
Sao Tomé and Príncipe	CACAO	80.0%

Percentage of Total Exports

Many places rely on a single natural resource or crop for 80 percent or more of their exports. They run the risk of becoming dependent on other countries for goods and services. Their economies also are vulnerable to sudden changes in international prices and demands for their key commodity.

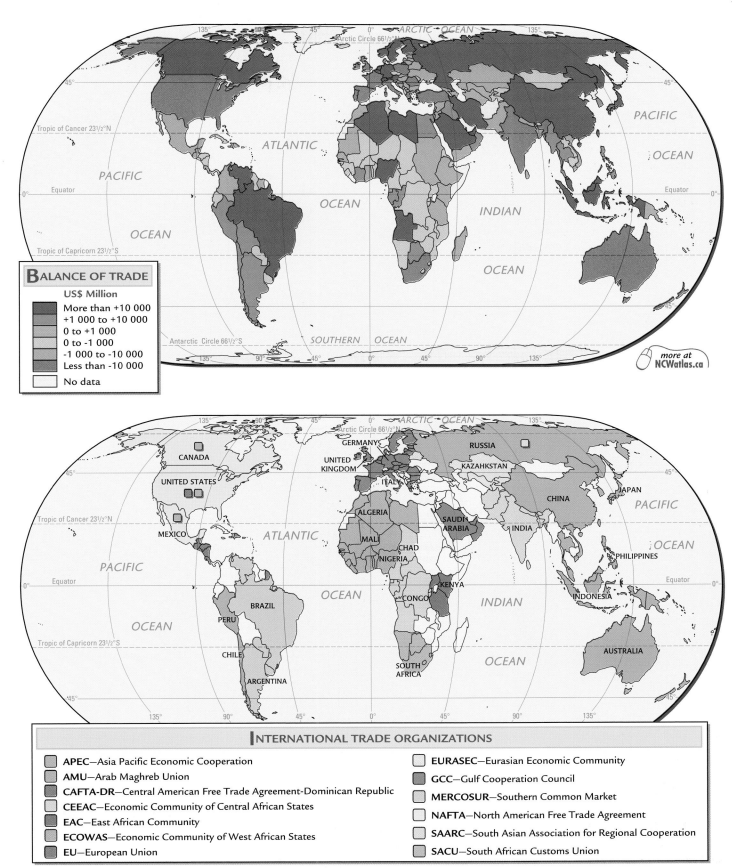

BALANCE OF TRADE

US$ Million

- More than +10 000
- +1 000 to +10 000
- 0 to +1 000
- 0 to -1 000
- -1 000 to -10 000
- Less than -10 000
- No data

more at NCWatlas.ca

INTERNATIONAL TRADE ORGANIZATIONS

- **APEC**—Asia Pacific Economic Cooperation
- **AMU**—Arab Maghreb Union
- **CAFTA-DR**—Central American Free Trade Agreement-Dominican Republic
- **CEEAC**—Economic Community of Central African States
- **EAC**—East African Community
- **ECOWAS**—Economic Community of West African States
- **EU**—European Union

- **EURASEC**—Eurasian Economic Community
- **GCC**—Gulf Cooperation Council
- **MERCOSUR**—Southern Common Market
- **NAFTA**—North American Free Trade Agreement
- **SAARC**—South Asian Association for Regional Cooperation
- **SACU**—South African Customs Union

Trade organizations are established by agreements between governments to increase free trade.
NAFTA and EU are among the wealthiest and most influential trade organizations in the world.
(For more information, see page 113.)

World Matters

CULTURAL DIVERSITY

Culture is the way of life of a given human society. Every society in the world has a unique culture.

▶ Aspects of culture include a society's language, religion, art, customs, ethnicity, institutions, technology, and other traits.

▶ Countries can have multiple cultures, and cultures can cross national boundaries.

▶ Language and religion are two distinguishing features of a culture. Thousands of religions are practiced and about 6000 languages are spoken in the world today.

▶ **Language families** are groups of related languages that developed slowly over time from a single earlier **parent language**.

Mother Teresa was a Roman Catholic nun who helped the poor in India. Indians of all faiths now revere her. Girls hold symbols of Hinduism, Islam, and Christianity during a rally in her honour.

MAJOR RELIGIONS

Predominant Belief
- Judaism
- Buddhism
- Christianity
- Hinduism
- Islam
- Traditional or folk
- Nonreligious or atheist

Other Significant Belief
- ⊛ Buddhism
- ✝ Christianity
- ॐ Hinduism
- ☾ Islam
- ◆ Traditional or folk
- ● Nonreligious or atheist
- ✳ Urban area with large Jewish population

more at NCWatlas.ca

MAJOR RELIGIONS

Each of these religions can be broken down into smaller groups. For example, there are three major groups of Christians: Roman Catholics, Protestants, and Eastern Orthodox. Among Protestants alone, there are hundreds of denominations.

Who Are You?

Ethnicity is complex. For example, if your ethnic background is Chinese, you might speak Mandarin at home and celebrate Chinese New Year. At the same time, you might speak English at school and celebrate Canadian holidays such as Canada Day and Thanksgiving.

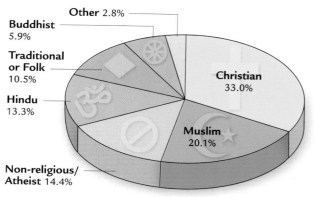

Other 2.8%
Buddhist 5.9%
Traditional or Folk 10.5%
Hindu 13.3%
Non-religious/Atheist 14.4%
Christian 33.0%
Muslim 20.1%

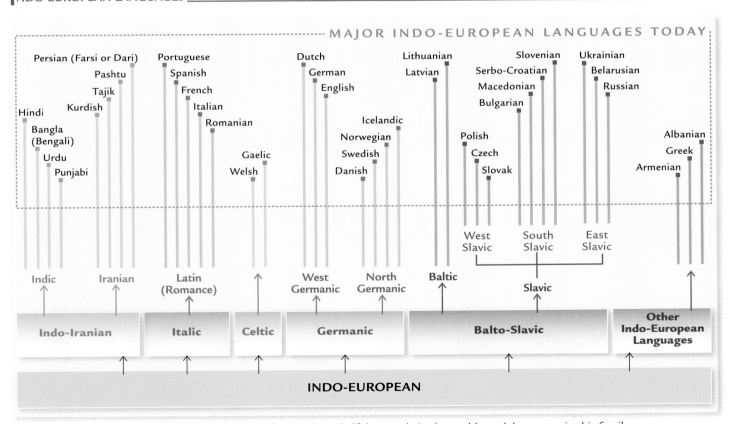

LANGUAGE FAMILIES

- Afro-Asian
- American Indian
- Australian
- Dravidian
- Indo-European
- Inuktitut
- Japanese and Korean
- Khoisan
- Malayo-Polynesian
- Mon-Khmer
- Niger-Congo (Bantu)
- Nilo-Saharan
- Papuan
- Sino Tibetan
- Uralic and Altaic

Unclassifiable

more at NCWatlas.ca

INDO-EUROPEAN LANGUAGES

MAJOR INDO-EUROPEAN LANGUAGES TODAY

Persian (Farsi or Dari)
Pashtu
Tajik
Hindi
Kurdish
Bangla (Bengali)
Urdu
Punjabi

Portuguese
Spanish
French
Italian
Romanian
Gaelic
Welsh

Dutch
German
English
Icelandic
Norwegian
Swedish
Danish

Lithuanian
Latvian

Slovenian
Serbo-Croatian
Macedonian
Bulgarian
Polish
Czech
Slovak

Ukrainian
Belarusian
Russian

Albanian
Greek
Armenian

West Slavic | South Slavic | East Slavic

Indic | **Iranian** | **Latin (Romance)** | | **West Germanic** | **North Germanic** | **Baltic** | **Slavic**

Indo-Iranian | **Italic** | **Celtic** | **Germanic** | **Balto-Slavic** | **Other Indo-European Languages**

INDO-EUROPEAN

Indo-European is the most widely spoken language family. About half the people in the world speak languages in this family, which originated in an area that extended from northern India to western Europe.

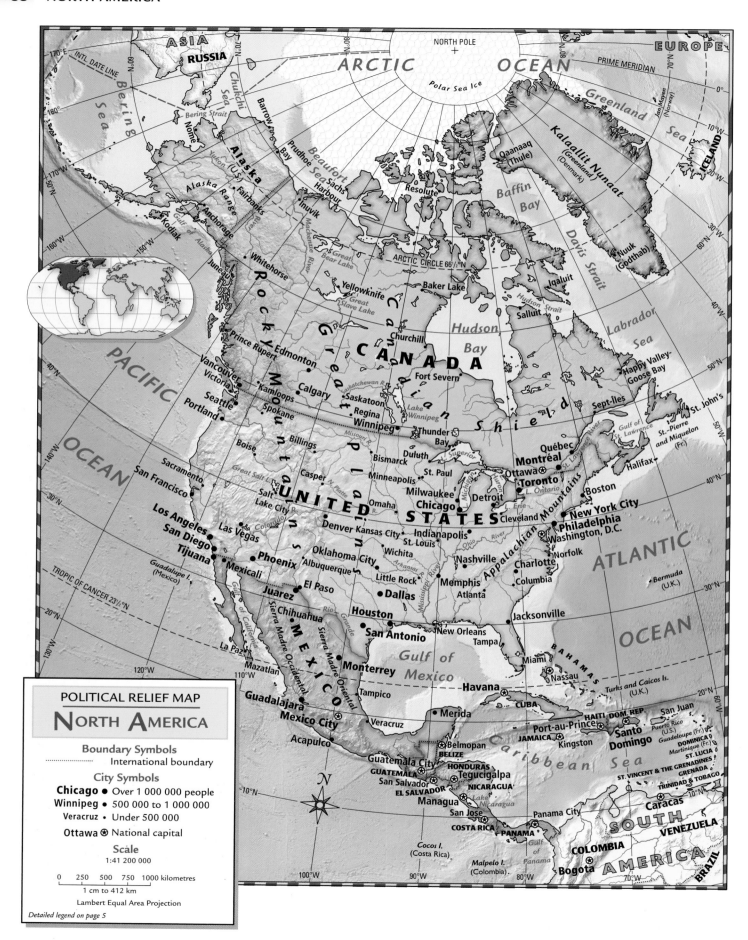

POLITICAL RELIEF MAP

NORTH AMERICA

Boundary Symbols
.... International boundary

City Symbols
Chicago ● Over 1 000 000 people
Winnipeg ● 500 000 to 1 000 000
Veracruz ● Under 500 000

Ottawa ⊗ National capital

Scale
1:41 200 000

0   250   500   750   1000 kilometres

1 cm to 412 km

Lambert Equal Area Projection

Detailed legend on page 5

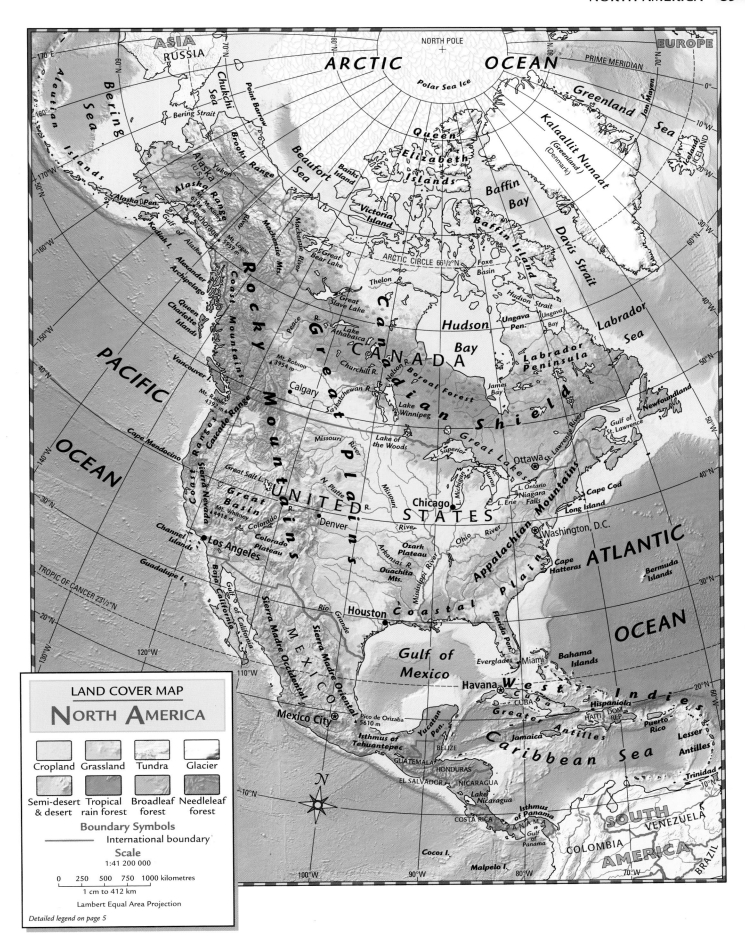

ASIA
RUSSIA
ARCTIC OCEAN
EUROPE
PRIME MERIDIAN
NORTH POLE
Polar Sea Ice

Aleutian Islands
Bering Sea
Chukchi Sea
Point Barrow
Bering Strait
Greenland Sea
Jan Mayen
Iceland
ICELAND

Brooks Range
Beaufort Sea
Banks Island
Queen Elizabeth Islands
Kalaallit Nunaat
(Greenland)
(Denmark)

Alaska Pen.
Alaska Range
Mt. McKinley
6194 m
Yukon River
Mackenzie Mts.
Victoria Island
Baffin Bay
Davis Strait

Kodiak I.
Gulf of Alaska
Anchorage
Mt. Logan 5959 m
Mackenzie River
Great Bear Lake
ARCTIC CIRCLE 66½°N
Baffin Island
Foxe Basin

Alexander Archipelago
Queen Charlotte Islands
Great Slave Lake
Thelon
Hudson Strait
Ungava Pen.
Ungava Bay
Labrador Sea

Vancouver I.
Coast Mountains
Peace R.
Lake Athabasca
CANADA
Hudson Bay
Labrador Peninsula

PACIFIC OCEAN
Cape Mendocino
Rocky Mountains
Mt. Robson 3954 m
Calgary
Churchill R.
Nelson River
Boreal Forest
James Bay
Labrador
Newfoundland

Coast Ranges
Cascade Range
Sierra Nevada
Great Salt L.
Saskatchewan R.
Lake Winnipeg
Great Lakes
Gulf of St. Lawrence

Mt. Rainier 4392 m
Missouri River
Lake of the Woods
L. Superior
St. Lawrence River
Ottawa
Cape Cod

Great Basin
Mt. Whitney 4418 m
N. Platte R.
UNITED STATES
L. Michigan
L. Huron
L. Ontario
Niagara Falls
L. Erie
Long Island

Channel Islands
Los Angeles
Colorado R.
Denver
Missouri River
Chicago
Ohio River
Appalachian Mountains
Washington, D.C.
ATLANTIC OCEAN
Bermuda Islands

Guadalupe I.
TROPIC OF CANCER 23½°N
Colorado Plateau
Ozark Plateau
Arkansas R.
Ouachita Mts.
Mississippi River
Cape Hatteras

Baja California
Gulf of California
Sierra Madre Occidental
Rio Grande
Houston
Coastal Plain
Florida Pen.
Everglades
Miami
Bahama Islands

MEXICO
Sierra Madre Oriental
Gulf of Mexico
Havana
West Indies
CUBA

Mexico City
Pico de Orizaba 5610 m
Yucatan Pen.
Greater Antilles
HAITI
HISPANIOLA
DOM. REP.
Puerto Rico
Lesser Antilles

Isthmus of Tehuantepec
BELIZE
Jamaica
Caribbean Sea

GUATEMALA
HONDURAS
EL SALVADOR
NICARAGUA
Lake Nicaragua
COSTA RICA
Isthmus of Panama
PANAMA
Gulf of Panama
SOUTH AMERICA
VENEZUELA
COLOMBIA
BRAZIL

Cocos I.
Malpelo I.
Trinidad

LAND COVER MAP
NORTH AMERICA

Cropland Grassland Tundra Glacier

Semi-desert & desert Tropical rain forest Broadleaf forest Needleleaf forest

Boundary Symbols
International boundary

Scale
1:41 200 000

0 250 500 750 1000 kilometres

1 cm to 412 km

Lambert Equal Area Projection

Detailed legend on page 5

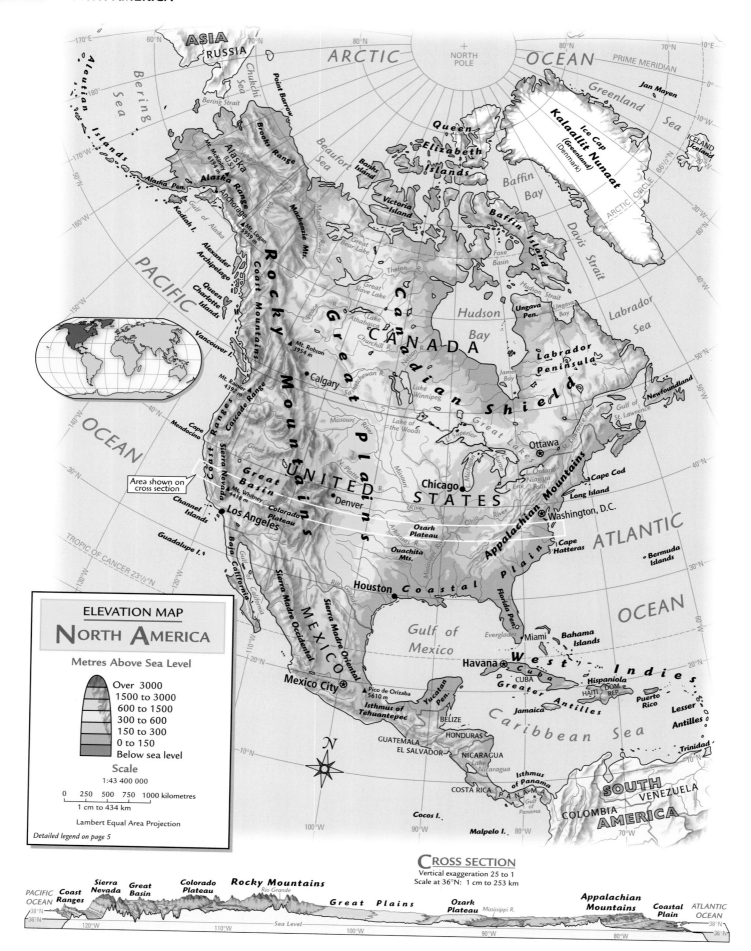

ASIA
RUSSIA
ARCTIC OCEAN
NORTH POLE
PRIME MERIDIAN

Aleutian Islands
Bering Sea
Chukchi Sea
Bering Strait
Point Barrow
Beaufort Sea
Queen Elizabeth Islands
Banks Island
Greenland
Jan Mayen
ICELAND
Iceland

Alaska Pen.
Alaska (U.S.)
Brooks Range
Mt. McKinley 6194 m
Anchorage
Alaska Range
Mt. Logan 5959 m
Mackenzie River
Victoria Island
Baffin Bay
Foxe Basin
Ice Cap
Kalaallit Nunaat
(Greenland)
(Denmark)
ARCTIC CIRCLE 66½°N

Kodiak I.
Gulf of Alaska
Alexander Archipelago
Queen Charlotte Islands
Coast Mountains
Great Bear Lake
Thelon R.
Great Slave Lake
Baffin Island
Hudson Strait
Davis Strait
Labrador Sea

PACIFIC
Vancouver I.
Rocky Mountains
Mt. Robson 3954 m
Peace River
Lake Athabasca
Churchill R.
Great Plains
CANADA
Canadian Shield
Hudson Bay
James Bay
Ungava Pen.
Ungava Bay
Labrador Peninsula
Newfoundland

Cape Mendocino
Coast Ranges
Cascade Range
Mt. Rainier 4392 m
Calgary
Saskatchewan R.
Missouri River
Lake Winnipeg
Lake of the Woods
Lake Superior
Great Lakes
L. Michigan
L. Huron
Gulf of St. Lawrence
St. Lawrence River

OCEAN
Area shown on cross section
Sierra Nevada
Great Basin
Great Salt Lake
UNITED STATES
N. Platte R.
Missouri R.
Ottawa
L. Ontario
Niagara Falls
L. Erie
Appalachian Mountains
Cape Cod
Long Island

Channel Islands
Mt. Whitney 4418 m
Colorado Plateau
Denver
Chicago
Ohio River
Washington, D.C.
ATLANTIC

Los Angeles
Colorado R.
Arkansas River
Ozark Plateau
Mississippi River
Cape Hatteras
Bermuda Islands

Guadalupe I.
TROPIC OF CANCER 23½°N
Baja California
Gulf of California
Sierra Madre Occidental
Rio Grande
Houston
Ouachita Mts.
Coastal Plain
Florida Pen.
OCEAN

ELEVATION MAP
NORTH AMERICA

Metres Above Sea Level

Over 3000
1500 to 3000
600 to 1500
300 to 600
150 to 300
0 to 150
Below sea level

Scale
1:43 400 000

0   250   500   750   1000 kilometres
1 cm to 434 km

Lambert Equal Area Projection

Detailed legend on page 5

MEXICO
Sierra Madre Oriental
Mexico City
Pico de Orizaba 5610 m
Isthmus of Tehuantepec
Yucatan Pen.
BELIZE
Gulf of Mexico
Everglades
Miami
Bahama Islands
Havana
West Indies
CUBA
Greater Antilles
Jamaica
Hispaniola
HAITI
DOM. REP.
Puerto Rico
Lesser Antilles
Caribbean Sea
Trinidad

N
GUATEMALA
EL SALVADOR
HONDURAS
NICARAGUA
Lake Nicaragua
Isthmus of Panama
COSTA RICA
PANAMA
Gulf of Panama
Cocos I.
Malpelo I.
COLOMBIA
SOUTH AMERICA
VENEZUELA

CROSS SECTION

Vertical exaggeration 25 to 1
Scale at 36°N: 1 cm to 253 km

PACIFIC OCEAN
Coast Ranges
Sierra Nevada
Great Basin
Colorado Plateau
Rocky Mountains
Rio Grande
Great Plains
Ozark Plateau
Mississippi R.
Appalachian Mountains
Coastal Plain
ATLANTIC OCEAN
Sea Level
38°N
36°N
120°W
110°W
100°W
90°W
80°W
38°N
36°N

RAIN SHADOW EFFECT

When moist warm air meets a mountain range, it rises, cools, and creates clouds that rain on the **windward** side of the mountain. The air then becomes drier as it descends the opposite **leeward** side of the mountain. Few clouds reach the leeward side, so it is relatively dry. Pachema Point lies near the Pacific Coast on the windward side of the Coast Mountains, while Penticton lies on the leeward side.

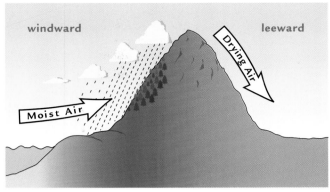

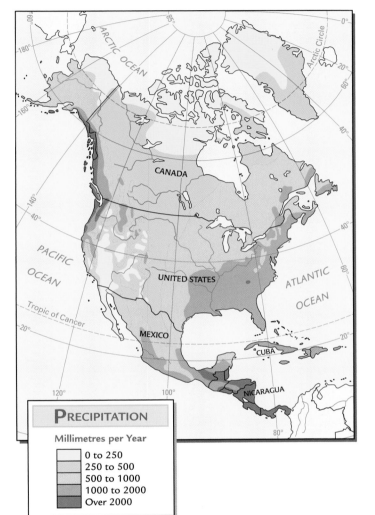

CLIMOGRAPHS

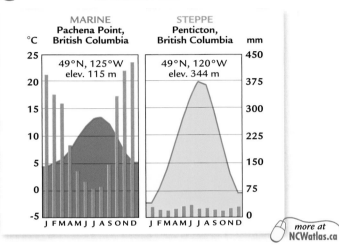

more at NCWatlas.ca

PRECIPITATION

Millimetres per Year

- 0 to 250
- 250 to 500
- 500 to 1000
- 1000 to 2000
- Over 2000

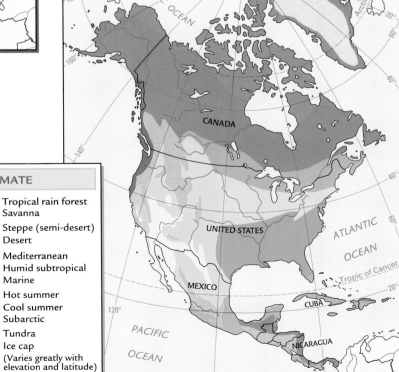

From the Greatest Height

Stretching from the Gaspé Peninsula in Québec to the southern United States, the Appalachians are some of the oldest mountains in the world. Three hundred million years ago, before the earliest dinosaurs, the Appalachians were taller than the Himalayas are today. Since then, erosion has reduced them to their present height.

CLIMATE

Tropical		Tropical rain forest
		Savanna
Dry		Steppe (semi-desert)
		Desert
Mild		Mediterranean
		Humid subtropical
		Marine
Continental		Hot summer
		Cool summer
		Subarctic
Polar		Tundra
		Ice cap
Highland		(Varies greatly with elevation and latitude)

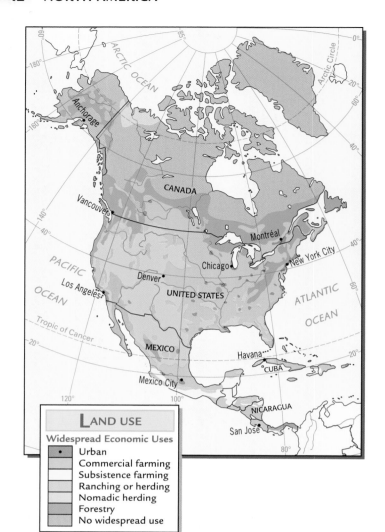

Wheat grows throughout the Interior Plains of Canada and the United States, making North America one of the world's leading wheat producers.

Waves of Grain

North America is one of the world's leading agricultural exporters, shipping corn, soybeans, wheat, and other crops to Europe, Japan, and China. The United States and Canada rank first and third in wheat exports, while the United States ranks first in soybean exports.

Mexico is rich in oil. Its largest oil field, in the Gulf of Mexico, produces over 2 million barrels of oil per day. It is the second largest oil field in the world. Mexico exports half of its oil. Forty percent of Mexico's national budget is funded by oil revenues.

ENERGY RESOURCES AND METALS
- Coal
- Oil (petroleum)
- Natural gas
- Uranium
- Aluminum (bauxite)
- Copper
- Gold
- Iron
- Lead
- Manganese
- Nickel
- Silver
- Tin
- Zinc

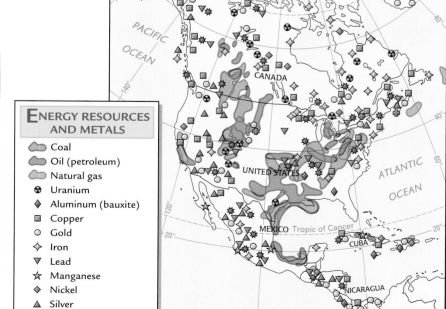

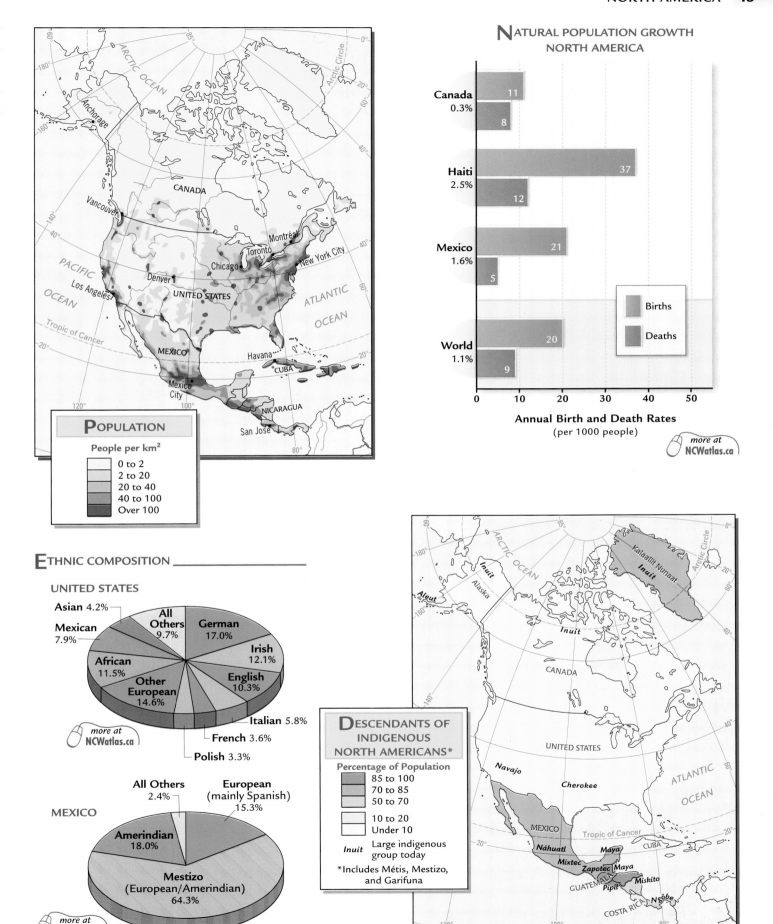

POPULATION

People per km²

- 0 to 2
- 2 to 20
- 20 to 40
- 40 to 100
- Over 100

NATURAL POPULATION GROWTH
NORTH AMERICA

Canada 0.3%
- Births: 11
- Deaths: 8

Haiti 2.5%
- Births: 37
- Deaths: 12

Mexico 1.6%
- Births: 21
- Deaths: 5

World 1.1%
- Births: 20
- Deaths: 9

Births / Deaths

Annual Birth and Death Rates
(per 1000 people)

more at NCWatlas.ca

ETHNIC COMPOSITION

UNITED STATES

- Asian 4.2%
- Mexican 7.9%
- African 11.5%
- Other European 14.6%
- All Others 9.7%
- German 17.0%
- Irish 12.1%
- English 10.3%
- Italian 5.8%
- French 3.6%
- Polish 3.3%

more at NCWatlas.ca

MEXICO

- All Others 2.4%
- European (mainly Spanish) 15.3%
- Amerindian 18.0%
- Mestizo (European/Amerindian) 64.3%

more at NCWatlas.ca

DESCENDANTS OF INDIGENOUS NORTH AMERICANS*

Percentage of Population

- 85 to 100
- 70 to 85
- 50 to 70
- 10 to 20
- Under 10

Inuit — Large indigenous group today

*Includes Métis, Mestizo, and Garifuna

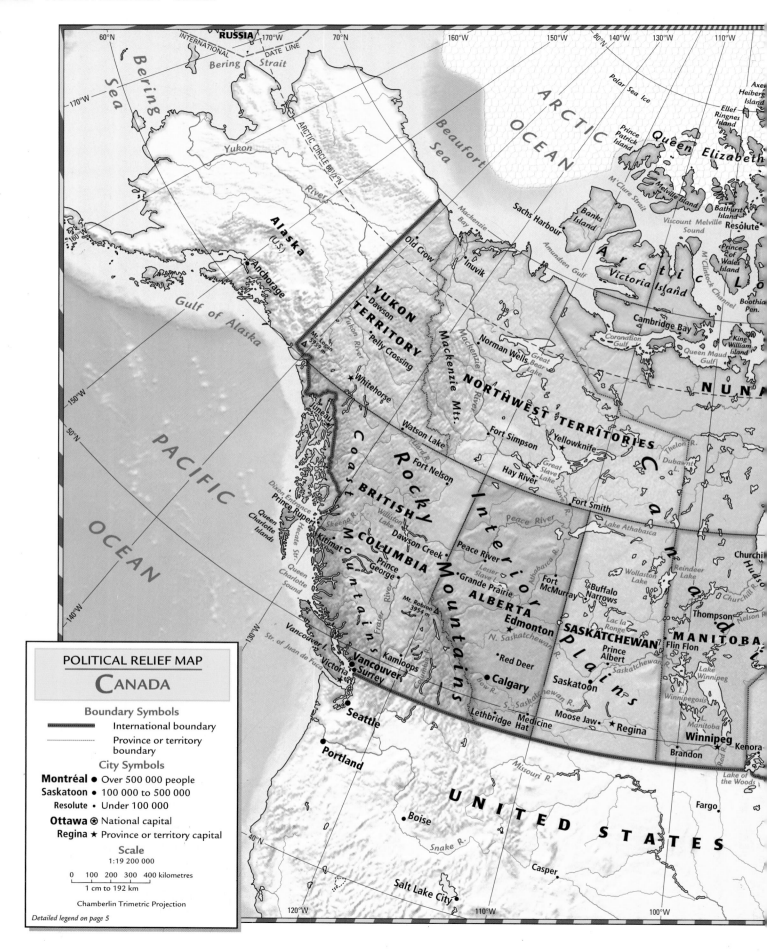

ICELAND

Kalaallit Nunaat
(Greenland)
(Denmark)

Baffin
Bay

Denmark Strait

ARCTIC CIRCLE 66½°N

Ellesmere Island

Islands

Qaanaaq (Thule)

Devon Island

Kane
Basin

Lancaster Sound

omerset
Island

Clyde River

Davis Strait

Nuuk (Godthab)

Baffin Island

wlands

Gulf of
Boothia

Kugaaruk

Prince
Charles I.

Melville
Peninsula

Foxe

Cape Farewell

ATLANTIC

Foxe
Basin

Southampton
Island

Foxe
Peninsula

Cumberland Sound

Iqaluit

Frobisher Bay

UT

N

OCEAN

Foxe Channel

Hudson Strait

Cape
Chidley

Labrador

Sea

Chesterfield
Inlet

Rankin Inlet

Coats
Island

Salluit

Mansel
Island

Ungava
Peninsula

Ungava
Bay

R. George

Kuujjuaq

Hudson

Bay

Labrador

NEWFOUNDLAND
AND
LABRADOR

Fort Severn

Belcher
Islands

Kuujjuarapik

Peninsula

R. Feuilles

Smallwood
Res.

Happy Valley-
Goose Bay

Churchill R.

Labrador City

St. John's

ay

Lowlands

Severn R.

Winisk R.

James
Bay

Akimiski
I.

QUÉBEC

Rés.
Manicouagan

Corner Brook

Newfoundland

Cape Race

Strait of Belle Isle

Albany R.

Moosonee

L.
Mistassini

Sept-Îles

Anticosti
Island

Gulf of
St. Lawrence

St.-Pierre and
Miquelon
(France)

50°N

a

NTARIO

S

h

i

e

l

d

Saguenay

St. Lawrence River

PRINCE
EDWARD
ISLAND

Charlottetown

Cape
Breton
Island

Sable Island
(Nova Scotia)

L.
Nipigon

Val-d'Or

NEW
BRUNSWICK

Fredericton

NOVA SCOTIA

Halifax

Thunder Bay

Sault
Ste. Marie

Sudbury

Ottawa R.

Gatineau

Québec

St. John R.

Saint John

Montréal

Bay of Fundy

Cape Sable

Lake Superior

L.
Nipissing

Ottawa

Yarmouth

Georgian
Bay

L. Simcoe

Kingston

Boston

nneapolis

Lake Michigan

Lake Huron

Toronto

L. Ontario

Mississauga

Hamilton

London

Buffalo

Detroit

Windsor

Niagara
Falls

New York City

ssissippi R.

Chicago

Lake Erie

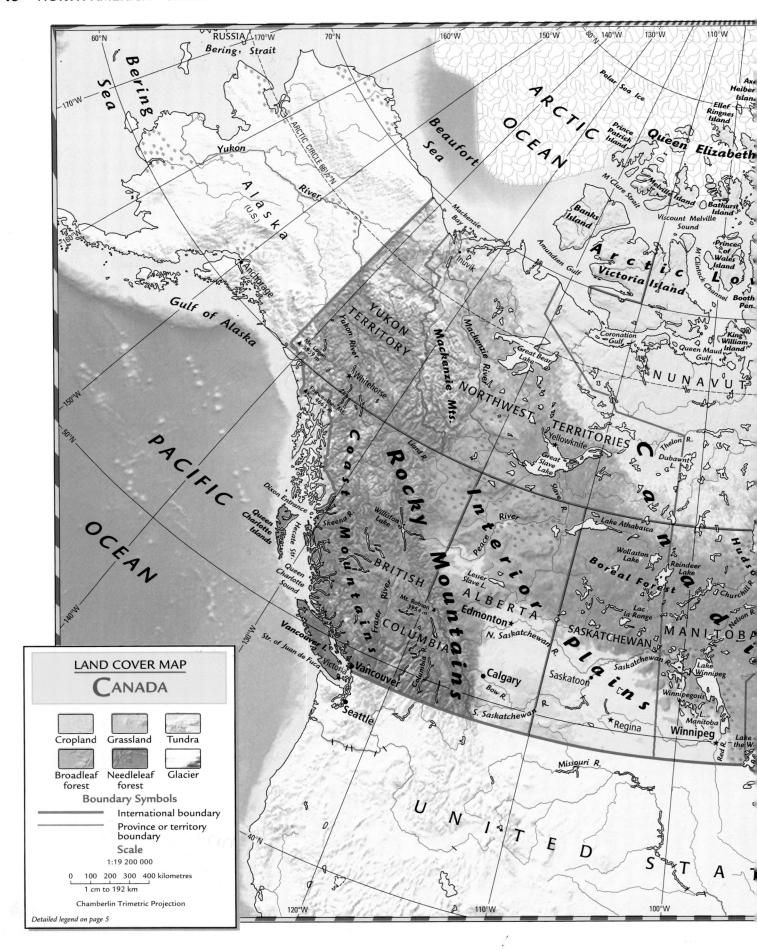

60°N
RUSSIA
Bering Strait
170°W
70°N
160°W
150°W
140°W
130°W
110°W
80°N

Bering Sea

ARCTIC OCEAN

Polar Sea Ice

Axel Heiberg Island

Ellef Ringnes Island

Prince Patrick Island

Queen Elizabeth

170°W

Yukon

ARCTIC CIRCLE 66½°N

M'Clure Strait

Melville Island

Bathurst Island

160°W

Alaska (U.S.)

River

Beaufort Sea

Mackenzie Bay

Viscount Melville Sound

Banks Island

Prince of Wales Island

Anchorage

Inuvik

Amundsen Gulf

A r c t i c   L o

Booth Pen.

Victoria Island

M'Clintock Channel

Gulf of Alaska

Mt. Logan 5959 m

YUKON TERRITORY

Yukon River

Whitehorse

Mackenzie Mts.

Mackenzie River

NORTHWEST

Great Bear Lake

Coronation Gulf

King William Island

Queen Maud Gulf

50°N

Fairweather Mt. 4663 m

Coast Mountains

Liard R.

TERRITORIES

Yellowknife

Thelon R.

Dubawnt L.

NUNAVUT

PACIFIC

Dixon Entrance

Queen Charlotte Islands

Hecate Str.

Skeena R.

Williston Lake

Rocky Mountains

Peace River

Interior

River

Great Slave Lake

Slave R.

Lake Athabasca

Wollaston Lake

Boreal Forest

Reindeer Lake

Hud

Churchill R.

Nelson R.

OCEAN

Queen Charlotte Sound

BRITISH COLUMBIA

Mt. Robson 3954 m

River

Fraser

Plains

ALBERTA

Edmonton

Lesser Slave L.

N. Saskatchewan

Lac la Ronge

SASKATCHEWAN

MANITOBA

C a n a d

Vancouver I.

Victoria

Vancouver

Columbia R.

Calgary

Bow R.

Saskatoon

Saskatchewan R.

Lake Winnipeg

Str. of Juan de Fuca

Seattle

S. Saskatchewan

Winnipegosis

Winnipeg

L. Manitoba

Regina

Red R.

Lake the W

130°W

120°W

Missouri R.

UNITED STA

110°W

100°W

40°N

Detailed legend on page 5

LAND COVER MAP
Canada

Cropland   Grassland   Tundra

Broadleaf forest   Needleleaf forest   Glacier

Boundary Symbols

International boundary

Province or territory boundary

Scale

1:19 200 000

0   100   200   300   400 kilometres

1 cm to 192 km

Chamberlin Trimetric Projection

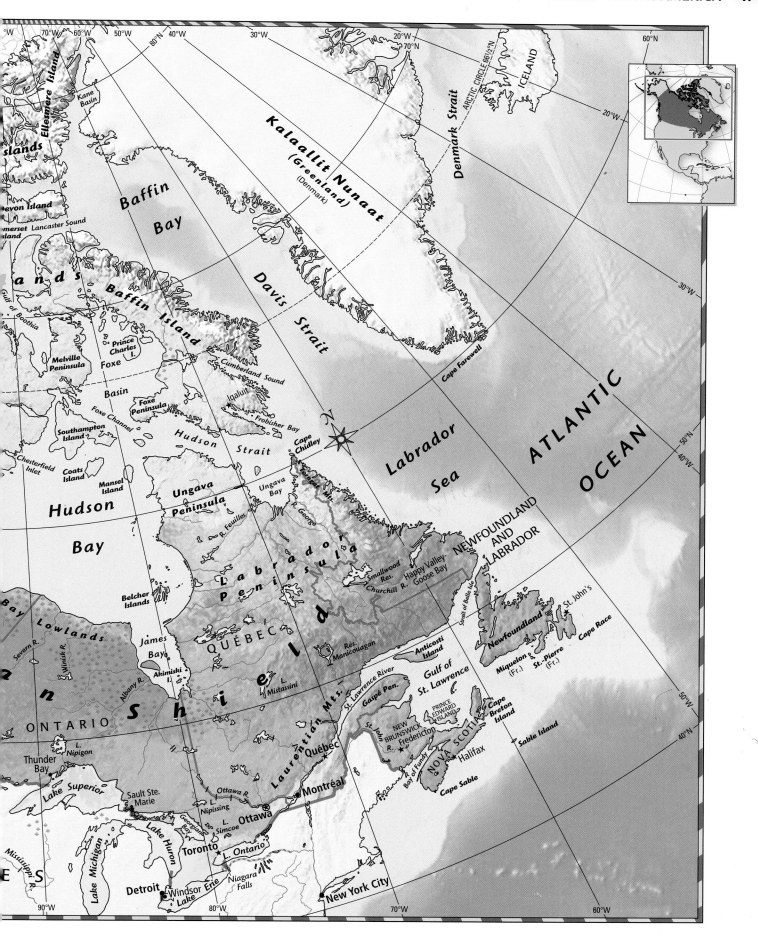

70°W   60°W   50°W   40°W   30°W   20°W   70°N   60°N

slands
Ellesmere Island
Kane Basin
Devon Island
merset Island
Lancaster Sound
Gulf of Boothia
ands

Baffin Bay

Baffin Island

Prince Charles I.
Melville Peninsula
Foxe
Foxe Basin
Foxe Peninsula
Foxe Channel
Southampton Island
Hudson Strait
Cumberland Sound
Iqaluit
Frobisher Bay
Cape Chidley

Davis Strait

Kalaallit Nunaat (Greenland) (Denmark)

ARCTIC CIRCLE 66½°N

ICELAND

Denmark Strait

Cape Farewell

Labrador Sea

ATLANTIC OCEAN

Chesterfield Inlet
Coats Island
Mansel Island
Ungava Peninsula
Ungava Bay
R. aux Feuilles
R. George
Torngat Mts.

Hudson Bay

Belcher Islands

Labrador Peninsula

Smallwood Res.
Churchill R.
Happy Valley-Goose Bay

NEWFOUNDLAND AND LABRADOR

Strait of Belle Isle

Newfoundland
St. John's
Cape Race

Bay
Lowlands
Severn R.
Winisk R.
James Bay
Akimiski
Albany R.
QUÉBEC
Rés. Manicouagan
Mistassini
L.
Anticosti Island
Gulf of St. Lawrence
Miquelon (Fr.)
St.-Pierre (Fr.)

ONTARIO
Shield
Thunder Bay
L. Nipigon
Lake Superior
Sault Ste. Marie
St. Lawrence River
Gaspé Pen.
NEW BRUNSWICK
Fredericton
St. John R.
PRINCE EDWARD ISLAND
Cape Breton Island
NOVA SCOTIA
Halifax
Sable Island

Ottawa R.
L. Nipissing
Georgian Bay
L. Simcoe
Ottawa
Québec
Montréal
Bay of Fundy
Cape Sable

Mississippi R.
Lake Michigan
Lake Huron
Toronto
L. Ontario
Detroit
Windsor
Lake Erie
Niagara Falls
New York City

90°W   80°W   70°W   60°W

50°N   40°W   50°N   40°N

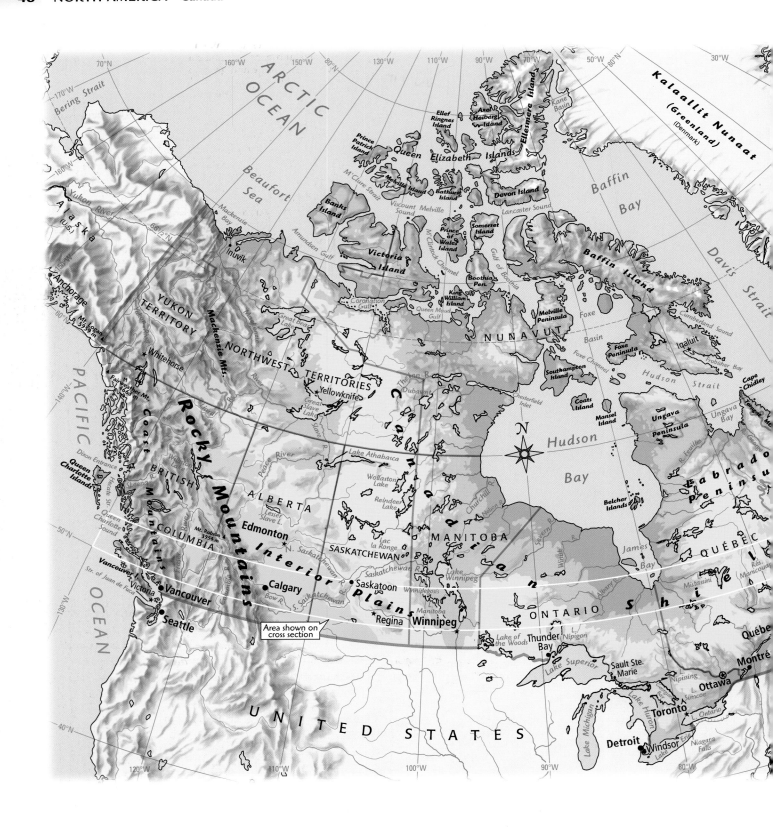

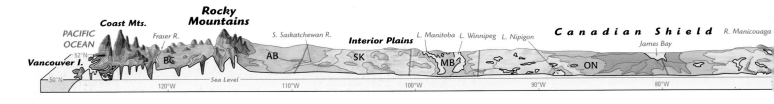

Vancouver I.

PACIFIC OCEAN

Coast Mts.

Rocky Mountains

Fraser R.

BC

S. Saskatchewan R.

Interior Plains

AB

SK

L. Manitoba L. Winnipeg L. Nipigon

MB

Canadian Shield

R. Manicouaga

James Bay

ON

52°N

Sea Level

120°W

110°W

100°W

90°W

80°W

50°N

HYDROELECTRICITY

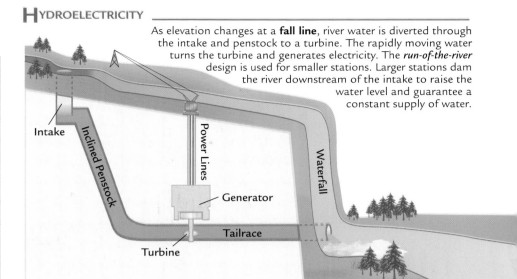

As elevation changes at a **fall line**, river water is diverted through the intake and penstock to a turbine. The rapidly moving water turns the turbine and generates electricity. The *run-of-the-river* design is used for smaller stations. Larger stations dam the river downstream of the intake to raise the water level and guarantee a constant supply of water.

Labels in diagram: Intake, Inclined Penstock, Power Lines, Generator, Turbine, Tailrace, Waterfall

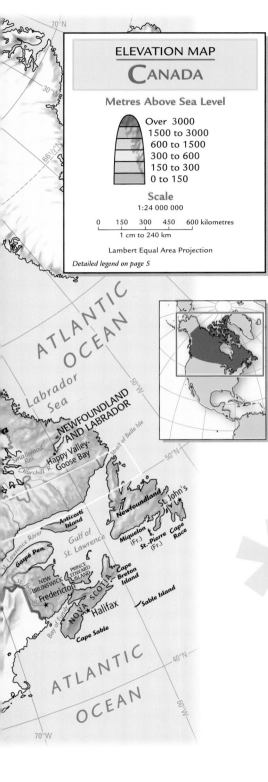

ELEVATION MAP

CANADA

Metres Above Sea Level

Over 3000
1500 to 3000
600 to 1500
300 to 600
150 to 300
0 to 150

Scale
1:24 000 000

0   150   300   450   600 kilometres
1 cm to 240 km

Lambert Equal Area Projection

Detailed legend on page 5

Canada leads the world in hydroelectric production. Hydroelectricity is Canada's main renewable energy source. Provincially-owned electric utilities have built massive stations along Canada's rivers. British Columbia, Québec, and the Atlantic Provinces rely heavily on hydro-electricity as a source of electrical energy. (For more information, see page 67.)

On the Rebound

A glacier covered Hudson Bay about 70 000 years ago. The crushing weight of the glacier caused the land to sink, much like a ship sinks when it is loaded with cargo. As the ice melted, the land gradually sprang back—a phenomenon known as isostatic rebound. The land in the region has rebounded about 250 metres since the glacier started to retreat about 12 000 years ago. (See page 50 for information about continental glaciation.)

The Canadian Rockies stretch across British Columbia and Alberta. The Rockies are part of a chain of mountain ranges that extends the length of the Americas.

CROSS SECTION
Vertical exaggeration 47 to 1
Scale at 50° N: 1 cm to 219 km

ATLANTIC OCEAN

QC   NL

ECOZONES

Canada has 15 different ecozones, which contain unique plants and animals. An ecozone's biology is determined by its land and water, called **physiographic**, features as well as by its climate. The plants and animals found in each ecozone are distinctly suited to survive in that region.

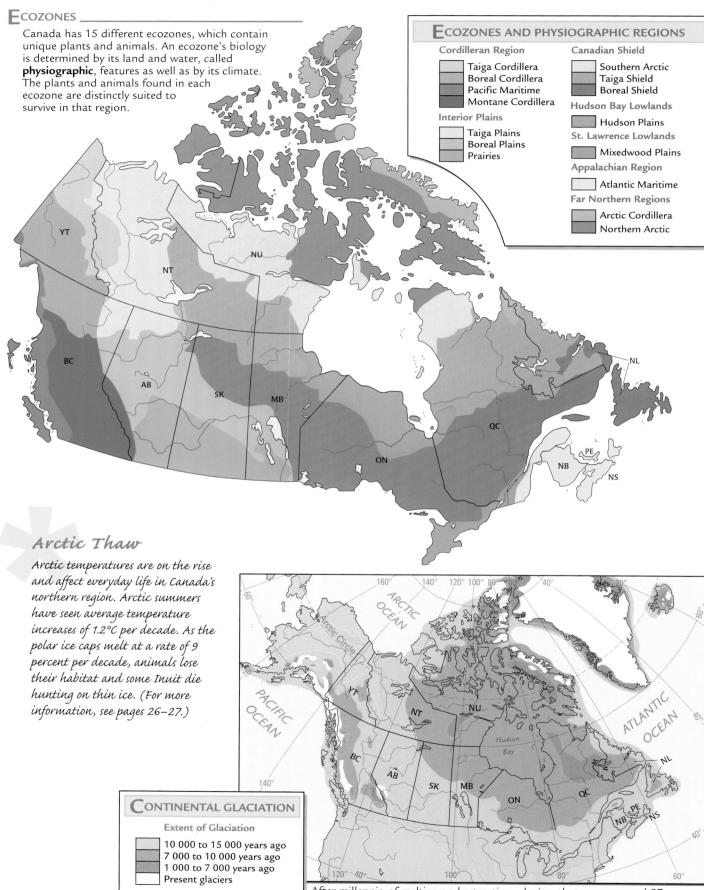

ECOZONES AND PHYSIOGRAPHIC REGIONS

Cordilleran Region
- Taiga Cordillera
- Boreal Cordillera
- Pacific Maritime
- Montane Cordillera

Interior Plains
- Taiga Plains
- Boreal Plains
- Prairies

Canadian Shield
- Southern Arctic
- Taiga Shield
- Boreal Shield

Hudson Bay Lowlands
- Hudson Plains

St. Lawrence Lowlands
- Mixedwood Plains

Appalachian Region
- Atlantic Maritime

Far Northern Regions
- Arctic Cordillera
- Northern Arctic

Arctic Thaw

Arctic temperatures are on the rise and affect everyday life in Canada's northern region. Arctic summers have seen average temperature increases of 1.2°C per decade. As the polar ice caps melt at a rate of 9 percent per decade, animals lose their habitat and some Inuit die hunting on thin ice. (For more information, see pages 26–27.)

CONTINENTAL GLACIATION

Extent of Glaciation
- 10 000 to 15 000 years ago
- 7 000 to 10 000 years ago
- 1 000 to 7 000 years ago
- Present glaciers

After millennia of melting and retreating, glaciers that once covered 97 percent of Canada now cover only 2 percent of the country. Abrasive ice sheets scraped the bedrock of the Canadian Shield, formed vast lakes, and created Hudson Bay.

SOILS

Chernozem—rich, black, fertile soil—covers much of the Prairie Provinces, which contain Canada's most productive cropland. Other soil types can also be productive especially with modern fertilizers. Many of Canada's rocky soils are vulnerable to the effects of acid rain.

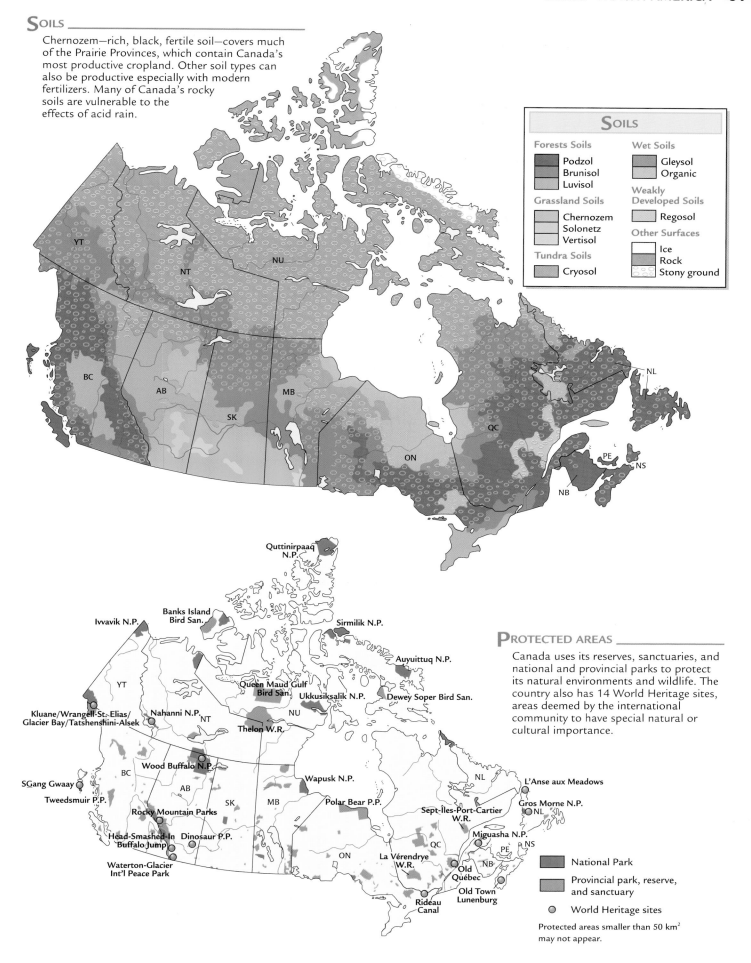

SOILS

Forests Soils
- Podzol
- Brunisol
- Luvisol

Grassland Soils
- Chernozem
- Solonetz
- Vertisol

Tundra Soils
- Cryosol

Wet Soils
- Gleysol
- Organic

Weakly Developed Soils
- Regosol

Other Surfaces
- Ice
- Rock
- Stony ground

PROTECTED AREAS

Canada uses its reserves, sanctuaries, and national and provincial parks to protect its natural environments and wildlife. The country also has 14 World Heritage sites, areas deemed by the international community to have special natural or cultural importance.

- National Park
- Provincial park, reserve, and sanctuary
- ○ World Heritage sites

Protected areas smaller than 50 km² may not appear.

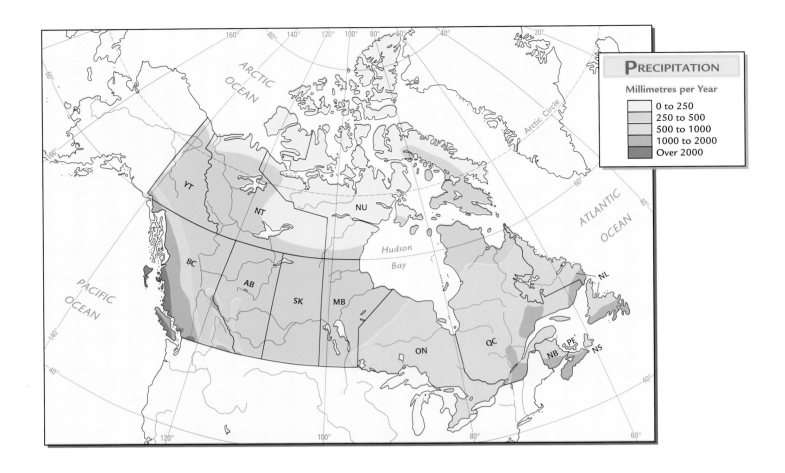

PRECIPITATION

Millimetres per Year

- 0 to 250
- 250 to 500
- 500 to 1000
- 1000 to 2000
- Over 2000

ACID RAIN

Sulphur dioxide (SO_2) and nitrogen oxides (NO_X) react with air and water, forming acids that fall as acid rain. These gases can travel thousands of kilometres before they fall to earth. (For more information, see pages 26–27.)

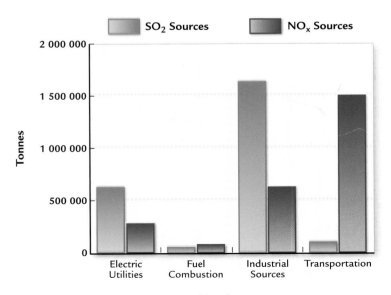

SO$_2$ Sources   NO$_x$ Sources

Acid Rain Sources

Tonnes

- 2 000 000
- 1 500 000
- 1 000 000
- 500 000
- 0

Electric Utilities   Fuel Combustion   Industrial Sources   Transportation

This stand of trees in Québec has been damaged by acid rain. More than half of the emissions that cause acid rain in eastern Canada originate in the United States.

TORNADOES

On average, Canada is hit by 80 tornadoes a year, which cause millions of dollars in damage. June and July are peak months for tornadoes.

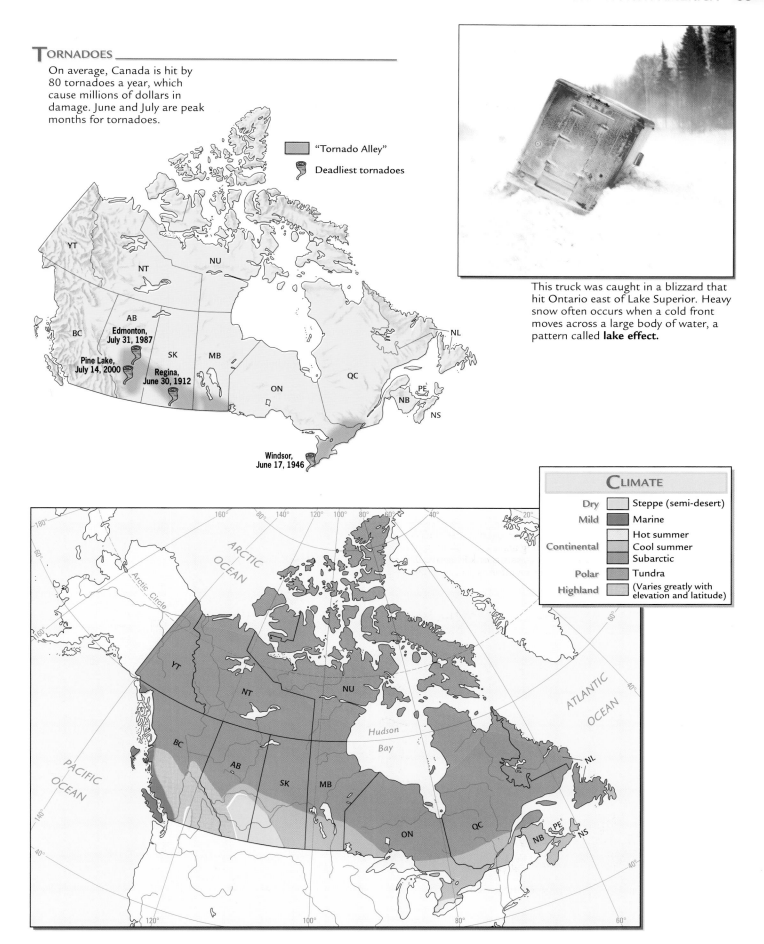

"Tornado Alley"

Deadliest tornadoes

YT

NT

NU

AB

Edmonton,
July 31, 1987

BC

Pine Lake,
July 14, 2000

SK

MB

Regina,
June 30, 1912

NL

QC

ON

PE

NB

NS

Windsor,
June 17, 1946

This truck was caught in a blizzard that hit Ontario east of Lake Superior. Heavy snow often occurs when a cold front moves across a large body of water, a pattern called **lake effect.**

CLIMATE

Dry		Steppe (semi-desert)
Mild		Marine
Continental		Hot summer
		Cool summer
		Subarctic
Polar		Tundra
Highland		(Varies greatly with elevation and latitude)

ARCTIC OCEAN

Arctic Circle

YT

NT

NU

BC

Hudson Bay

AB

SK

MB

ATLANTIC OCEAN

NL

PACIFIC OCEAN

ON

QC

NB

PE

NS

160° 140° 120° 100° 80° 60° 40° 20°

180°

120° 100° 80° 60°

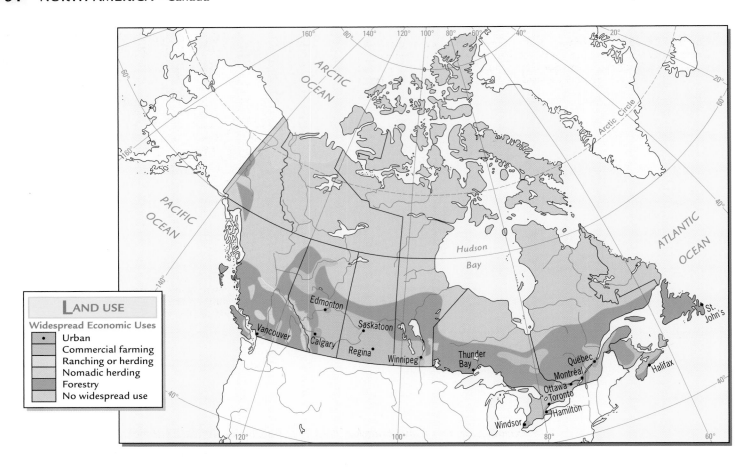

LAND USE

Widespread Economic Uses
- • Urban
- Commercial farming
- Ranching or herding
- Nomadic herding
- Forestry
- No widespread use

CHANGE IN CANADIAN FARMS

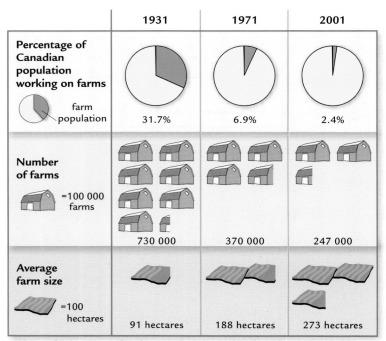

	1931	1971	2001
Percentage of Canadian population working on farms (farm population)	31.7%	6.9%	2.4%
Number of farms (=100 000 farms)	730 000	370 000	247 000
Average farm size (=100 hectares)	91 hectares	188 hectares	273 hectares

Due to advances in technology and more sophisticated methods of farming, fewer people are needed to operate larger farms. Thus, the number of Canadian farmers has decreased, while the size of the average farm in Canada has increased.

VALUE OF AGRICULTURE BY PROVINCE

Nearly all of Canada's cropland is located within 500 kilometres of the southern border, where the climate is warmest. Most of Canada's farmland is in the Prairie Provinces, though the greatest crop variety grows in southern Ontario.

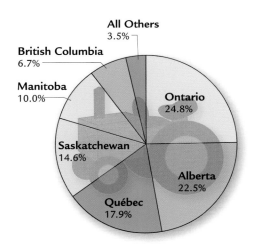

All Others 3.5%
British Columbia 6.7%
Manitoba 10.0%
Saskatchewan 14.6%
Québec 17.9%
Alberta 22.5%
Ontario 24.8%

CANADIAN AGRICULTURE

Currently Canada is one of the world's top wheat producers. However, as the global warming trend continues, more wheat production will move into new northern areas. Some agricultural scientists speculate that by 2050 Canada will become the leading producer of wheat, making it the new *World's Breadbasket*.

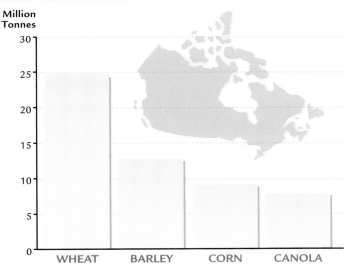

Canola, which is grown mainly for its oil, has become both valuable and widespread. The canola grown each year is now worth about 70 percent as much as Canada's annual wheat crop.

Forests—Canada's Surplus Crop

Short growing seasons throughout much of Canada make farming difficult, but not forestry. Forests cover nearly 40 percent of the country. Two-thirds of British Columbia is forested. The forest industry is Canada's single largest net exporter, contributing approximately US$ 35 billion to the country's trade surplus.

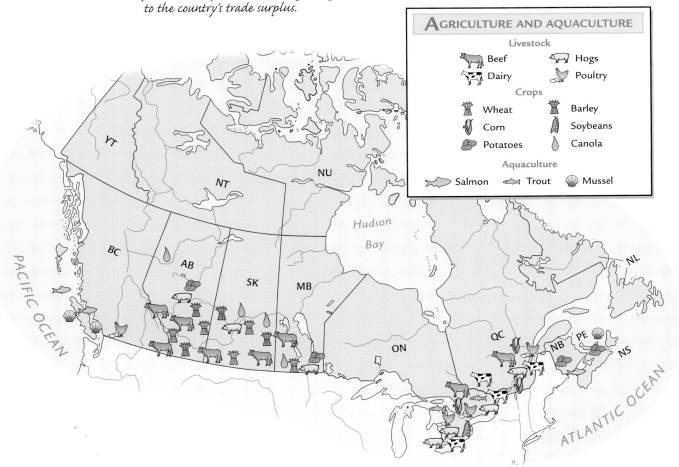

AGRICULTURE AND AQUACULTURE

Livestock

- Beef
- Dairy
- Hogs
- Poultry

Crops

- Wheat
- Corn
- Potatoes
- Barley
- Soybeans
- Canola

Aquaculture

- Salmon
- Trout
- Mussel

Only 26 percent of Canada's energy comes from sustainable resources, such as hydroelectricity or wind. Here ships are working offshore in the frozen Beaufort Sea, drilling for oil.

This street in Toronto serves as a snapshot of energy resources and how they are used. Oil is used for transportation, electricity provides power for lights, and heating oil or natural gas supplies heat.

SOURCES OF CONSUMED ENERGY

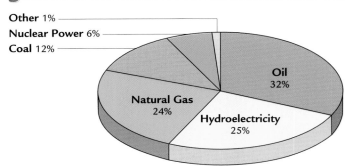

Other 1%
Nuclear Power 6%
Coal 12%

Oil 32%
Natural Gas 24%
Hydroelectricity 25%

USES OF CONSUMED ENERGY

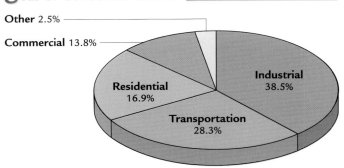

Other 2.5%
Commercial 13.8%

Industrial 38.5%
Residential 16.9%
Transportation 28.3%

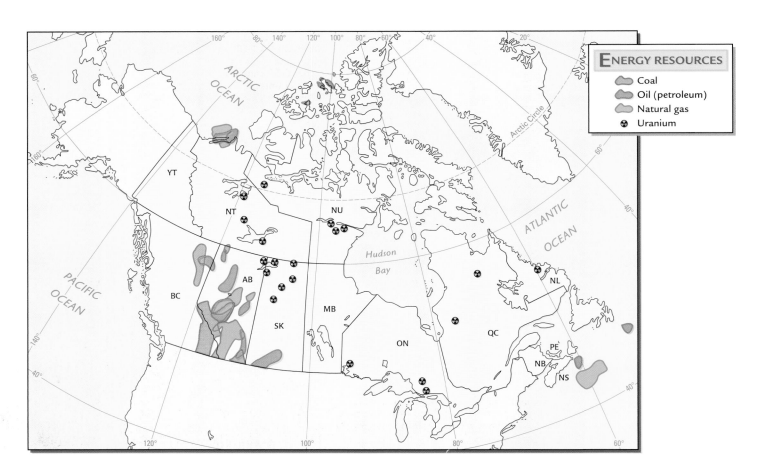

ENERGY RESOURCES

- Coal
- Oil (petroleum)
- Natural gas
- Uranium

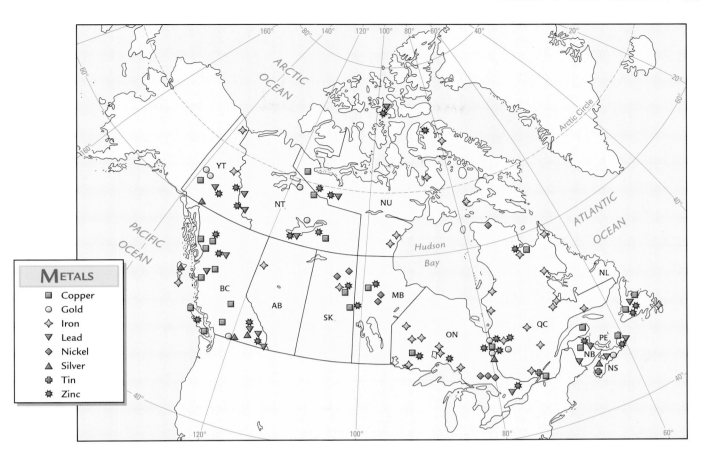

METALS

▣	Copper
○	Gold
◇	Iron
▽	Lead
◆	Nickel
▲	Silver
✛	Tin
✳	Zinc

MINING IN CANADA

Canada produces more than 70 minerals and metals. Communities shown on the map depend on mining or metal processing for 50 percent of their economies or more.

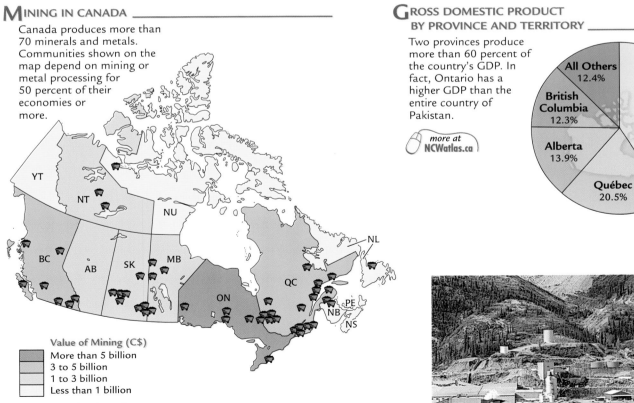

Value of Mining (C$)

▦	More than 5 billion
▦	3 to 5 billion
▦	1 to 3 billion
▢	Less than 1 billion

⛏ Community dependent on mining

Tungsten and copper are mined at this facility in the Northwest Territories. Because of its vast natural resources and low population, the Northwest Territories has the highest GDP per capita in all Canada, over C$ 95 000.

GROSS DOMESTIC PRODUCT BY PROVINCE AND TERRITORY

Two provinces produce more than 60 percent of the country's GDP. In fact, Ontario has a higher GDP than the entire country of Pakistan.

🖰 *more at* **NCWatlas.ca**

- All Others 12.4%
- British Columbia 12.3%
- Alberta 13.9%
- Québec 20.5%
- Ontario 40.9%

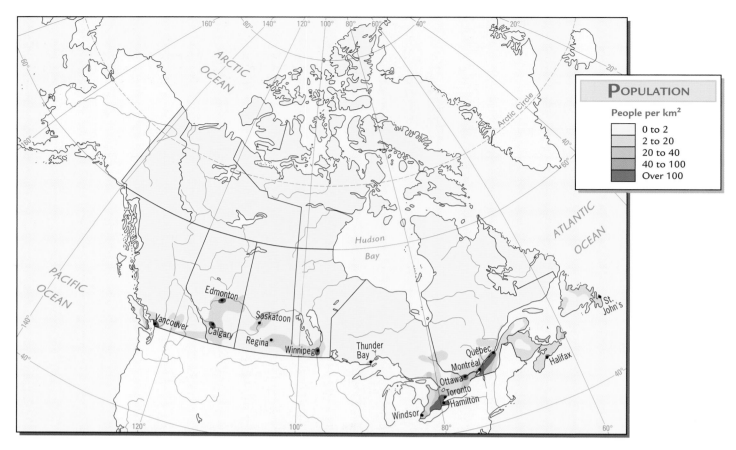

POPULATION

People per km²

- 0 to 2
- 2 to 20
- 20 to 40
- 40 to 100
- Over 100

ANNUAL NET MIGRATION

Immigration refers to the movement of people into a new country of residence. **Emigration** refers to the movement of people away from their native country to a new home elsewhere. Canada has the highest net immigration rate in North America.

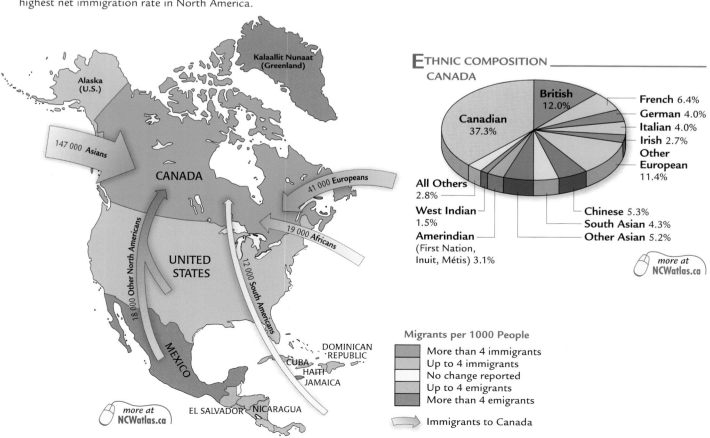

147 000 Asians

41 000 Europeans

19 000 Africans

18 000 Other North Americans

12 000 South Americans

ETHNIC COMPOSITION
CANADA

- **Canadian** 37.3%
- **British** 12.0%
- **French** 6.4%
- **German** 4.0%
- **Italian** 4.0%
- **Irish** 2.7%
- **Other European** 11.4%
- **Chinese** 5.3%
- **South Asian** 4.3%
- **Other Asian** 5.2%
- **Amerindian** (First Nation, Inuit, Métis) 3.1%
- **West Indian** 1.5%
- **All Others** 2.8%

more at **NCWatlas.ca**

Migrants per 1000 People

- More than 4 immigrants
- Up to 4 immigrants
- No change reported
- Up to 4 emigrants
- More than 4 emigrants

➔ Immigrants to Canada

more at **NCWatlas.ca**

Major Highways and Airports

Canada has more than 300 airports and over 1.4 million kilometres of road. The Trans-Canada Highway is the world's longest highway. It runs through all 10 Canadian provinces.

Airline Passengers per Year

✈ 20 to 35 million

✈ 10 to 20 million

✈ 2 to 10 million

• Other airport

— Trans-Canada and other major highways

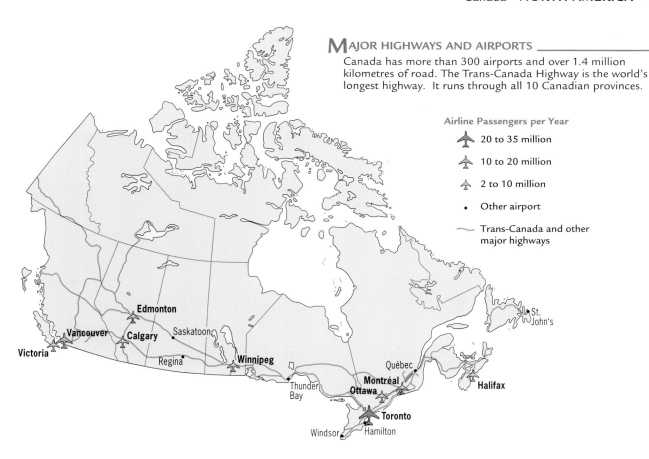

Great Lakes and St. Lawrence Seaway

The St. Lawrence Seaway enables freighters to reach the Great Lakes from the Atlantic Ocean. The waterway stretches 3700 kilometres from the Gulf of St. Lawrence to Lake Superior. The Seaway carries about 50 million tonnes of cargo per year, while the Great Lakes move about 200 million tonnes.

Alien Invasions by Sea

Invasive species *spread quickly in non-native environments where they have few or no natural enemies. In the St. Lawrence Seaway, some exotic species travel in the ballast water of ships. The zebra mussel, from Russia, alone has caused billions of dollars in damage and threatens several native species.*

more at
NCWatlas.ca

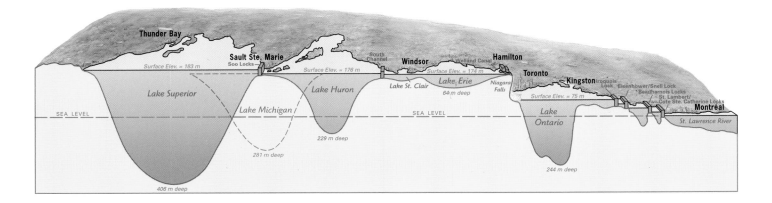

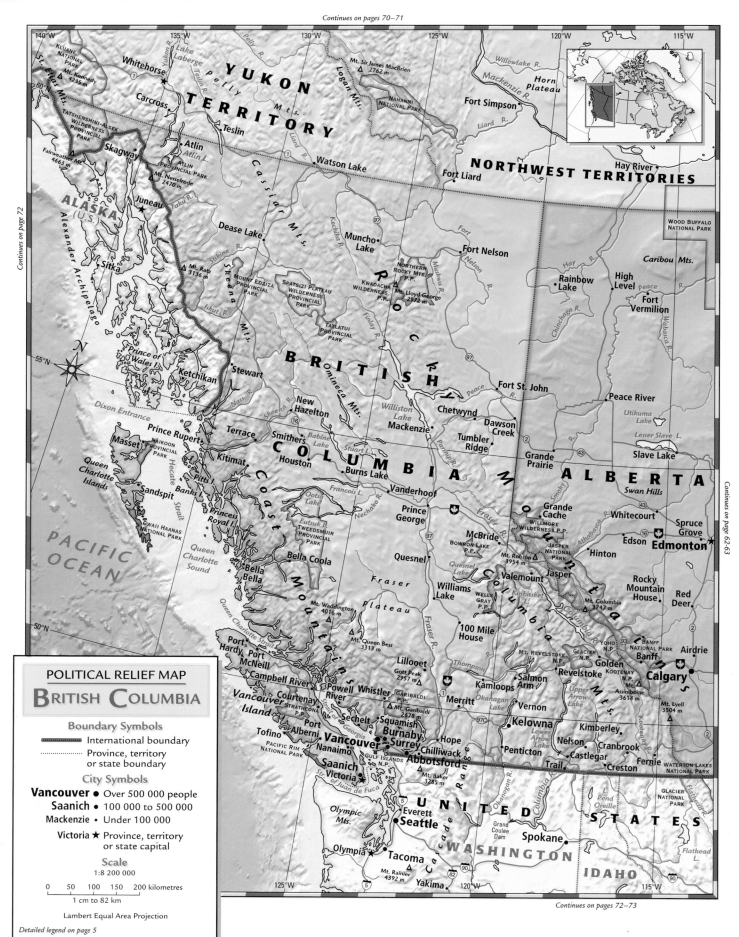

Continues on pages 70–71

Continues on page 72

Continues on page 62–63

POLITICAL RELIEF MAP
BRITISH COLUMBIA

Boundary Symbols
International boundary
Province, territory or state boundary

City Symbols
Vancouver • Over 500 000 people
Saanich • 100 000 to 500 000
Mackenzie • Under 100 000

Victoria ★ Province, territory or state capital

Scale
1:8 200 000

0   50   100   150   200 kilometres

1 cm to 82 km

Lambert Equal Area Projection

Detailed legend on page 5

Continues on pages 72–73

FOREST PRODUCTION BY PROVINCE OR TERRITORY

British Columbia accounts for nearly 40 percent of Canada's forest production. However, forestry in the province has declined by about 15 percent since 1987.

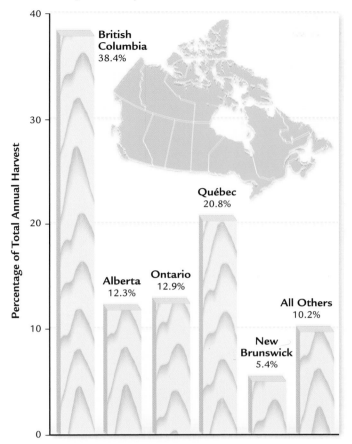

Percentage of Total Annual Harvest

- British Columbia 38.4%
- Québec 20.8%
- Alberta 12.3%
- Ontario 12.9%
- New Brunswick 5.4%
- All Others 10.2%

The Aboriginal peoples of British Columbia carve elaborate totem poles like these at SGang Gwaay, a UNESCO World Heritage Site in Gwaii Haanas National Park. Totem poles are inspired by history, lineage, and community identity of the band.

Hollywood North

Vancouver is now the third largest film production centre in North America, after Los Angeles and New York. The area's diverse geography allows British Columbia to represent just about any location, from bustling cities to remote rain forests. Major films and television shows shot in Vancouver include *Smallville*, *Elf*, and *Are We Done Yet?*

more at **NCWatlas.ca**

FORESTRY EXPORTS

Canada is the world's largest exporter of forest products. More than three-quarters of these exports go to the United States. Most of the others go to the European Union, Japan, and China.

more at **NCWatlas.ca**

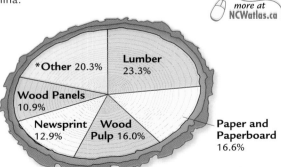

- Lumber 23.3%
- *Other 20.3%
- Wood Panels 10.9%
- Newsprint 12.9%
- Wood Pulp 16.0%
- Paper and Paperboard 16.6%

Total exports: $42 billion

*Other: converted paper, maple products, and Christmas trees.

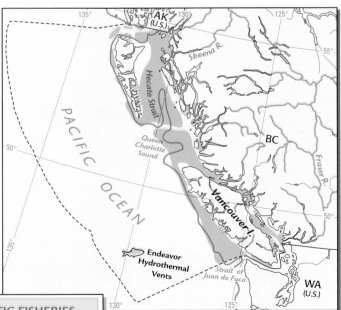

PACIFIC FISHERIES

- Pacific salmon
- Pacific herring
- Salmon spawning grounds
- Marine Protected Area
- 200-mile fishing limit
- 200-metre water depth

Canada exports over C$ 4 billion worth of fish and seafood products, making Canada the fifth-largest fish exporter in the world. Pacific-coast fisheries in Canada account for 20 percent of the country's fish production.

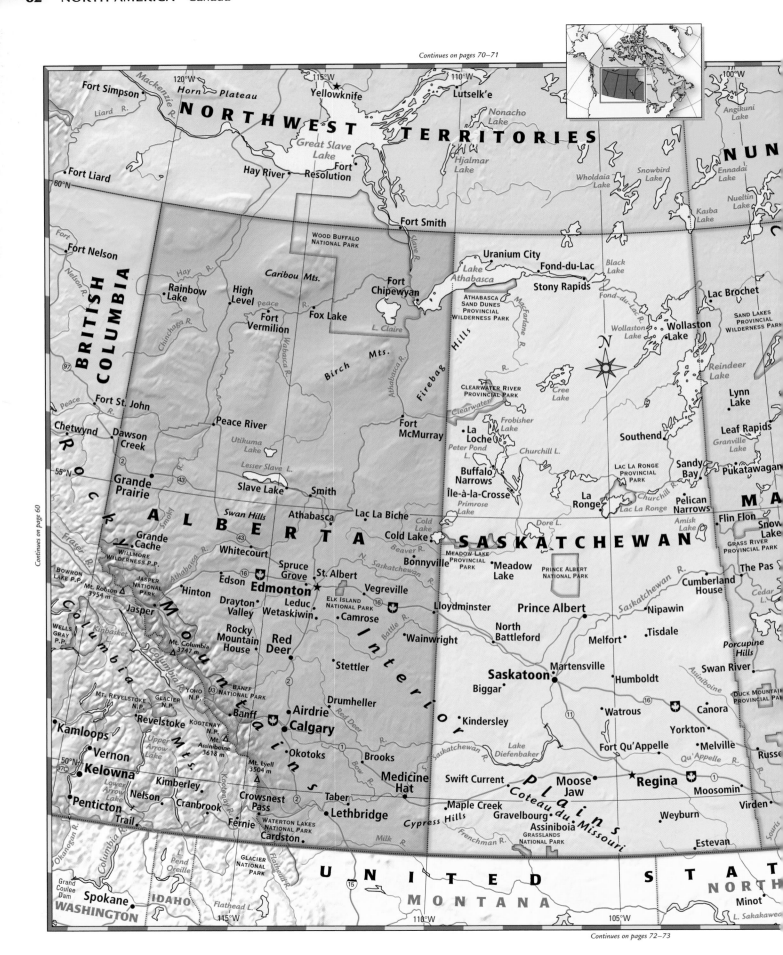

Continues on pages 70–71

NORTHWEST   TERRITORIES   NUN

Fort Simpson
Mackenzie R.
Horn   Plateau
120°W
115°W
Yellowknife
110°W
Lutselk'e
100°W
Angikuni
Lake
Liard R.
Nonacho
Lake
Great Slave
Lake
Fort
Resolution
Hay River
Hjalmar
Lake
Snowbird
Lake
Ennadai
Lake
60°N
Fort Liard
Wholdaia
Lake
Nueltin
Lake
Fort Smith
Kasba
Lake
Fort Nelson
Nelson R.
WOOD BUFFALO
NATIONAL PARK
Slave R.
Fort
Hay R.
Uranium City
Fond-du-Lac
Black
Lake
Rainbow
Lake
High
Level
Caribou Mts.
Lake
Athabasca
Stony Rapids
Fond-du-Lac R.
Lac Brochet
BRITISH COLUMBIA
Peace R.
Chinchaga R.
Fort
Vermilion
Fox Lake
Fort
Chipewyan
ATHABASCA
SAND DUNES
PROVINCIAL
WILDERNESS PARK
Macfarlane R.
SAND LAKES
PROVINCIAL
WILDERNESS PARK
L. Claire
Birch Mts.
Athabasca R.
Firebag Hills
Wollaston
Lake
Wollaston
Lake
Reindeer
Lake
97
Fort St. John
Peace
R.
Peace River
CLEARWATER RIVER
PROVINCIAL PARK
Cree
Lake
Lynn
Lake
Chetwynd
Dawson
Creek
Utikuma
Lake
Clearwater R.
Fort
McMurray
Frobisher
Lake
Churchill L.
Leaf Rapids
55°N
ROCK
43
Grande
Prairie
Lesser Slave L.
Slave Lake
Smith
La
Loche
Peter Pond
L.
Southend
Granville
Lake
Pukatawagan
Smoky
Swan Hills
Athabasca
Lac La Biche
Buffalo
Narrows
Île-à-la-Crosse
Primrose
Lake
LAC LA RONGE
PROVINCIAL
PARK
Sandy
Bay
Pelican
Narrows
MA
ALBERTA
Grande
Cache
WILLMORE
WILLMORE
WILDERNESS P.P.
43
Whitecourt
Cold
Lake
Cold Lake
Beaver R.
N. Saskatchewan R.
SASKATCHEWAN
Dore L.
La
Ronge
Lac La Ronge
Churchill R.
Amisk
Lake
Flin Flon
Snow
BOWRON
LAKE P.P.
Fraser R.
JASPER
NATIONAL
PARK
Mt. Robson
3954 m
Edson
Hinton
Spruce
Grove
Edmonton
St. Albert
MEADOW LAKE
PROVINCIAL PARK
Meadow
Lake
PRINCE ALBERT
NATIONAL PARK
GRASS RIVER
PROVINCIAL PARK
The Pas
Cedar
L.
WELLS
GRAY
P.P.
Kinbasket
Lake
Mt. Columbia
3747 m
Drayton
Valley
Leduc
Wetaskiwin
Vegreville
ELK ISLAND
NATIONAL
PARK
16
Bonnyville
Lloydminster
Prince Albert
Saskatchewan R.
Cumberland
House
Nipawin
Columbia
Columbia R.
Mountains
Rocky
Mountain
House
Red
Deer
Camrose
Battle R.
Wainwright
North
Battleford
Melfort
Tisdale
Porcupine
Hills
Swan River
Kamloops
MT. REVELSTOKE
N.P.
GLACIER
N.P.
YOHO
N.P.
BANFF
NATIONAL PARK
Stettler
Martensville
Saskatoon
Humboldt
DUCK MOUNTAIN
PROVINCIAL PAR
Vernon
Revelstoke
93
KOOTENAY
N.P.
Mt.
Assiniboine
3618 m
Banff
2
Airdrie
Calgary
Drumheller
Red Deer R.
Biggar
11
Watrous
Canora
Kelowna
Upper
Arrow
Lake
Okotoks
1
Brooks
Kindersley
16
Yorkton
Kimberley
Mt. Lyell
3504 m
Bow R.
Lake
Diefenbaker
Watrous
Melville
Penticton
Lower
Arrow
Lake
Nelson
Medicine
Hat
Swift Current
Moose
Jaw
Fort Qu'Appelle
Russe
Trail
Kootenay R.
Crowsnest
Pass
2
Taber
Maple Creek
Coteau
du
Missouri
Gravelbourg
Assiniboia
Regina
1
Moosomin
Fernie
Lethbridge
Cypress Hills
Frenchman R.
GRASSLANDS
NATIONAL PARK
Plains
Weyburn
Virden
Cardston
WATERTON LAKES
NATIONAL PARK
Milk R.
Estevan
Souris
GLACIER
NATIONAL
PARK
Flathead R.
UNITED   STAT
NORTH
Grand
Coulee
Dam
Spokane
IDAHO
15
MONTANA
Minot
WASHINGTON
115°W
Flathead L.
110°W
105°W
L. Sakakawea

Continues on page 60

Continues on pages 72–73

POLITICAL RELIEF MAP
PRAIRIE PROVINCES

Boundary Symbols

━━━━ International boundary

⋯⋯⋯ Province, territory or state boundary

City Symbols

Calgary ● Over 100 000 people

Brandon ● 25 000 to 100 000

Weyburn • Under 25 000

Edmonton ★ Province, territory or state capital

Scale
1:7 200 000

0   50   100   150   200 kilometres

1 cm to 72 km

Lambert Equal Area Projection

Detailed legend on page 5

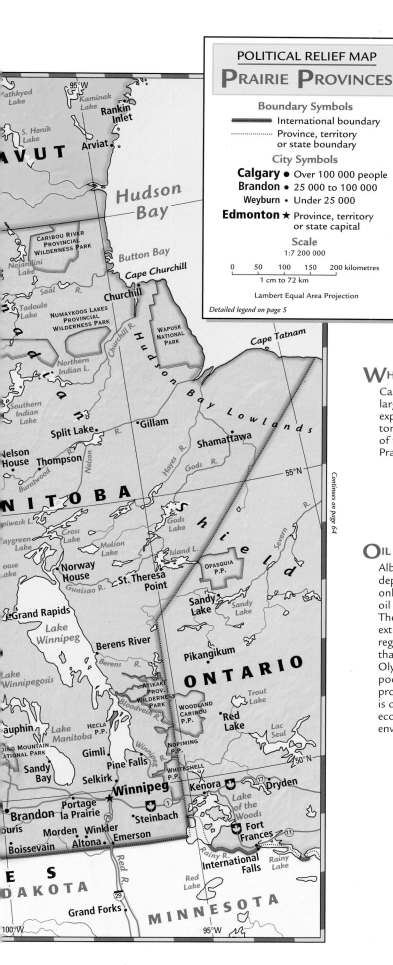

Continues on page 64

The Canadian Shield is a circular area of bedrock that extends from the Great Lakes to the Arctic Ocean, covering about half of Canada. This region is rich in minerals, such as iron, copper, and gold.

WHEAT PRODUCTION BY PROVINCE

Canada is one of the world's largest producers of wheat, exporting about 20 million tonnes a year. Over 95 percent of that wheat comes from the Prairie Provinces.

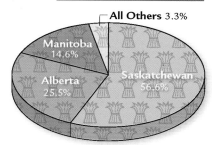

All Others 3.3%
Manitoba 14.6%
Alberta 25.5%
Saskatchewan 56.6%

OIL SANDS

Alberta's oil sands deposits are second only to Saudi Arabia's oil reserves in volume. The oil that can be extracted from this region could fill more than nine million Olympic swimming pools. However, processing the sands is costly both economically and environmentally.

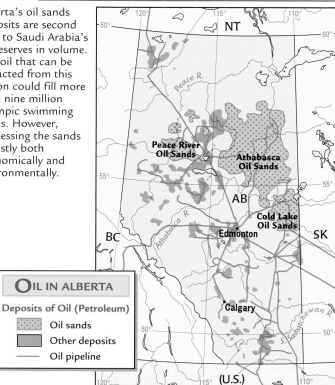

OIL IN ALBERTA

Deposits of Oil (Petroleum)

▦ Oil sands

▬ Other deposits

— Oil pipeline

Continues on pages 70–71

POLITICAL RELIEF MAP
CENTRAL CANADA
ONTARIO

Boundary Symbols

International boundary
Province or state boundary

City Symbols

Mississauga ● Over 500 000 people
Sudbury • 100 000 to 500 000
Nipigon • Under 100 000
Ottawa ⊗ National capital
Toronto ★ Province or state capital

Scale
1:9 000 000

0   50   100   150   200 kilometres
1 cm to 90 km

Albers Equal Area Projection

Detailed legend on page 5

60°N

90°W   85°W   80°W

Hudson

Bay

Ottawa Islands (Nunavut)

CANADIAN SHIELD

Cape Churchill
Churchill
Churchill R.

SAND LAKES PROVINCIAL WILDERNESS PARK

95°W

NUMAYKOOS LAKES PROVINCIAL WILDERNESS PARK

WAPUSK NATIONAL PARK

Port Nelson

Cape Tatnam

Nelson R.

Stephens Lake
Gillam

MANITOBA

Hayes R.   Gods R.

Shamattawa

Hudson Bay Lowlands

55°N

Fort Severn

Peawanuck   Wabuk Point

Cape Henrietta Maria

55°N

Gods Lake

Sachigo R.

Winisk R.

POLAR BEAR PROVINCIAL PARK

Bear I. (Nunavut)

75°W

St. Theresa Point

OPASQUIA P.P.

Sachigo Lake

Severn R.

Big Trout Lake

Fawn R.

Sutton Lake

Ekwan R.

James Bay

Chisasibi

R. la Grande

Réservoir de la Grande 2

Réservoir de la Grande 3

Réservoir de la Grande 4

Island Lake

Sandy Lake
Sandy Lake

WINISK RIVER P.P.

Winisk Lake

Atheweig R.

Attawapiskat

Akimiski I. (Nunavut)

Wemindji

L. Sakami

L. Boyd   R. Opinaca

R. Eastmain

Pikangikum

Berens R.

Trout L.

Otoskwin R.

Attawapiskat R.

Kapiskau R.

Fort Albany

Charlton I. (Nunavut)

Eastmain

Rés. de Eastmain Un

Réservoir Opinaca

L. Mistassini

Central Patricia

WOODLAND CARIBOU P.P.

Red Lake
Red Lake

Lake St. Joseph

WABAKIMI P.P.

Albany R.

Albany R.

Missinaibi R.

Moosonee

Moose R.

R. de Rupert

Waskaganish

NOPIMING P.P.

L. Seul

ONTARIO

L. Evans

R. Nottaway

QUÉBEC

50°N

WHITESHELL P.P.

Sioux Lookout

Armstrong

Kenogami R.

Kesagami Lake

Abitibi R.

Chibougamau

50°N

Kenora

Dryden

Lake of the Woods

Rainy Lake

Lake Nipigon

Longlac

Hearst

Kapuskasing

Matagami

R. Bell

Réservoir Gouin

95°W

Fort Frances

Atikokan

QUETICO P.P.

Nipigon

Schreiber

Kabinakagami R.

Oba

Kapuskasing R.

Iroquois Falls

Cochrane

La Sarre

Rouyn-Noranda

Senneterre

Parent

International Falls

Thunder Bay

St. Ignace Island

Marathon

White River

Mattagami R.

Timmins

L. Abitibi

Val-d'Or

Réservoir Cabonga

Rainy R.

Red Lake

MINNESOTA

Pigeon R.

PUKASKWA N.P.

Wawa

Chapleau

Kirkland Lake

Témiscaming

L. Kipawa

Maniwaki

MONT-TREMBLANT P.P.

Isle Royale

Michipicoten Island

LAKE SUPERIOR P.P.

Biscotasi

Ramsey

△ Ishpatina Ridge 693 m

Cobalt

Temiskaming

L. Gatineau

Duluth

Lake   Superior

Whitefish Bay

Mississagi R.

Indian

Temagami

Ottawa R. (R. des Outaouais)

L. Baskatong

Superior

Marquette

Sault Ste. Marie
Sault Ste. Marie

Sudbury

Elliot Lake

Blind River

KILLARNEY P.P.

North Channel

North Bay

Nipissing

ALGONQUIN P.P.

Pembroke

Gatineau

417

Cornwall

St. Lawrence R.

20

St. Cloud

WISCONSIN

MICHIGAN

Cockburn Island

Manitoulin I.

Georgian Bay

Parry Sound

Huntsville

BRUCE PENINSULA N.P.

Bancroft

Ottawa

401

45°N

St. Paul

Minneapolis

Alpena

GEORGIAN BAY IS. N.P.

Orillia

Simcoe

Kawartha Lakes

Brockville

ST. LAWRENCE IS. NATIONAL PARK

Owen Sound

Barrie

Peterborough

Belleville

Kingston

Rochester

Wausau

Traverse City

Markham

Oshawa

Green Bay

Saginaw Bay

Brampton

Toronto

L. Ontario

La Crosse

Waterloo

Mississauga

Rochester

Syracuse

Mason City

Saginaw

Kitchener

Niagara Falls

Erie Canal

Milwaukee

Grand Rapids

Flint

London

Hamilton

Buffalo

NEW

Madison ★

Lansing

Sarnia

St. Catharines

Welland Canal

YORK

Waterloo

IOWA

Dubuque

Lake St. Clair

Lake Erie

PT. PELEE N.P.

Cedar Rapids

Rockford

Detroit

Windsor

Chatham

Erie

Des Moines

Davenport

ILLINOIS

Chicago

UNITED

STATES

PENNSYLVANIA

Moline

90°W

Gary **INDIANA**   85°W

Toledo

OHIO

Cleveland

80°W

79

81

75°W

VALUE OF MANUFACTURING BY PROVINCE

Aptly nicknamed the *Manufacturing Heartland of Canada*, Ontario produces about half of the country's manufactured goods each year. Ontario also employs about half of Canada's industrial workers in the automotive, steel, and food and beverage industries.

more at NCWatlas.ca

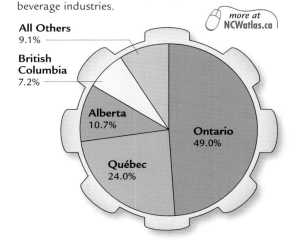

All Others 9.1%
British Columbia 7.2%
Alberta 10.7%
Québec 24.0%
Ontario 49.0%

Total manufacturing: C$ 610.2 billion

POPULATION BY PROVINCE

Over 12 million people live in Ontario, more people than any other Canadian province. The majority live in southern Ontario, near Canada's industrial centres and the Great Lakes. Québec, Canada's largest province in area, has the country's second largest population.

more at NCWatlas.ca

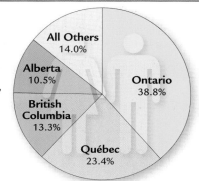

All Others 14.0%
Alberta 10.5%
British Columbia 13.3%
Ontario 38.8%
Québec 23.4%

Canada shares Niagara Falls with the United States, but 85 percent of the water flows over Horseshoe Falls in Ontario. More than 14 million tourists visit Niagara Falls each year.

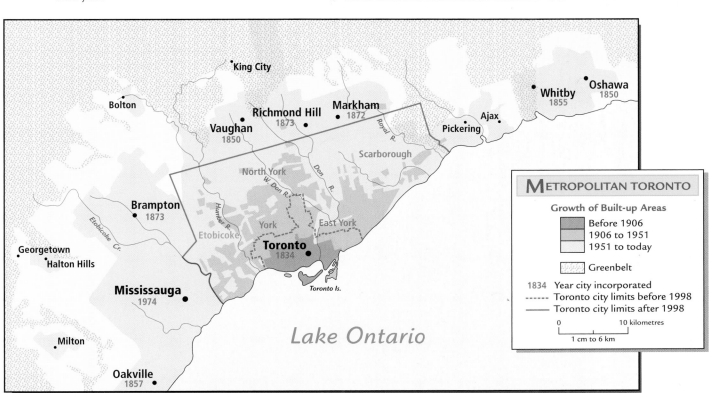

METROPOLITAN TORONTO
Growth of Built-up Areas
- Before 1906
- 1906 to 1951
- 1951 to today
- Greenbelt
- 1834 Year city incorporated
- Toronto city limits before 1998
- Toronto city limits after 1998

0 — 10 kilometres
1 cm to 6 km

As Toronto and the surrounding communities have grown, farms and forests have been replaced with businesses, housing developments, and roads. To prevent the farms and natural areas from disappearing entirely, the government of Ontario created the Greenbelt, which protects the countryside from **urbanization**.

Continues on pages 70–71

POLITICAL RELIEF MAP

CENTRAL CANADA
QUÉBEC

Boundary Symbols
━━━━━ International boundary
·············· Province or state boundary

City Symbols
Montréal ● Over 500 000 people
Saguenay ● 100 000 to 500 000
Kuujjuaq • Under 100 000
Ottawa ⊛ National capital
Québec ★ Province, territory, or state capital

Scale
1:10 000 000

0 50 100 150 200 kilometres

1 cm to 100 km

Lambert Equal Area Projection

Detailed legend on page 5

Continues on page 64

Continues on page 68

LANGUAGES OF CANADA

Québec has been unique in terms of ethnicity and language since before the founding of Canada. Compare the the language graph for all of Canada to the graph for just Québec.

CANADA

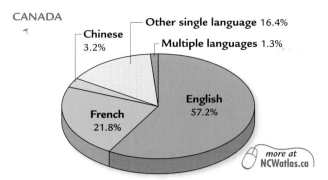

Other single language 16.4%
Chinese 3.2%
Multiple languages 1.3%
French 21.8%
English 57.2%

more at NCWatlas.ca

QUÉBEC

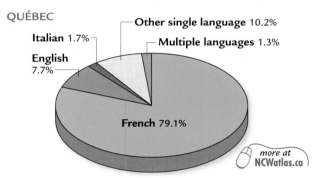

Other single language 10.2%
Italian 1.7%
Multiple languages 1.3%
English 7.7%
French 79.1%

more at NCWatlas.ca

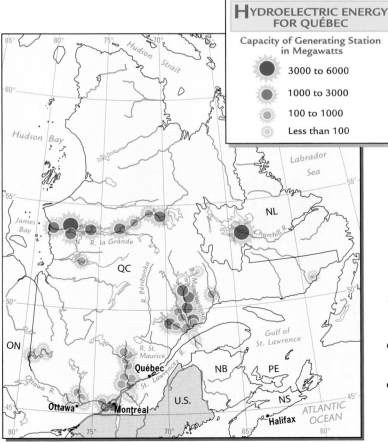

HYDROELECTRIC ENERGY FOR QUÉBEC

Capacity of Generating Station in Megawatts

- 3000 to 6000
- 1000 to 3000
- 100 to 1000
- Less than 100

Québec produces more hydropower than any other province. Plentiful electricity allows energy-intensive industries to thrive in Québec. For more information on hydroelectricity, see page 49.

For 17 days every year, half a million people enjoy the *Carnaval de Québec*, the largest winter festival in the world. The festival generates C$ 34 million a year for the Québec City area.

La Province Unique

Québec is culturally different from the other provinces. Its legal system is French rather than English. Since the 1960's, the Québecois have sought to protect their unique culture. Many in the province have demanded special autonomy or independence. No solution acceptable to Québec and the rest of the country has been found.

SOURCES OF ELECTRICITY

Different provinces take advantage of local resources to meet their electricity needs. Each energy source produces its own environmental problems. **Fossil fuels**, such as coal and natural gas, contribute to global warming. **Nuclear power** creates long-lasting toxic wastes. **Hydroelectricity** disrupts the ecosystem of the rivers. Compare Canadian electricity sources with European sources on page 114.

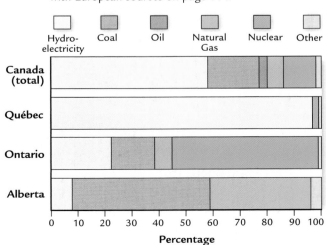

Hydro-electricity | Coal | Oil | Natural Gas | Nuclear | Other

Canada (total)
Québec
Ontario
Alberta

0 10 20 30 40 50 60 70 80 90 100

Percentage

Continues on pages 70–71

POLITICAL RELIEF MAP

ATLANTIC CANADA

Boundary Symbols
International boundary
Province or state boundary

City Symbols
Halifax ● Over 100 000 people
Moncton ● 25 000 to 100 000
Makkovik ● Under 25 000
St. John's ★ Province capital

Scale
1:8 000 000

0   50   100   150   200 kilometres
1 cm to 80 km

Lambert Equal Area Projection

Detailed legend on page 5

Killiniq Island (Nunavut)
Cape Chidley
TORNGAT MOUNTAINS NATIONAL PARK RESERVE
Ungava Bay
Torngat Mts.
Kangiqsualujjuaq
Mont d'Iberville △ 1652 m
Kuujjuaq
R. aux Feuilles
R. aux Mélèzes
R. Caniapiscau
R. George
R. de la Baleine
Fraser R.
Nain
Labrador Peninsula
QUÉBEC
Labrador Sea
Adlatok R.
Hopedale
Schefferville
Makkovik
Réservoir de Caniapiscau
Menihek Lakes
Smallwood Res.
Naskaupi R.
Kanairiktok R.
Rigolet
Hamilton Inlet
Canadian
Lac Opiscotéo
Churchill Falls
Churchill Falls
Lake Melville
Medly Mts.
Cartwright
Ross Bay Junction
Eagle R.
ATLANTIC OCEAN
Labrador City
Wabush
Little Mecatina
Churchill R.
Fermont
Happy Valley-Goose Bay
Otish Mts.
Shield
Lake Ashuanipi
L. Brule
Alexis R.
Port Hope Simpson
NEWFOUNDLAND AND LABRADOR
R. aux Outardes
Réservoir Manicouagan
R. Ste-Marguerite
R. Moisie
R. Romaine
R. Natashquan
R. du Petit Mecatina
R. St. Augustin
St. Paul R.
Blanc-Sablon
Strait of Belle Isle
St. Anthony
Baie-Comeau
Havre-Saint-Pierre
Sept-Îles
MINGAN ARCHIPELAGO NATIONAL PARK RESERVE
Long Range Mts.
White Bay
(138)
Pointe des Monts
Anticosti Island
GROS MORNE NATIONAL PARK
Notre Dame Bay
St. Lawrence River
Chic-Chocs Mts.
Gulf of St. Lawrence
Bay of Islands
Deer Lake
(1)
Windsor
Gander
Bonavista Bay
Bonavista
Notre Dame Mts.
Matane
GASPÉSIE P.P.
FORILLON N.P.
Gaspé
Corner Brook
Grand Lake
Grand Falls
TERRA NOVA N.P.
Rimouski
Gaspé Peninsula
Stephenville
Newfoundland
(132)
Chandler
St. George's Bay
Long Range Mts.
Lloyd's R.
Clarenville
Cape Spear
Campbellton
Chaleur Bay
Magdalen Islands (Québec)
Conception Bay
Trinity Bay
(185)
Bathurst
MOUNT CARLETON P.P.
Shippagan
Channel-Port aux Basques
Marystown
★ St. John's
Edmundston
St. John R.
Miramichi R.
Miramichi
KOUCHIBOUGUAC N.P.
PRINCE EDWARD ISLAND
CAPE BRETON HIGHLANDS N.P.
St.-Pierre and Miquelon (France)
Placentia
Avalon Peninsula
Grand
NEW
(11)
PRINCE EDWARD ISLAND N.P.
Fortune Bay
Placentia Bay
Cape Race
Falls
MAINE (U.S.)
Summerside
Charlottetown
(105)
Sydney
St. Mary's Bay
(95)
BRUNSWICK
(1)
★
St. Ann's Bay
Glace Bay
Fredericton
Moncton
Northumberland Str.
Cape Breton I.
Louisbourg
(2)
Amherst
Bras d'Or L.
Port Hawkesbury
FUNDY N.P.
New Glasgow
Saint John
(104)
Truro
Canso
Bay of Fundy
Sherbrooke
(101)
NOVA SCOTIA
Kentville
(102)
Grand Manan Island
KEJIMKUJIK NATIONAL PARK
Digby
(103)
★ **Halifax**
Lunenburg
Bridgewater
L. Rossignol
Sable I. (Nova Scotia)
Yarmouth
Shelburne
Gulf of Maine
Cape Sable
ATLANTIC OCEAN

Continues on page 66

Continues on pages 72–73

ATLANTIC COD

In 1976, to protect fish stocks, Canada extended its international fishing limit from 12 miles to 200 miles (19 km to 322 km). Seventeen years later, cod fishing was banned in Canada. Fishing has reopened in some areas, but stocks of cod continue to decline.

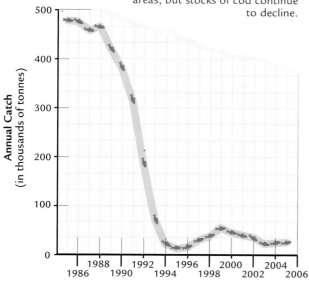

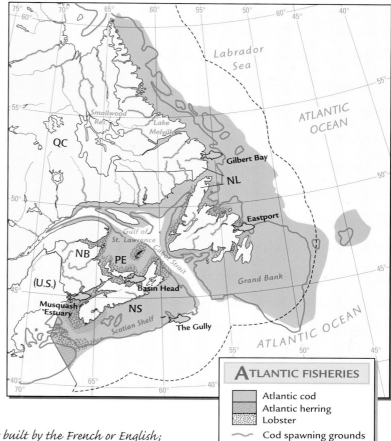

ATLANTIC FISHERIES

- Atlantic cod
- Atlantic herring
- Lobster
- Cod spawning grounds
- Marine Protected Area
- 200-mile fishing limit
- 200-metre water depth

Canada's First

The oldest European settlement in Canada wasn't built by the French or English; it was built by Norwegian Vikings. Few believed Norse sagas of a settlement in the New World over one thousand years ago, until remnants of a Viking village were found on the northern tip of Newfoundland in 1960. The village, now called L'Anse aux Meadows, is a World Heritage site.

HIGH TIDE

Twice a day 100 billion tonnes of water flow into and, later, out of the Bay of Fundy. The daily flow of these tides has carved the Hopewell Rocks into unusual shapes.

LOW TIDE

Water levels drop an average of 12 metres at Hopewell Rocks. Elsewhere around the Bay of Fundy tides can drop 16 metres, more than anywhere in the world. The world's average tide is only 1 metre.

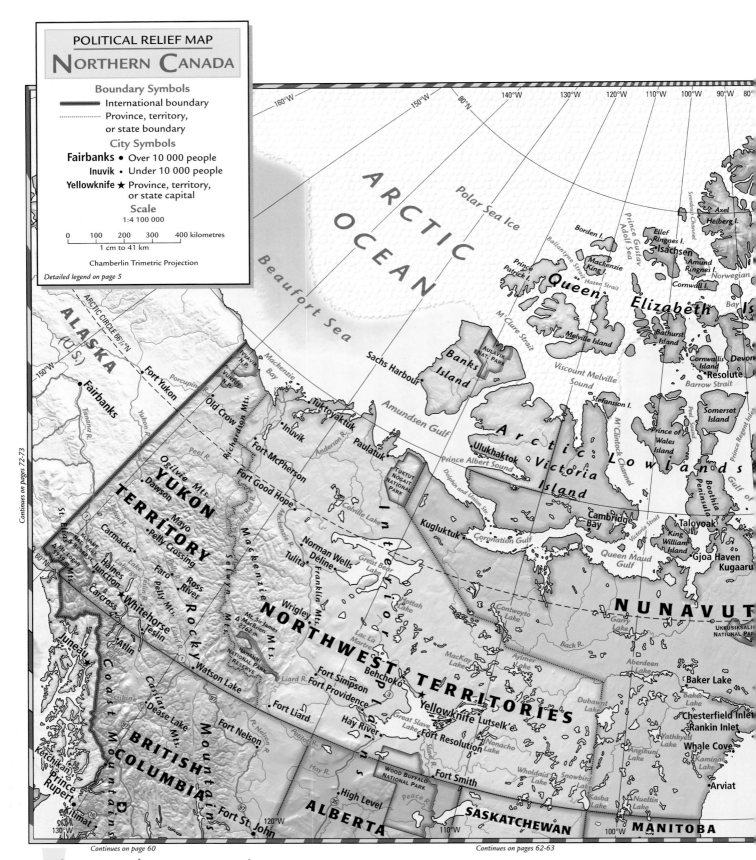

POLITICAL RELIEF MAP
Northern Canada

Boundary Symbols
International boundary
Province, territory,
or state boundary
City Symbols
Fairbanks • Over 10 000 people
Inuvik • Under 10 000 people
Yellowknife ★ Province, territory,
or state capital
Scale
1:4 100 000

0   100   200   300   400 kilometres
1 cm to 41 km

Chamberlin Trimetric Projection

Detailed legend on page 5

Continues on pages 72-73

Continues on page 60

Continues on pages 62-63

First People, Last Territory

Although the Aboriginal people were the first inhabitants of Canada, the government has always been run by European-descended people. That changed in 1999, when Nunavut was created for the Inuit. This marks the first time that a modern country in North America has established a regional government with an Aboriginal majority.

Continues on page 38

Continues on inset at right

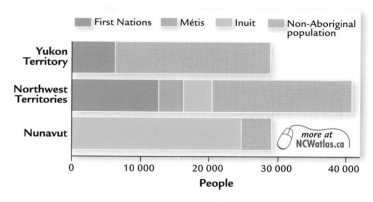

The Inuit build stone figures for many purposes, such as marking a place of respect. This *inukshuk* in the Northwest Territories provides direction to travelers in the vast Canadian North.

ABORIGINAL PEOPLE

Aboriginal people make up about three percent of Canada's population. The highest concentrations of Aboriginal people are found in the territories and the Prairie Provinces.

First Nations	Métis	Inuit	Non-Aboriginal population

more at NCWatlas.ca

People

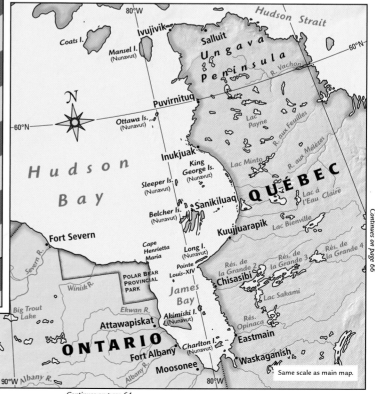

Continues on page 66

Same scale as main map.

Continues on page 64

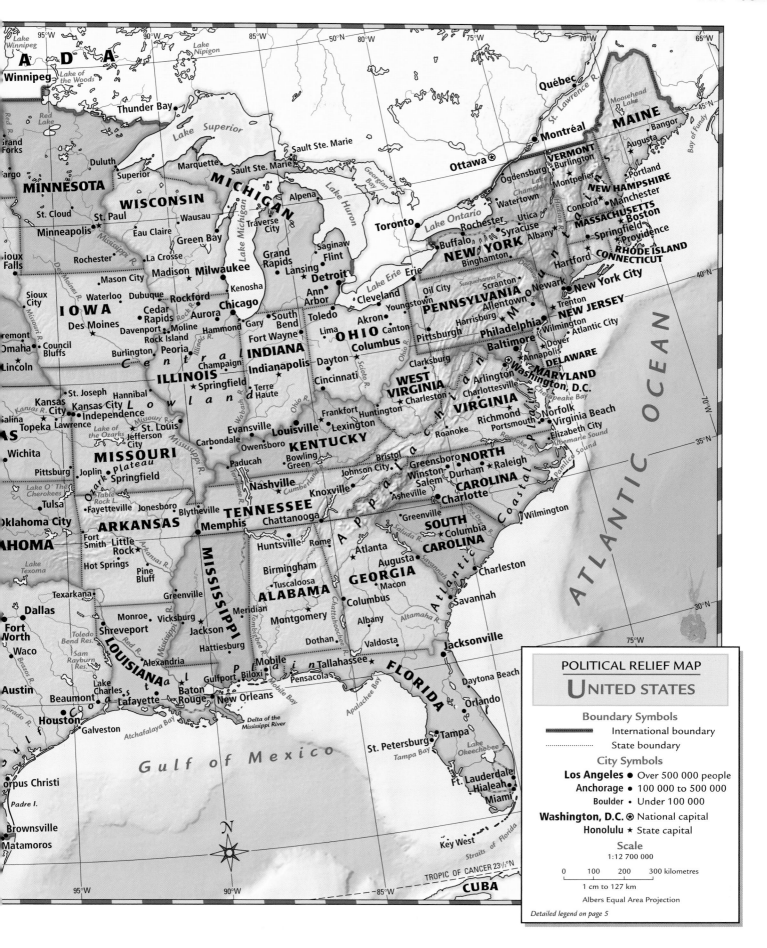

ADA
Winnipeg
Grand Forks
argo
ioux Falls
Lake Winnipeg
Red Lake
Red R.
Lake of the Woods
Lake Nipigon
Thunder Bay

MINNESOTA
Duluth
Superior
Marquette
St. Cloud
St. Paul
Minneapolis
Rochester
Mason City
Waterloo
Wausau
Eau Claire
Green Bay
Madison
Milwaukee

WISCONSIN
MICHIGAN
Sault Ste. Marie
Sault Ste. Marie
Alpena
Traverse City
Saginaw
Flint
Lansing
Grand Rapids
Detroit
Ann Arbor
Kenosha

Lake Superior
Lake Michigan
Lake Huron
Georgian Bay

IOWA
Sioux City
Des Moines
Cedar Rapids
Davenport
Moline
Rock Island
Dubuque
Rockford
Aurora
Chicago
Hammond
Gary
South Bend
Fort Wayne

Mississippi R.
Missouri R.
Des Moines R.

Omaha
Council Bluffs
Lincoln
remont
Burlington
Peoria
Champaign

ILLINOIS
Springfield
Terre Haute

INDIANA
Indianapolis

OHIO
Toledo
Lima
Canton
Columbus
Dayton
Cincinnati
Akron

Cleveland
Youngstown
Oil City
Pittsburgh

PENNSYLVANIA
Scranton
Harrisburg
Allentown
Newark

Erie
Lake Erie
Buffalo
Rochester
Syracuse
Utica
Binghamton

NEW YORK
Albany

Toronto
Lake Ontario

Ottawa
Québec
Montréal

VERMONT
Burlington
Montpelier
Ogdensburg
Watertown

St. Lawrence R.
Moosehead Lake

MAINE
Bangor
Augusta

NEW HAMPSHIRE
Concord
Manchester
Portland

MASSACHUSETTS
Boston
Springfield
RHODE ISLAND
Providence
Hartford
CONNECTICUT

Lake Champlain
Hudson R.

Newark
New York City
Trenton
NEW JERSEY
Atlantic City

Philadelphia
Wilmington
Dover
DELAWARE
Baltimore
Annapolis
MARYLAND
Washington, D.C.
Arlington
Charlottesville

Chesapeake Bay

Clarksburg
WEST VIRGINIA
Charleston

Frankfort
Huntington

KENTUCKY
Lexington
Louisville
Owensboro
Bowling Green
Paducah

Evansville
Carbondale

St. Joseph
Hannibal
MISSOURI
Jefferson City
St. Louis
Joplin
Springfield

Kansas City
Independence
Lawrence
Topeka
alina
Wichita
Pittsburg

Kansas R.
Lake of the Ozarks

KANSAS / AS

OKLAHOMA / HOMA
Oklahoma City
Tulsa

ARKANSAS
Fort Smith
Little Rock
Hot Springs
Fayetteville
Jonesboro
Blytheville

Lake O' The Cherokees
Ozark Plateau
Table Rock L.

Mississippi R.
Arkansas R.

Ozark Plateau

TENNESSEE
Memphis
Nashville
Chattanooga
Knoxville
Johnson City
Bristol

Cumberland R.

VIRGINIA
Roanoke
Richmond
Portsmouth
Norfolk
Virginia Beach
Elizabeth City

Albemarle Sound
Pamlico Sound

NORTH CAROLINA
Greensboro
Winston Salem
Durham
Raleigh
Charlotte
Asheville
Greenville

Roanoke R.

SOUTH CAROLINA
Columbia
Charleston
Wilmington

Atlantic Coastal Plain

Saluda R.

Appalachian

Huntsville
Rome
GEORGIA
Atlanta
Augusta
Macon
Columbus
Albany
Savannah
Valdosta

Savannah R.
Altamaha R.
Chattahoochee R.

ALABAMA
Birmingham
Tuscaloosa
Montgomery
Dothan

Texarkana
Greenville
MISSISSIPPI
Meridian
Jackson
Vicksburg
Hattiesburg
Monroe
Shreveport
Alexandria

Tombigbee R.

Dallas
Fort Worth
Waco
Austin
Houston
Galveston
Beaumont

Toledo Bend Res.
Sam Rayburn Res.
Brazos R.
Colorado R.

LOUISIANA
Lake Charles
Lafayette
Baton Rouge
New Orleans
Gulfport
Biloxi
Mobile
Pensacola

Mobile Bay
Delta of the Mississippi River
Atchafalaya Bay

Tallahassee
FLORIDA
Daytona Beach
Orlando
Tampa
St. Petersburg
Ft. Lauderdale
Hialeah
Miami

Apalachee Bay
Lake Okeechobee
Tampa Bay

Corpus Christi
Padre I.
Brownsville
Matamoros

Gulf of Mexico

Key West
Straits of Florida

ATLANTIC OCEAN

CUBA

TROPIC OF CANCER 23½°N

Coordinates: 95°W, 90°W, 85°W, 80°W, 50°N, 75°W, 70°W, 65°W, 45°N, 40°N, 35°N, 30°N, 70°W, 75°W

POLITICAL RELIEF MAP
UNITED STATES

Boundary Symbols
━━━━ International boundary
·········· State boundary

City Symbols
Los Angeles • Over 500 000 people
Anchorage • 100 000 to 500 000
Boulder • Under 100 000
Washington, D.C. ⊗ National capital
Honolulu ★ State capital

Scale
1:12 700 000

0   100   200   300 kilometres

1 cm to 127 km

Albers Equal Area Projection

Detailed legend on page 5

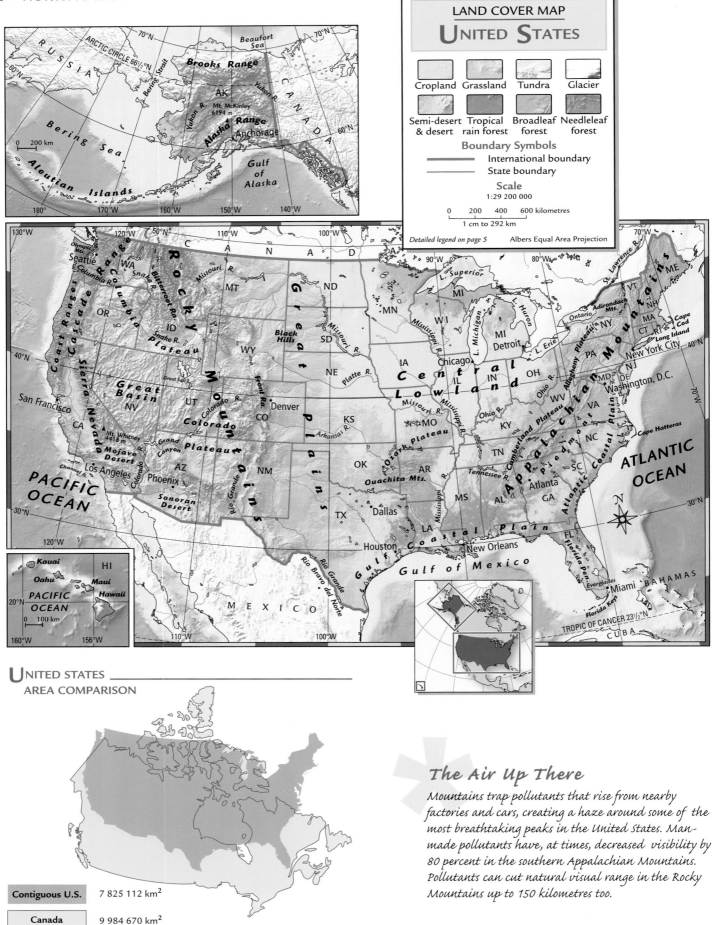

LAND COVER MAP
UNITED STATES

Cropland Grassland Tundra Glacier

Semi-desert Tropical Broadleaf Needleleaf
& desert rain forest forest forest

Boundary Symbols

International boundary

State boundary

Scale
1:29 200 000

0 200 400 600 kilometres

1 cm to 292 km

Detailed legend on page 5   Albers Equal Area Projection

UNITED STATES
AREA COMPARISON

Contiguous U.S.	7 825 112 km²
Canada	9 984 670 km²

The Air Up There

Mountains trap pollutants that rise from nearby
factories and cars, creating a haze around some of the
most breathtaking peaks in the United States. Man-
made pollutants have, at times, decreased visibility by
80 percent in the southern Appalachian Mountains.
Pollutants can cut natural visual range in the Rocky
Mountains up to 150 kilometres too.

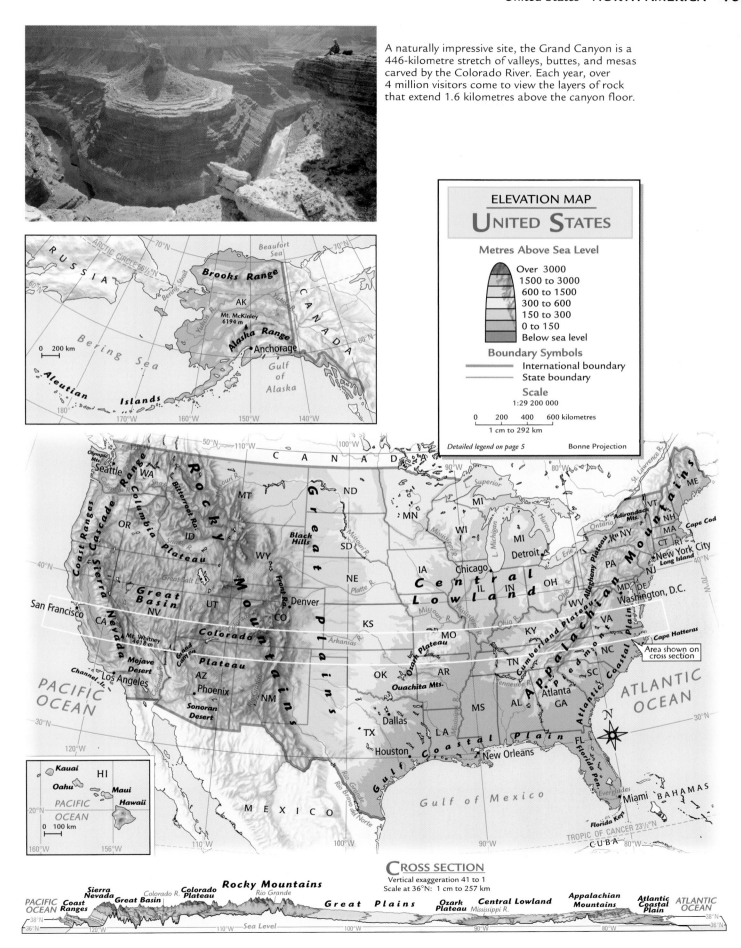

A naturally impressive site, the Grand Canyon is a 446-kilometre stretch of valleys, buttes, and mesas carved by the Colorado River. Each year, over 4 million visitors come to view the layers of rock that extend 1.6 kilometres above the canyon floor.

ELEVATION MAP
UNITED STATES

Metres Above Sea Level

Over 3000
1500 to 3000
600 to 1500
300 to 600
150 to 300
0 to 150
Below sea level

Boundary Symbols

International boundary
State boundary

Scale
1:29 200 000

0   200   400   600 kilometres
1 cm to 292 km

Detailed legend on page 5   Bonne Projection

CROSS SECTION
Vertical exaggeration 41 to 1
Scale at 36°N: 1 cm to 257 km

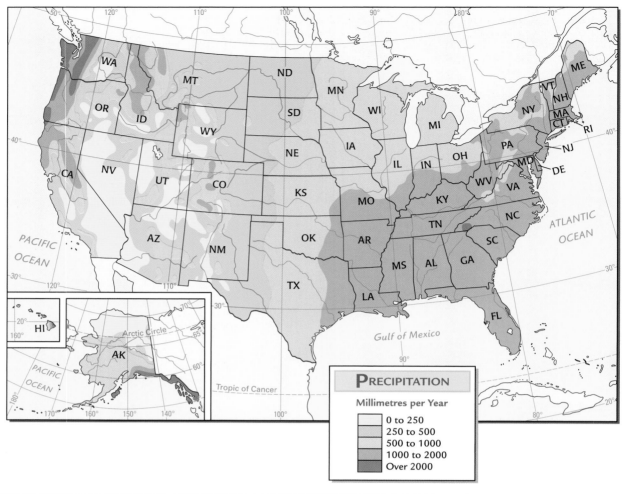

PRECIPITATION

Millimetres per Year

- 0 to 250
- 250 to 500
- 500 to 1000
- 1000 to 2000
- Over 2000

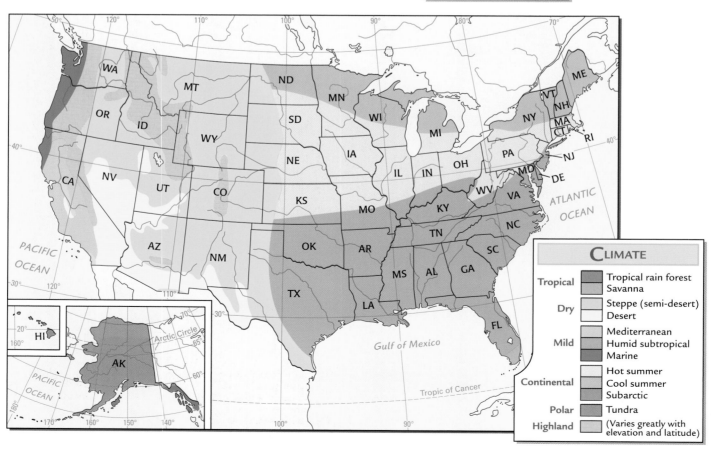

CLIMATE

Tropical	Tropical rain forest
	Savanna
Dry	Steppe (semi-desert)
	Desert
Mild	Mediterranean
	Humid subtropical
	Marine
Continental	Hot summer
	Cool summer
	Subarctic
Polar	Tundra
Highland	(Varies greatly with elevation and latitude)

CROP IRRIGATION

Different crops require different systems of irrigation. Cotton fields are often sprayed. Spraying can be inefficient; up to a third of the water can be lost to evaporation and blowing wind. Potato and tomato crops can be drip irrigated, which uses much less water.

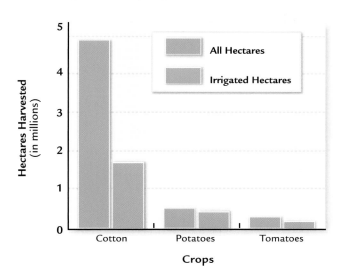

Hectares Harvested (in millions)

■ All Hectares

■ Irrigated Hectares

Crops: Cotton, Potatoes, Tomatoes

This irrigated cotton field in California is located in an arid, mountainous region. California has more irrigated farmland than any other state, over 4 million hectares.

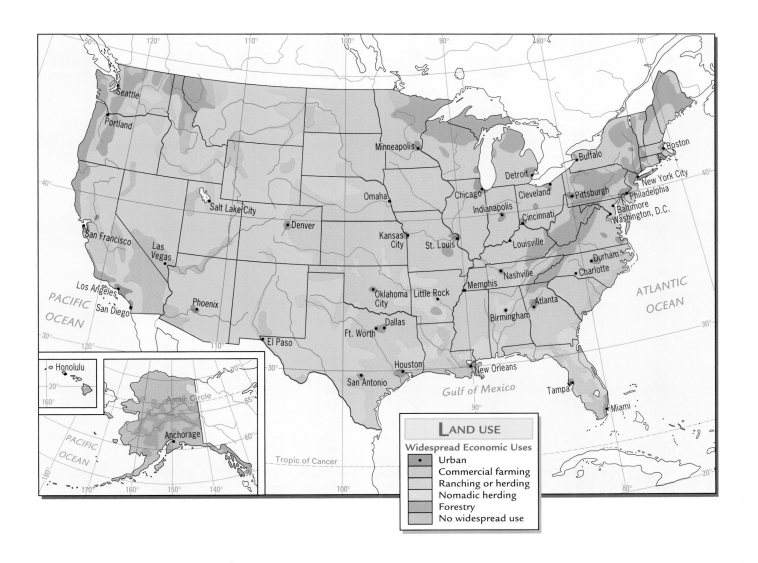

LAND USE

Widespread Economic Uses

- Urban
- Commercial farming
- Ranching or herding
- Nomadic herding
- Forestry
- No widespread use

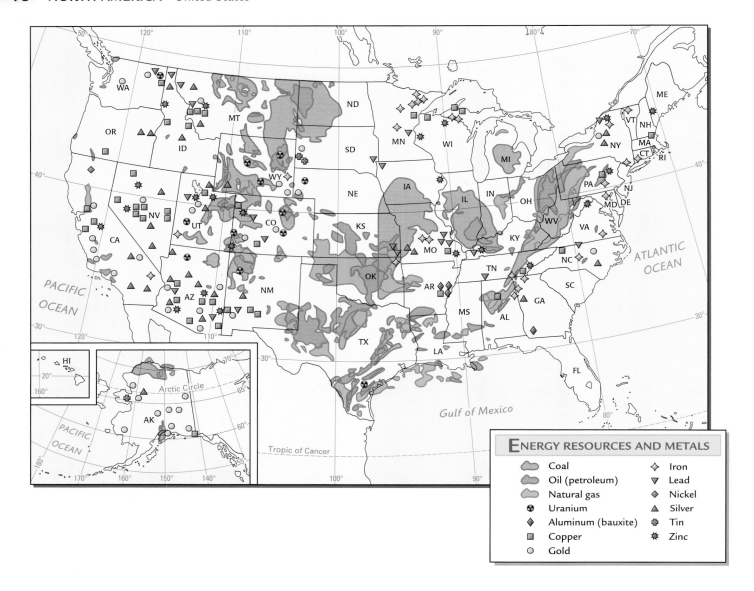

ENERGY RESOURCES AND METALS

Coal		Iron	
Oil (petroleum)		Lead	
Natural gas		Nickel	
Uranium		Silver	
Aluminum (bauxite)		Tin	
Copper		Zinc	
Gold			

BALANCE OF TRADE
UNITED STATES

U.S. consumers demand far more foreign goods than the rest of the world demands U.S.-made products. Over 35 percent of the deficit is from consumer goods such as electronics and household goods. The U.S. trade deficit from clothing alone is more than twice Canada's entire trade surplus. The total U.S. trade deficit is ten times that of any other country in the world.

more at NCWatlas.ca

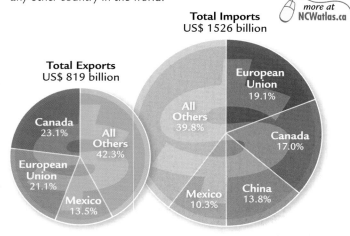

Total Exports
US$ 819 billion

Canada 23.1%
All Others 42.3%
European Union 21.1%
Mexico 13.5%

Total Imports
US$ 1526 billion

European Union 19.1%
All Others 39.8%
Canada 17.0%
China 13.8%
Mexico 10.3%

MAJOR HIGHWAYS AND AIRPORTS

The U.S. highway network consists of 6.4 million kilometres of streets and roads. Air travel is the fastest-growing means of transportation in the United States. In 1975 less than 50 percent of all Americans had flown, while today that number has climbed to 80 percent.

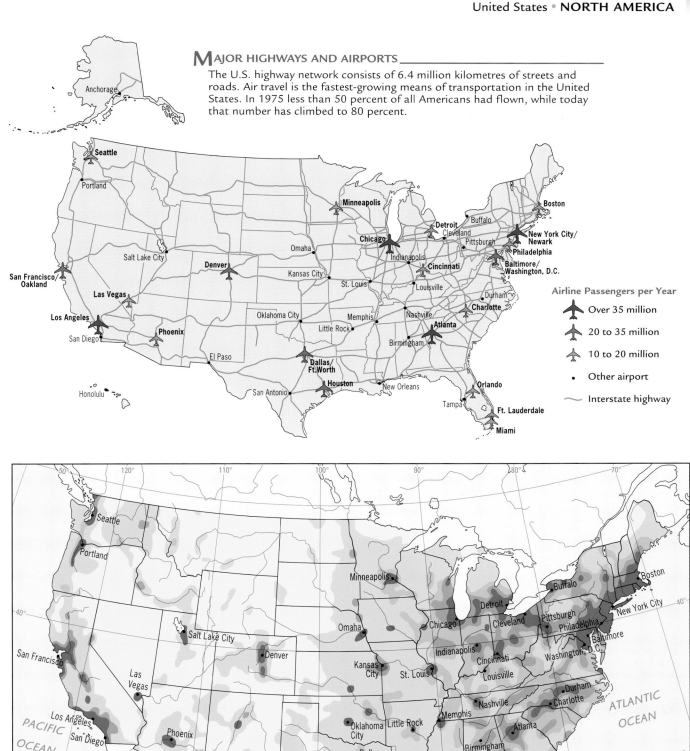

Airline Passengers per Year
- Over 35 million
- 20 to 35 million
- 10 to 20 million
- Other airport
- Interstate highway

POPULATION

People per km²
- 0 to 2
- 2 to 20
- 20 to 40
- 40 to 100
- Over 100

UNITED STATES

NORTH AMERICA

MEXICO

Gulf of Mexico

PACIFIC

OCEAN

Los Angeles
San Diego
Phoenix
Memphis
Tijuana
Mexicali
Dallas
Nogales
Nogales
Juarez
El Paso
Colorado R.
Salada Lagoon
Baja California
Angel de la Guarda I.
Hermosillo
Rio Grande
Amistad Res.
New Orleans
Cedros I.
Sebastian
Vizcaino Bay
Tiburon I.
Alvaro Obregon Res.
Ciudad Obregon
Chihuahua
Conchos R.
Rio Bravo del Norte
Houston
Point Eugenia
Gulf of California (Sea of Cortes)
Sierra Madre Occidental
Sierra
Laredo
Fuerte R.
Nuevo Laredo
Santa Margarita I.
San Jose I.
Torreon
Sierra Madre Oriental
Matamoros
Brownsville
Gulf of Mexico
Saltillo
Monterrey
La Paz
TROPIC OF CANCER 23½°N
Madre Lagoon
Cape San Lucas
Mazatlan
Ciudad Victoria
Gulf
Coastal Plain
Plateau of Mexico
San Luis Potosi
Tampico
Cape Rojo
Cancun
Tres Marias Is.
Tepic
Leon
Panuco R.
Merida
Puerto Vallarta
Guadalajara
Cape Corrientes
L. Chapala
Morelia
Campeche
Yucatan Peninsula
Revillagigedo Is. (Mex.)
Paricutin Volcano 2808 m
Mexico City
Netzahualcoyotl
Puebla
Veracruz
Bay of Campeche
Popocatepetl 5452 m
Pico de Orizaba 5610 m
Terminos Lagoon
Hondo R.
Villahermosa
El Chichon 1060 m
BELIZE
Chetumal Bay
Sierra Madre del Sur
Balsas R.
Oaxaca
Sierra Madre
Angostura Res.
Belmopan
Acapulco
L. Izabal
San Pedro S
Gulf
Gulf of Tehuantepec
Tajumulco 4220 m
GUATEMALA
Guatemala City
San Salvador
Tegucigal
EL SALVADOR
Gulf of Fonseca

Cocos I. (Costa Rica)

110°W
100°W
90°W
30°N
20°N
10°N
110°W
100°W
90°W

N

POLITICAL RELIEF MAP
CENTRAL AMERICA AND CARIBBEAN SEA

Boundary Symbols
.... International boundary
City Symbols
Monterrey ● Over 500 000 people
Veracruz ● 100 000 to 500 000
Limon • Under 100 000
Mexico City ⊗ National capital
Scale
1:15 300 000

0   100   200   300 kilometres
1 cm to 153 km
Albers Equal Area Projection

Detailed legend on page 5

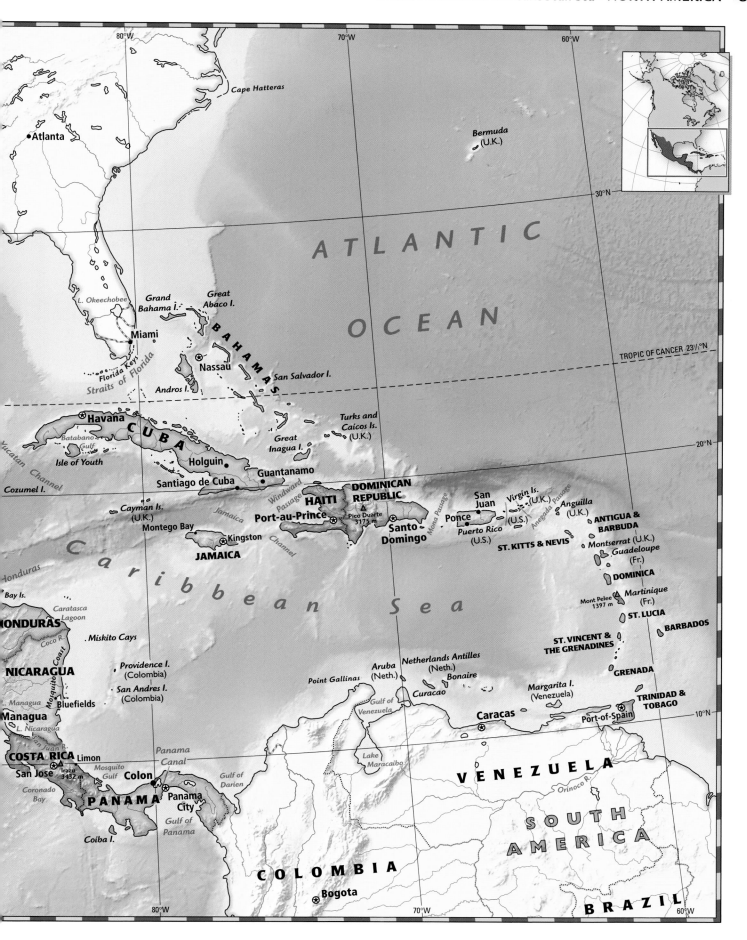

ATLANTIC OCEAN

Cape Hatteras

Bermuda (U.K.)

•Atlanta

30°N

L. Okeechobee
Grand Bahama I.
Great Abaco I.

Miami

TROPIC OF CANCER 23½°N

Florida Keys
Straits of Florida

Nassau

San Salvador I.

Andros I.

BAHAMAS

Havana
CUBA

Turks and Caicos Is. (U.K.)

Batabano Gulf

Great Inagua I.

20°N

Isle of Youth

Holguin

Yucatan Channel

Santiago de Cuba

Guantanamo

Cozumel I.

Cayman Is. (U.K.)

Montego Bay

Jamaica

Windward Passage

HAITI
Port-au-Prince

DOMINICAN REPUBLIC

Pico Duarte 3175 m

Santo Domingo

San Juan

Virgin Is. (U.K.)

Anguilla (U.K.)

Mona Passage

Ponce

Puerto Rico (U.S.)

Anegada Passage

ANTIGUA & BARBUDA

Kingston

ST. KITTS & NEVIS

Montserrat (U.K.)

JAMAICA

Jamaica Channel

Guadeloupe (Fr.)

DOMINICA

Honduras

Bay Is.

Caribbean Sea

Mont Pelee 1397 m

Martinique (Fr.)

Caratasca Lagoon

ST. LUCIA

HONDURAS

Coco R.

Miskito Cays

BARBADOS

NICARAGUA

Providence I. (Colombia)

ST. VINCENT & THE GRENADINES

Mosquito Coast

San Andres I. (Colombia)

GRENADA

Managua
Bluefields

Point Gallinas

Aruba (Neth.)

Netherlands Antilles (Neth.)

Bonaire

Margarita I. (Venezuela)

Managua
L. Nicaragua

Curacao

TRINIDAD & TOBAGO

Caracas

Port-of-Spain

10°N

COSTA RICA

Limon

Panama Canal

Gulf of Venezuela

San Jose

Irazu 3432 m

Mosquito Gulf

Colon

Gulf of Darien

Lake Maracaibo

VENEZUELA

Coronado Bay

PANAMA

Panama City

Orinoco R.

Coiba I.

Gulf of Panama

SOUTH AMERICA

COLOMBIA

•Bogota

BRAZIL

80°W

70°W

60°W

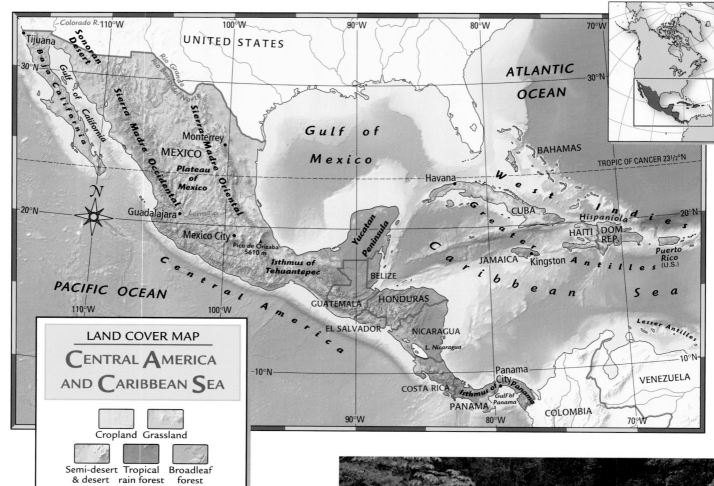

LAND COVER MAP

CENTRAL AMERICA
AND CARIBBEAN SEA

Cropland Grassland

Semi-desert Tropical Broadleaf
& desert rain forest forest

Boundary Symbols

International boundary

Scale

1:28 000 000

0   150 300 450 600 kilometres

1 cm to 280 km

Albers Equal Area Projection

Detailed legend on page 5

Ecotourism helps protect approximately two-thirds of Costa Rica's undisturbed tropical rain forests. Hanging bridges, like the one above, are used to protect the rain forest floors while tourists admire the landscape. (For more on tropical rain forests, see pages 26 and 92.)

The Sonoran Desert is wetter than most deserts, receiving up to 300 millimetres of rain each year. Its summer rainy season sustains a variety of plants and animals, over 20 percent of Mexico's plant species.

Trickle Down

The Colorado River is the main river in the southwestern United States and northwestern Mexico. Much of the river's water is diverted to Los Angeles. Hydroelectric dams and irrigation for agriculture have also reduced the amount of water reaching the river's delta. Some years the river never reaches its mouth at the Gulf of California.

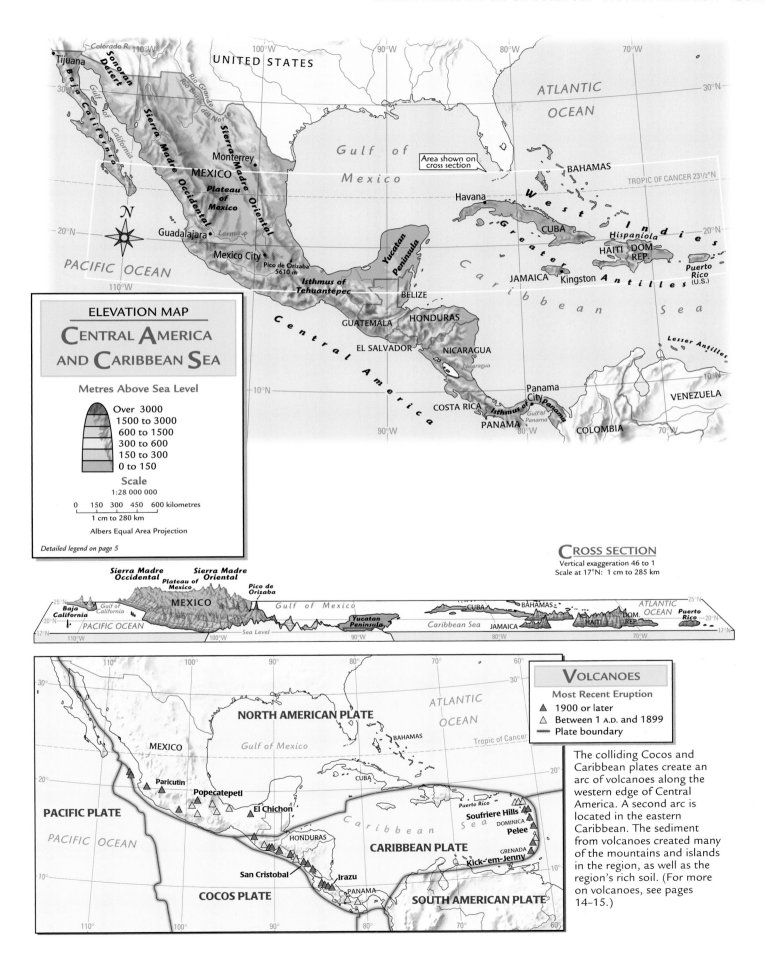

ELEVATION MAP

CENTRAL AMERICA AND CARIBBEAN SEA

Metres Above Sea Level

Over 3000
1500 to 3000
600 to 1500
300 to 600
150 to 300
0 to 150

Scale
1:28 000 000

0   150 300 450 600 kilometres

1 cm to 280 km

Albers Equal Area Projection

Detailed legend on page 5

UNITED STATES

Tijuana

Sonoran Desert

Baja California

Gulf of California

Sierra Madre Occidental

Colorado R.

Rio Bravo del Norte

Rio Grande

Monterrey

MEXICO

Sierra Madre Oriental

Plateau of Mexico

Guadalajara

Lerma R.

Mexico City

Pico de Orizaba 5610 m

PACIFIC OCEAN

Isthmus of Tehuantepec

Yucatan Peninsula

BELIZE

GUATEMALA

HONDURAS

EL SALVADOR

NICARAGUA

Lake Nicaragua

Central America

COSTA RICA

Panama City

Isthmus of Panama

Gulf of Panama

PANAMA

Gulf of Mexico

Area shown on cross section

ATLANTIC OCEAN

BAHAMAS

TROPIC OF CANCER 23½°N

Havana

West Indies

CUBA

Greater Antilles

Hispaniola

HAITI DOM. REP.

Puerto Rico (U.S.)

JAMAICA Kingston

Caribbean Sea

Lesser Antilles

VENEZUELA

COLOMBIA

CROSS SECTION

Vertical exaggeration 46 to 1
Scale at 17°N: 1 cm to 285 km

Sierra Madre Occidental

Sierra Madre Oriental

Plateau of Mexico

Pico de Orizaba

Baja California

Gulf of California

MEXICO

Gulf of Mexico

Yucatan Peninsula

Caribbean Sea

PACIFIC OCEAN

Sea Level

CUBA

BAHAMAS

ATLANTIC OCEAN

JAMAICA

HAITI

DOM. REP.

Puerto Rico

VOLCANOES

Most Recent Eruption

▲ 1900 or later
△ Between 1 A.D. and 1899
— Plate boundary

NORTH AMERICAN PLATE

MEXICO

Gulf of Mexico

BAHAMAS

ATLANTIC OCEAN

Tropic of Cancer

CUBA

Paricutin

Popocatepetl

El Chichon

PACIFIC PLATE

PACIFIC OCEAN

HONDURAS

San Cristobal

Irazu

PANAMA

COCOS PLATE

Puerto Rico

Caribbean Sea

Soufriere Hills

DOMINICA

Pelee

CARIBBEAN PLATE

GRENADA

Kick-'em-Jenny

SOUTH AMERICAN PLATE

The colliding Cocos and Caribbean plates create an arc of volcanoes along the western edge of Central America. A second arc is located in the eastern Caribbean. The sediment from volcanoes created many of the mountains and islands in the region, as well as the region's rich soil. (For more on volcanoes, see pages 14–15.)

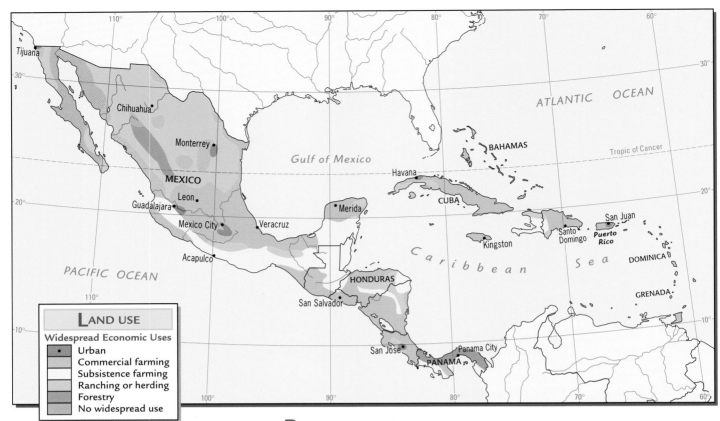

LAND USE

Widespread Economic Uses
- Urban
- Commercial farming
- Subsistence farming
- Ranching or herding
- Forestry
- No widespread use

From Bananas to Beaches

Central American and Caribbean countries were once called **banana republics** *because of their heavy reliance on one major export, such as bananas or coffee. Large land owners and foreign fruit companies dominated both politics and the economy. Now tourism provides much of the economic growth for this region. About 43 percent of the GDP in the Bahamas is from tourism.*

more at NCWatlas.ca

BALANCE OF TRADE

MEXICO

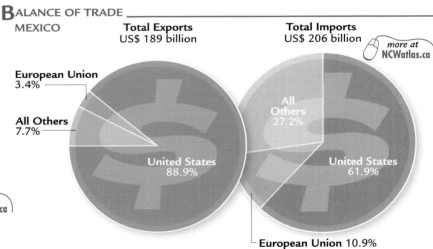

Total Exports
US$ 189 billion

Total Imports
US$ 206 billion

more at NCWatlas.ca

European Union 3.4%

All Others 7.7%

United States 88.9%

All Others 27.2%

United States 61.9%

European Union 10.9%

PANAMA CANAL

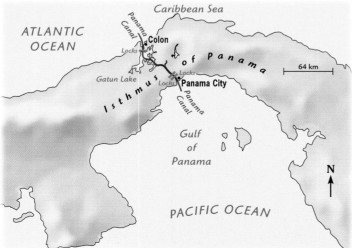

The Panama Canal is vital to world trade, providing a relatively inexpensive passageway between the Atlantic and Pacific Oceans. Vessels save thousands of kilometres by travelling through the canal, rather than sailing around South America.

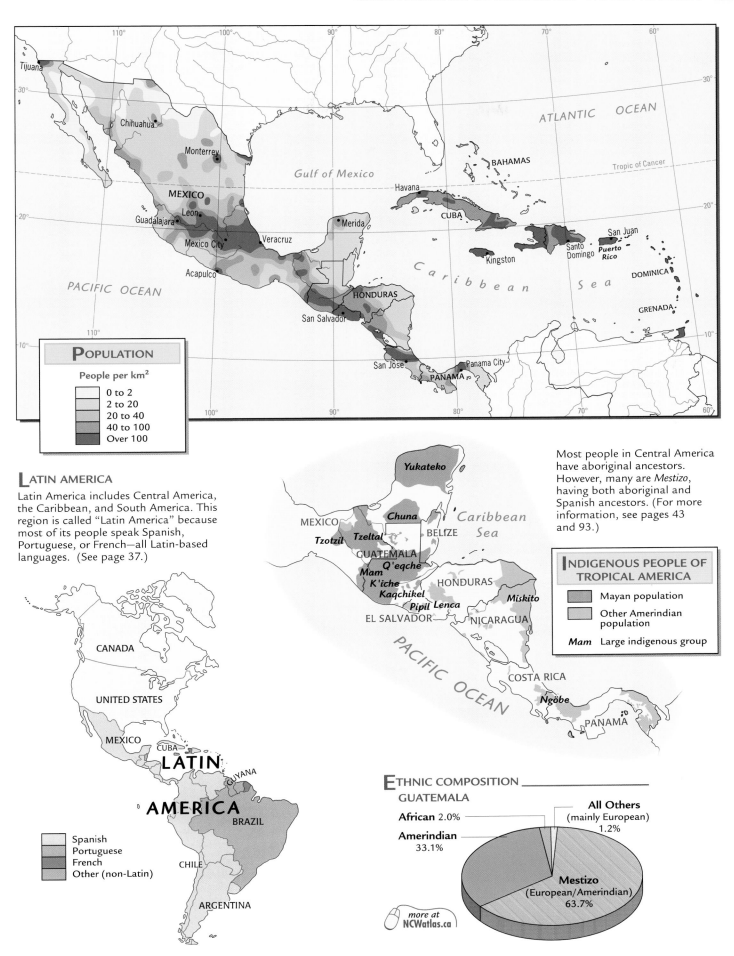

POPULATION

People per km²

- 0 to 2
- 2 to 20
- 20 to 40
- 40 to 100
- Over 100

LATIN AMERICA

Latin America includes Central America, the Caribbean, and South America. This region is called "Latin America" because most of its people speak Spanish, Portuguese, or French—all Latin-based languages. (See page 37.)

Spanish
Portuguese
French
Other (non-Latin)

Most people in Central America have aboriginal ancestors. However, many are *Mestizo*, having both aboriginal and Spanish ancestors. (For more information, see pages 43 and 93.)

INDIGENOUS PEOPLE OF TROPICAL AMERICA

Mayan population

Other Amerindian population

Mam Large indigenous group

ETHNIC COMPOSITION

GUATEMALA

African 2.0%

Amerindian 33.1%

All Others (mainly European) 1.2%

Mestizo (European/Amerindian) 63.7%

more at NCWatlas.ca

Continues on pages 72–73

NORTH AMERICA
UNITED STATES

• Los Angeles
Salton Sea
• San Diego
Mexicali
• Tijuana
Ensenada
Salada Lagoon
San Luis Rio Colorado
Sonoran Desert
Colorado R.
• Phoenix
• Tucson
Nogales
El Paso
Juarez
Rio Bravo del Norte
Rio Grande
Chihuahuan Desert

• Fort Worth   • Dallas
• Atlanta
• Austin
• San Antonio
• Houston
New Orleans

Gulf Coastal Plain
Mississippi River

BAJA CALIFORNIA

Guadalupe I.
Angel de la Guarda I.
Sebastian Vizcaino Bay
Cedros I.

SONORA
★ Hermosillo
Sierra Madre Occidental
• Ciudad Obregon
Yaqui R.
Fuerte R.

Chihuahua
★ CHIHUAHUA
Conchos R.

Ciudad Acuna
Piedras Negras
COAHUILA
Monclova
Nuevo Laredo

Gulf of Mexico

30°N
Gulf of California (Sea of Cortez)
Baja California

BAJA CALIFORNIA SUR
• La Paz
Cape San Lucas

Los Mochis
• Culiacan
Mazatlan
SINALOA

Gomez Palacio
Ciudad Lerdo
• Torreon
DURANGO
★ Durango
Plateau of Mexico

Saltillo
Sierra Madre Oriental
NUEVO LEON
• Guadalupe
Monterrey

Reynosa
Matamoros

TAMAULIPAS
• Ciudad Victoria
Ciudad Madero
Tampico

TROPIC OF CANCER 23½°N

PACIFIC OCEAN

ZACATECAS
★ Zacatecas
NAYARIT
Aguascalientes
Tepic
Tres Marias Is.
Zapopan
Guadalajara
Tlaquepaque
JALISCO
Colima
COLIMA
MICHOACAN
Morelia

SAN LUIS POTOSI
San Luis Potosi
Leon
Irapuato
Guanajuato
Querétaro
Pachuca
Mexico City
Toluca
Cuernavaca
Netzahualcoyotl

Gulf Coastal Plain
VERACRUZ
Jalapa
Veracruz
Tlaxcala
Puebla
Tehuacan

Bay of Campeche

Ciudad del Carmen

Merida
YUCATAN
Yucatan Peninsula
Campeche

Cancun
Cozumel I.

QUINTANA ROO
Chetumal
Chetumal Bay

GUERRERO
• Chilpancingo
Acapulco
Oaxaca
OAXACA
Tuxtla Gutierrez
Gulf of Tehuantepec

Coatzacoalcos
Minatitlan
CAMPECHE
Villahermosa
San Cristobal de las Casas
CHIAPAS

Belmopan
BELIZE
Gulf of Honduras
Bay Is.

GUATEMALA

Tapachula
Guatemala City

HONDURAS
Tegucigalpa

San Salvador
EL SALVADOR

NICARAGUA
Managua

Continues on page 87

Mexican States Not Named Above
① AGUASCALIENTES ⑥ FEDERAL DISTRICT
② GUANAJUATO   ⑦ MEXICO
③ QUERETARO   ⑧ MORELOS
④ HIDALGO   ⑨ PUEBLA
⑤ TLAXCALA   ⑩ TABASCO

POLITICAL RELIEF MAP
MEXICO

Boundary Symbols
—— International boundary
······ State boundary

City Symbols
Leon ● Over 1 000 000 people
Guadalupe ● 500 000 to 1 000 000
Nogales • Under 500 000

Mexico City ⊕ National capital
Villahermosa ★ State capital

Scale
1:17 700 000

0   125   250   375   500 kilometres
1 cm to 177 km

Albers Equal Area Projection

Detailed legend on page 5

Mexico's *maquiladoras* are industrial plants owned by foreign corporations. These factories often assemble American-made parts. The finished products are then usually exported back to the United States.

MEXICO
AREA COMPARISON

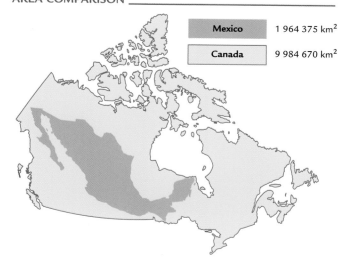

| Mexico | 1 964 375 km² |
| Canada | 9 984 670 km² |

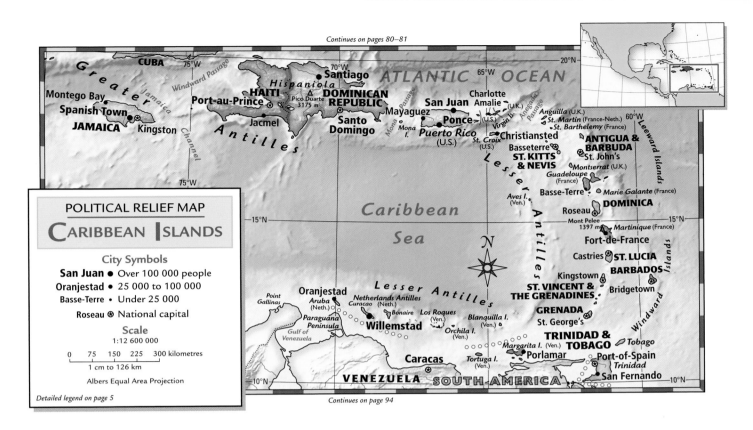

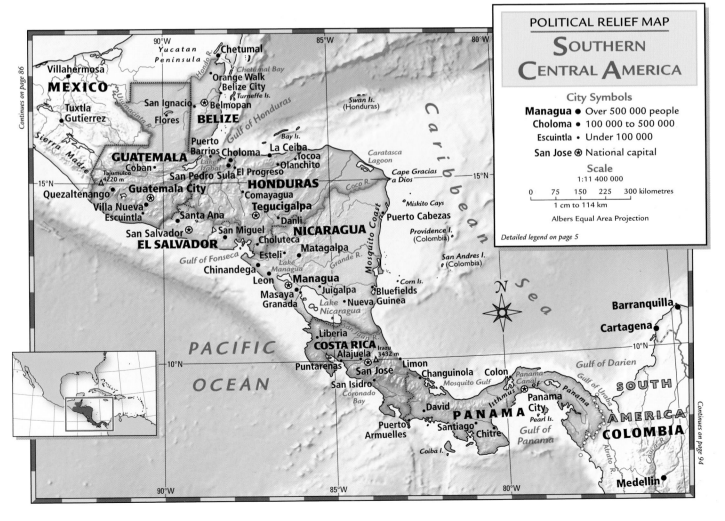

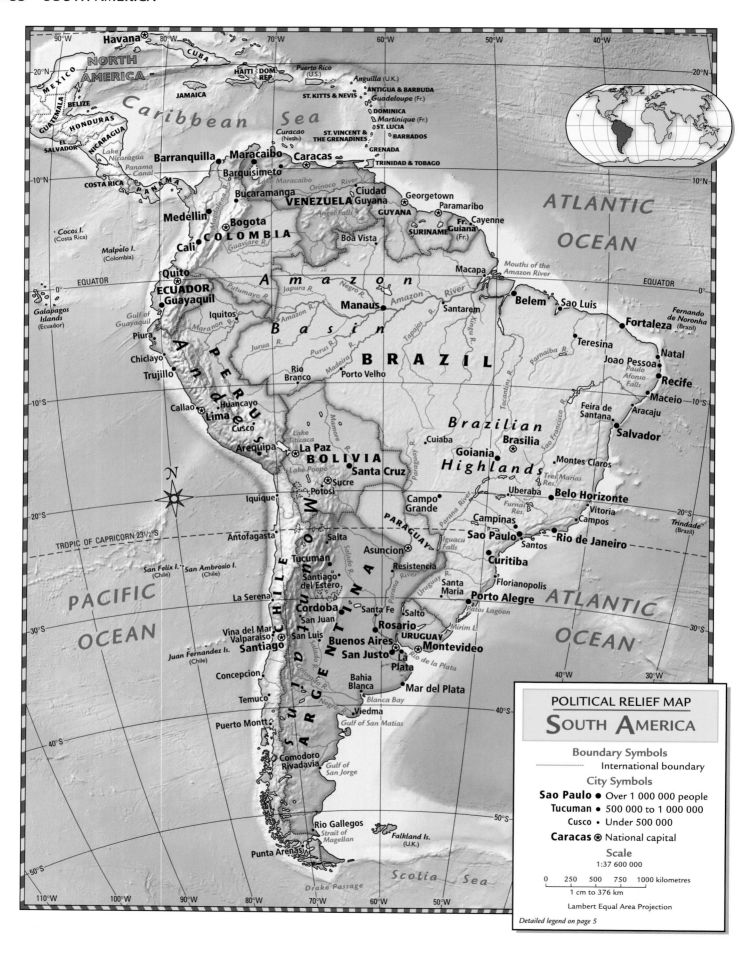

90°W   80°W   70°W   60°W   50°W   40°W

Havana ⊛   CUBA
20°N   20°N
NORTH   HAITI   DOM.   Puerto Rico
AMERICA   REP.   (U.S.)
MEXICO   Anguilla (U.K.)
BELIZE   JAMAICA   ANTIGUA & BARBUDA
GUATEMALA   Guadeloupe (Fr.)
HONDURAS   DOMINICA
EL   NICARAGUA   Martinique (Fr.)
SALVADOR   ST. VINCENT &   ST. LUCIA
COSTA RICA   Lake   Curacao   THE GRENADINES   BARBADOS
Nicaragua   (Neth.)   GRENADA
Panama   TRINIDAD & TOBAGO
Canal
Caribbean   Sea

Barranquilla   Maracaibo   Caracas ⊛
Barquisimeto
10°N   10°N
Bucaramanga   Orinoco   River
VENEZUELA   Ciudad   Georgetown
Lake Maracaibo   Guyana   Paramaribo
Medellin   Angel Falls   GUYANA   Fr.   Cayenne
Bogota ⊛   SURINAME   Guiana
COLOMBIA   (Fr.)
Cali   Boa Vista   ATLANTIC
Guaviare R.
OCEAN
Quito ⊛   A m a z o n   Mouths of the
EQUATOR   Macapa   Amazon River   EQUATOR
0°   ECUADOR   Putumayo R.   Japura R.   Negro R.   Amazon   0°
Guayaquil   River
Cocos I.   Manaus   Belem   Sao Luis
(Costa Rica)   Iquitos   B a s i n   Santarem   Fortaleza   Fernando
Gulf of   Amazon   de Noronha
Galapagos   Guayaquil   Maranon   Teresina   (Brazil)
Islands   Piura   Purus R.   Madeira   Tapajos R.   Xingu R.   Natal
(Ecuador)   Jurua R.   Joao Pessoa
Chiclayo   B R A Z I L   Recife
Rio   Porto Velho   Maceio
Trujillo   Branco   Parnaiba R.   10°S
10°S   Callao   Huancayo   Paulo
Lima ⊛   Cusco   B r a z i l i a n   Afonso   Feira de   Aracaju
Manore R.   Falls   Santana
Arequipa   Lake   Cuiaba   H i g h l a n d s   Salvador
Titicaca   Goiania   Sao Francisco R.
La Paz ⊛   Brasilia   Montes Claros   Trindade
Lake   BOLIVIA   Tres Marias   (Brazil)
Iquique   Poopo   Santa Cruz   Paraguay River   Res.   Belo Horizonte
Sucre ⊛   Uberaba   Furnas   Vitoria
Potosi   Campo   Res.   20°S
20°S   Grande   Campinas   Campos
TROPIC OF CAPRICORN 23½°S   Salta   P A R A G U A Y   Sao Paulo   Rio de Janeiro
Antofagasta   Santos
Asuncion ⊛   Iguacu   Curitiba
San Felix I.   San Ambrosio I.   Tucuman   Salado R.   Falls
(Chile)   (Chile)   Santiago   Resistencia   Florianopolis
del Estero   Parana River   Santa   Porto Alegre
PACIFIC   La Serena   Cordoba   Santa Fe   Maria   Patos Lagoon
Vina del Mar   San Juan   Salto   URUGUAY   30°S
30°S   Valparaiso   San Luis   Rosario   Montevideo
OCEAN   Santiago ⊛   Buenos Aires ⊛   Rio de la Plata   Mirim L.
Juan Fernandez Is.   San Justo   La   ATLANTIC
(Chile)   Concepcion   Salado R.   Plata   OCEAN
Colorado R.   Bahia   Mar del Plata
Temuco   Blanca
Negro R.   Blanca Bay   40°W   30°W
Viedma
40°S   40°S
Puerto Montt   Gulf of San Matias

Comodoro   Gulf of
Rivadavia   San Jorge

50°S   Rio Gallegos   50°S
Strait of   Falkland Is.
Magellan   (U.K.)
Punta Arenas
Scotia   Sea
Drake Passage
110°W   100°W   90°W   80°W   70°W   60°W   50°W

PACIFIC   OCEAN

ANDES   PERU   Mountains   CHILE   ARGENTINA

POLITICAL RELIEF MAP
SOUTH AMERICA

Boundary Symbols
.... International boundary

City Symbols

Sao Paulo ● Over 1 000 000 people
Tucuman ● 500 000 to 1 000 000
Cusco · Under 500 000
Caracas ⊛ National capital

Scale
1:37 600 000

0   250   500   750   1000 kilometres
1 cm to 376 km

Lambert Equal Area Projection

Detailed legend on page 5

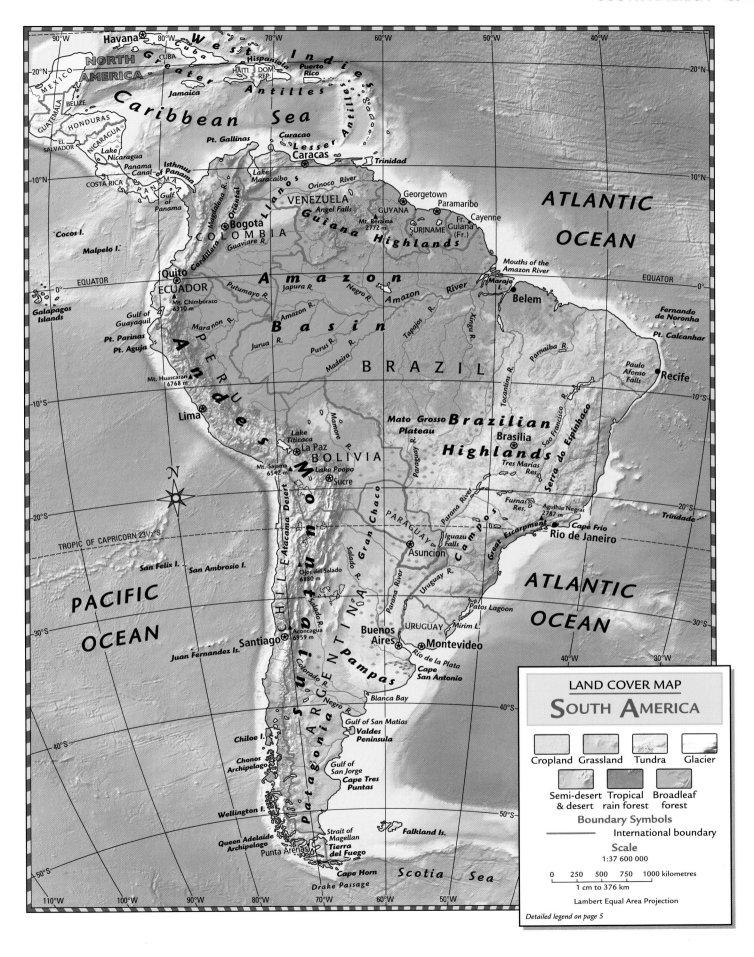

Havana ⊕ Cuba
NORTH West Indies
AMERICA Greater CUBA
MEXICO Jamaica HAITI Hispaniola DOM. REP. Puerto Rico
GUATEMALA Antilles Rico
BELIZE
HONDURAS Caribbean Sea
EL SALVADOR
NICARAGUA Pt. Gallinas Curacao Lesser Antilles
Lake Nicaragua Caracas Curacao Trinidad
COSTA RICA Isthmus of Panama Lake Maracaibo Orinoco River Georgetown Paramaribo
Panama Canal Llanos VENEZUELA Angel Falls GUYANA Cayenne
Gulf of Panama COLOMBIA Bogota Oriental Mt. Roraima 2772 m SURINAME Fr. Guiana (Fr.)
Cocos I. Guaviare R. Guiana Highlands ATLANTIC OCEAN
Malpelo I. Quito Putumayo R. Japura R. Negro R. Amazon River Mouths of the Amazon River
EQUATOR ECUADOR Amazon Basin Marajo I. EQUATOR
Galapagos Islands Mt. Chimborazo 6310 m Amazon R. Belem Fernando de Noronha
Gulf of Guayaquil Maranon R. Jurua R. Purus R. Madeira Tapajos R. Xingu R. Pt. Calcanhar
Pt. Parinas BRAZIL Parnaiba R.
Pt. Aguja ANDES Paulo Afonso Falls Recife
Mt. Huascaran 6768 m Mamore Mato Grosso Plateau Brazilian Sao Francisco
Lima Lake Titicaca La Paz BOLIVIA Highlands Brasilia Serra do Espinhaco
Mt. Sajama 6542 m Lake Poopo Sucre Tres Marias Res.
Gran Chaco Paraguay R. Agulhas Negras 2787 m Trindade
TROPIC OF CAPRICORN 23½°S PARAGUAY Furnas Res. Cape Frio
San Felix I. San Ambrosio I. Ojos del Salado 6880 m Salado R. Iguazu Falls Campos Great Escarpment Rio de Janeiro
Atacama Desert Parana River Asuncion ATLANTIC OCEAN
PACIFIC CHILE Salado R. Uruguay R.
OCEAN Aconcagua 6959 m Patos Lagoon
Juan Fernandez Is. Santiago ARGENTINA Buenos Aires URUGUAY Mirim L. OCEAN
Colorado R. Pampas Montevideo
Negro R. Rio de la Plata Cape San Antonio
Blanca Bay
Chiloe I. Gulf of San Matias Valdes Peninsula
Chonos Archipelago Patagonia Gulf of San Jorge Cape Tres Puntas
Wellington I. Falkland Is.
Queen Adelaide Archipelago Strait of Magellan Tierra del Fuego
Punta Arenas Cape Horn Scotia Sea
Drake Passage

LAND COVER MAP
SOUTH AMERICA

Cropland   Grassland   Tundra   Glacier

Semi-desert   Tropical   Broadleaf
& desert   rain forest   forest

Boundary Symbols
——————— International boundary

Scale
1:37 600 000

0 250 500 750 1000 kilometres
1 cm to 376 km

Lambert Equal Area Projection

Detailed legend on page 5

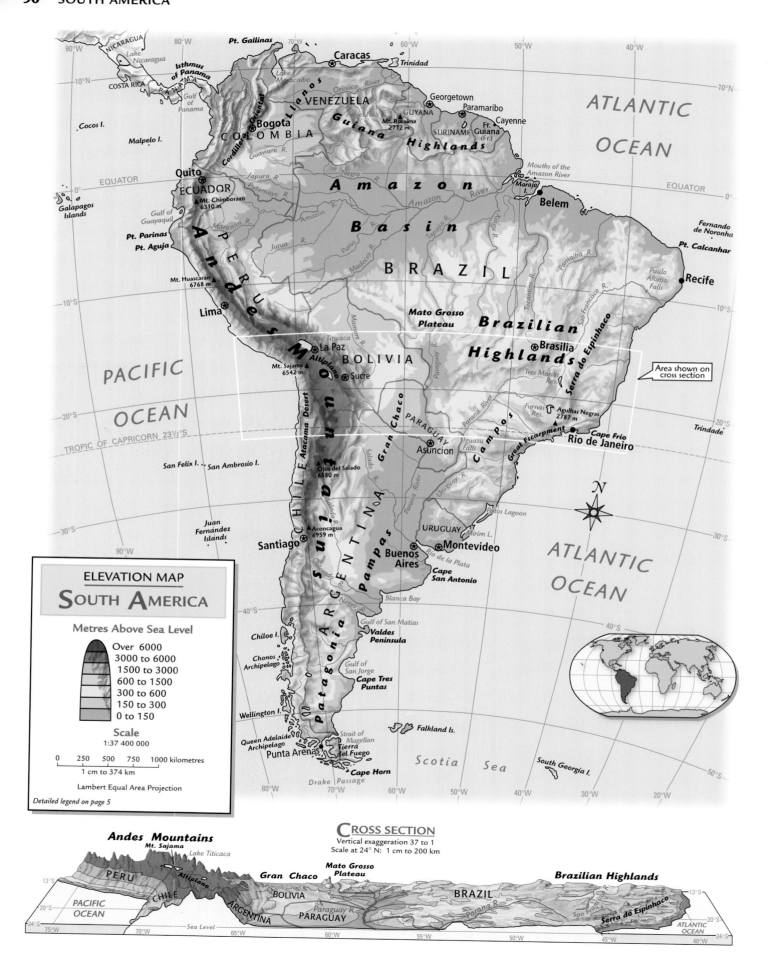

ATLANTIC OCEAN

PACIFIC OCEAN

ATLANTIC OCEAN

NICARAGUA
Lake Nicaragua
Pt. Gallinas
Caracas
Trinidad
Isthmus of Panama
COSTA RICA
PANAMA
Gulf of Panama
VENEZUELA
Orinoco River
Georgetown
Paramaribo
Cayenne
Cocos I.
Cordillera Oriental
Bogota
Llanos
Guiana
GUYANA
SURINAME
Fr. Guiana (Fr.)
COLOMBIA
Guaviare R.
Mt. Roraima 2772 m
Highlands
Malpelo I.
EQUATOR
Quito
ECUADOR
Japura R.
Putumayo R.
Negro
Mouths of the Amazon River
Marajo
EQUATOR
Galapagos Islands
Mt. Chimborazo 6310 m
Marañon R.
Amazon
Amazon River
Belem
A m a z o n
Gulf of Guayaquil
Jurua
Purus R.
Madeira R.
B a s i n
Tapajos R.
Xingu R.
Tocantins R.
Fernando de Noronha
Pt. Calcanhar
Pt. Parinas
Pt. Aguja
B R A Z I L
Parnaíba R.
Recife
Mt. Huascaran 6768 m
Paulo Afonso Falls
Lima
Mato Grosso Plateau
Brazilian
São Francisco R.
Lake Titicaca
La Paz
Altiplano
BOLIVIA
Highlands
Brasilia
Serra do Espinhaco
Mt. Sajama 6542 m
Sucre
Mamore R.
Paraguay R.
Tres Marias Res.
Area shown on cross section
Atacama Desert
Gran Chaco
PARAGUAY
Campos
Furnas Res.
Agulhas Negras 2787 m
TROPIC OF CAPRICORN 23½°S
Salado R.
Parana River
Great Escarpment
Cape Frio
Rio de Janeiro
Trindade
San Felix I.
San Ambrosio I.
Ojos del Salado 6880 m
Asuncion
Iguazu Falls
Salado R.
Uruguay R.
Juan Fernandez Islands
Aconcagua 6959 m
Pampas
URUGUAY
Patos Lagoon
Santiago
Colorado R.
Buenos Aires
Mirim L.
Montevideo
ARGENTINA
Negro R.
Cape San Antonio
Rio de la Plata
CHILE
Blanca Bay
Chiloe I.
Gulf of San Matias
Valdes Peninsula
Chonos Archipelago
Gulf of San Jorge
Cape Tres Puntas
Patagonia
Wellington I.
Queen Adelaide Archipelago
Strait of Magellan
Tierra del Fuego
Falkland Is.
Punta Arenas
Cape Horn
Scotia Sea
South Georgia I.
Drake Passage

ELEVATION MAP

SOUTH AMERICA

Metres Above Sea Level

Over 6000
3000 to 6000
1500 to 3000
600 to 1500
300 to 600
150 to 300
0 to 150

Scale
1:37 400 000

0   250   500   750   1000 kilometres

1 cm to 374 km

Lambert Equal Area Projection

Detailed legend on page 5

CROSS SECTION
Vertical exaggeration 37 to 1
Scale at 24° N: 1 cm to 200 km

Andes Mountains
Mt. Sajama
Lake Titicaca
PERU
Altiplano
Gran Chaco
Mato Grosso Plateau
Brazilian Highlands
CHILE
BOLIVIA
BRAZIL
PACIFIC OCEAN
ARGENTINA
PARAGUAY
Paraguay R.
Parana R.
São Francisco R.
Serra do Espinhaço
Sea Level
ATLANTIC OCEAN

ALTITUDE ZONES IN THE ANDES

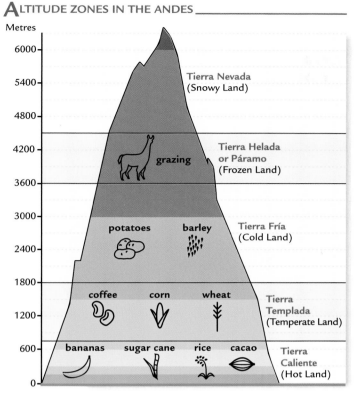

Metres

6000	Tierra Nevada (Snowy Land)
5400	
4800	
4200	Tierra Helada or Páramo (Frozen Land)
3600	grazing
3000	potatoes · barley — Tierra Fría (Cold Land)
2400	
1800	
1200	coffee · corn · wheat — Tierra Templada (Temperate Land)
600	bananas · sugar cane · rice · cacao — Tierra Caliente (Hot Land)
0	

As altitude in the Andes increases, the climate gets colder and drier. For centuries, indigenous people in the region have cultivated crops that grow well at each elevation zone and climate.

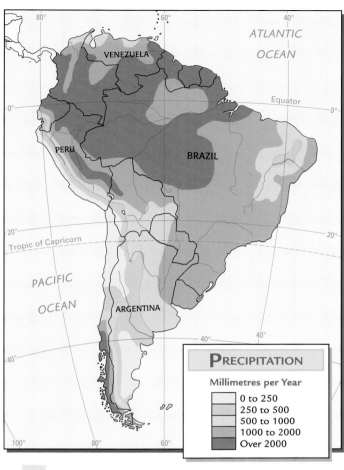

PRECIPITATION

Millimetres per Year

- 0 to 250
- 250 to 500
- 500 to 1000
- 1000 to 2000
- Over 2000

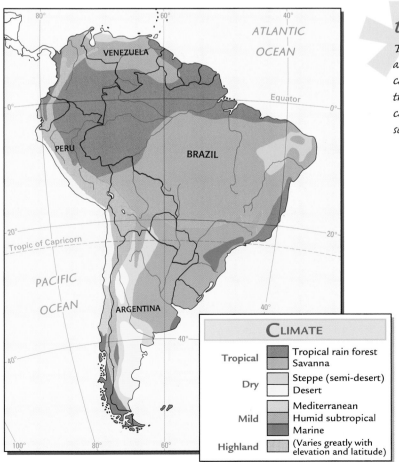

CLIMATE

Tropical	Tropical rain forest
	Savanna
Dry	Steppe (semi-desert)
	Desert
Mild	Mediterranean
	Humid subtropical
	Marine
Highland	(Varies greatly with elevation and latitude)

Desert by the Sea

The Atacama Desert along coastal Peru and Chile is among the driest places on Earth. Its dry conditions are caused by the cold Peru Current, which flows north along the western coast of the continent. This surface current cools the air, preventing it from holding much moisture, so very little rain falls in this region.

CLIMOGRAPHS

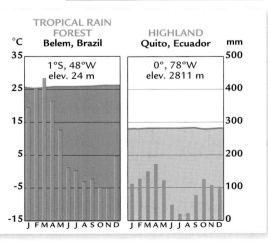

TROPICAL RAIN FOREST
Belem, Brazil
1°S, 48°W
elev. 24 m

HIGHLAND
Quito, Ecuador
0°, 78°W
elev. 2811 m

Both Quito and Belem are near the Equator. The difference in their elevations explains why Quito is colder and drier. Air temperature drops about 6.5°C for each rise of 1000 metres.

more at NCWatlas.ca

LAND USE

Widespread Economic Uses

- • Urban
- Commercial farming
- Subsistence farming
- Ranching or herding
- Forestry
- No widespread use

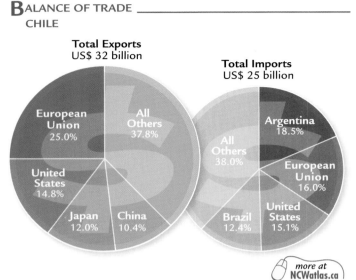

BALANCE OF TRADE
CHILE

Total Exports
US$ 32 billion

- European Union 25.0%
- All Others 37.8%
- United States 14.8%
- Japan 12.0%
- China 10.4%

Total Imports
US$ 25 billion

- Argentina 18.5%
- All Others 38.0%
- European Union 16.0%
- United States 15.1%
- Brazil 12.4%

more at NCWatlas.ca

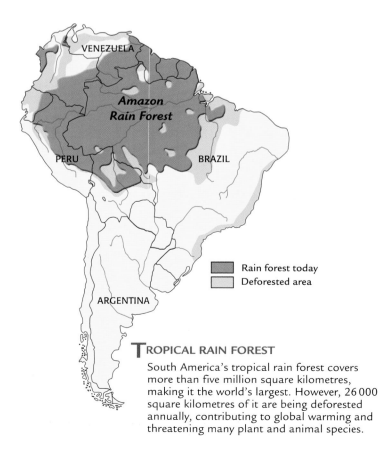

TROPICAL RAIN FOREST

South America's tropical rain forest covers more than five million square kilometres, making it the world's largest. However, 26 000 square kilometres of it are being deforested annually, contributing to global warming and threatening many plant and animal species.

- Rain forest today
- Deforested area

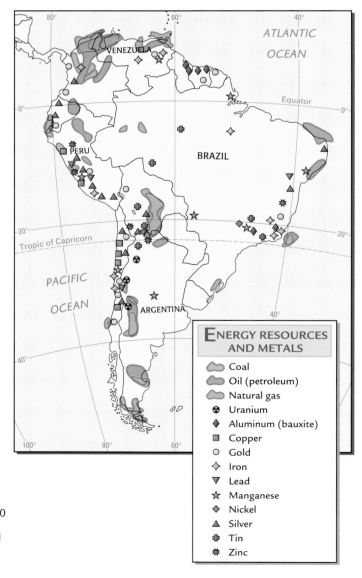

ENERGY RESOURCES AND METALS

- Coal
- Oil (petroleum)
- Natural gas
- Uranium
- Aluminum (bauxite)
- Copper
- Gold
- Iron
- Lead
- Manganese
- Nickel
- Silver
- Tin
- Zinc

Natural Population Growth
SOUTH AMERICA

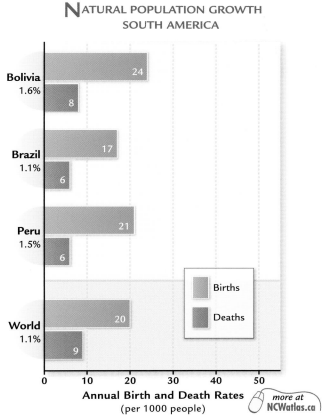

Bolivia
1.6%
24
8

Brazil
1.1%
17
6

Peru
1.5%
21
6

World
1.1%
20
9

Births
Deaths

Annual Birth and Death Rates
(per 1000 people)

more at
NCWatlas.ca

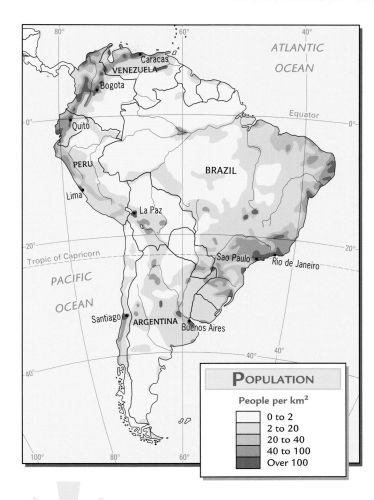

ATLANTIC OCEAN

Caracas
VENEZUELA
Bogota
Quito
Equator
PERU
BRAZIL
Lima
La Paz
Tropic of Capricorn
Sao Paulo
Rio de Janeiro
PACIFIC OCEAN
Santiago
ARGENTINA
Buenos Aires

Population
People per km²

	0 to 2
	2 to 20
	20 to 40
	40 to 100
	Over 100

Mixed Roots

Mestizo *is Spanish for* mixed. *In Latin America, the term is used to describe a person of mixed European and American Indian parentage.* **Mulatto** *describes a person of mixed European and African parentage. Over 85 percent of the people in Paraguay are mestizo, while over 35 percent of those in French Guiana are mulatto.*

more at
NCWatlas.ca

Goajiro
VENEZUELA
ATLANTIC OCEAN
Chibcha
COLOMBIA
Equator
Quechua
ECUADOR
Aymara
PERU
Quechua
BRAZIL
Quechua
BOLIVIA
Aymara
Guarani
PARAGUAY
Tropic of Capricorn
CHILE
PACIFIC OCEAN
ARGENTINA
Mapuche

Descendants of Indigenous South Americans*
Percentage of Population

	85 to 100
	70 to 85
	50 to 70
	Under 10

Aymara Large indigenous group today
*Includes Mestizo

Peru has one of the larger indigenous populations in South America. (For more information, see page 95.) Many Quechua and Aymara still farm and bring goods to market in the highlands.

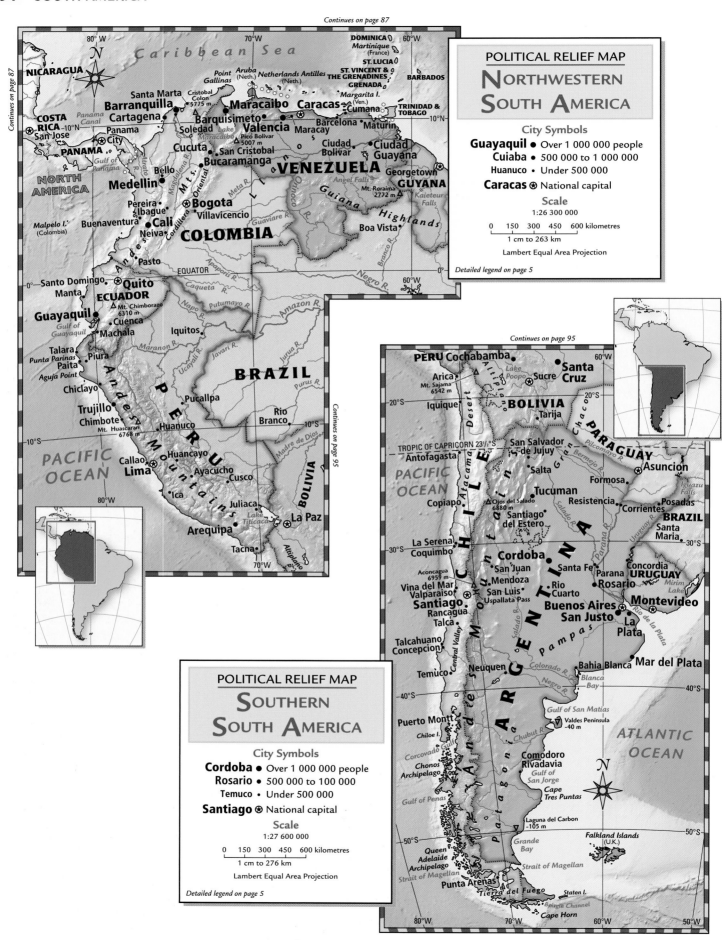

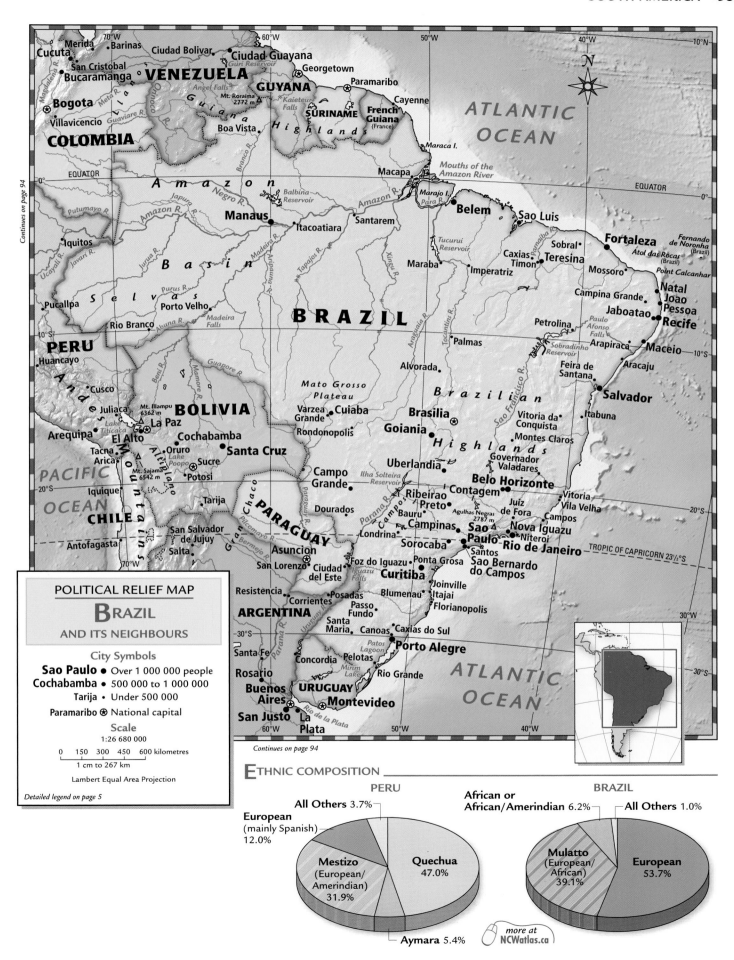

ATLANTIC OCEAN

PACIFIC OCEAN

Continues on page 94

Continues on page 94

POLITICAL RELIEF MAP

Brazil

AND ITS NEIGHBOURS

City Symbols

Sao Paulo ● Over 1 000 000 people
Cochabamba ● 500 000 to 1 000 000
Tarija • Under 500 000

Paramaribo ⊗ National capital

Scale

1:26 680 000

0   150   300   450   600 kilometres

1 cm to 267 km

Lambert Equal Area Projection

Detailed legend on page 5

ETHNIC COMPOSITION

PERU

All Others 3.7%

European (mainly Spanish) 12.0%

Mestizo (European/ Amerindian) 31.9%

Quechua 47.0%

Aymara 5.4%

BRAZIL

African or African/Amerindian 6.2%

All Others 1.0%

Mulatto (European/ African) 39.1%

European 53.7%

more at NCWatlas.ca

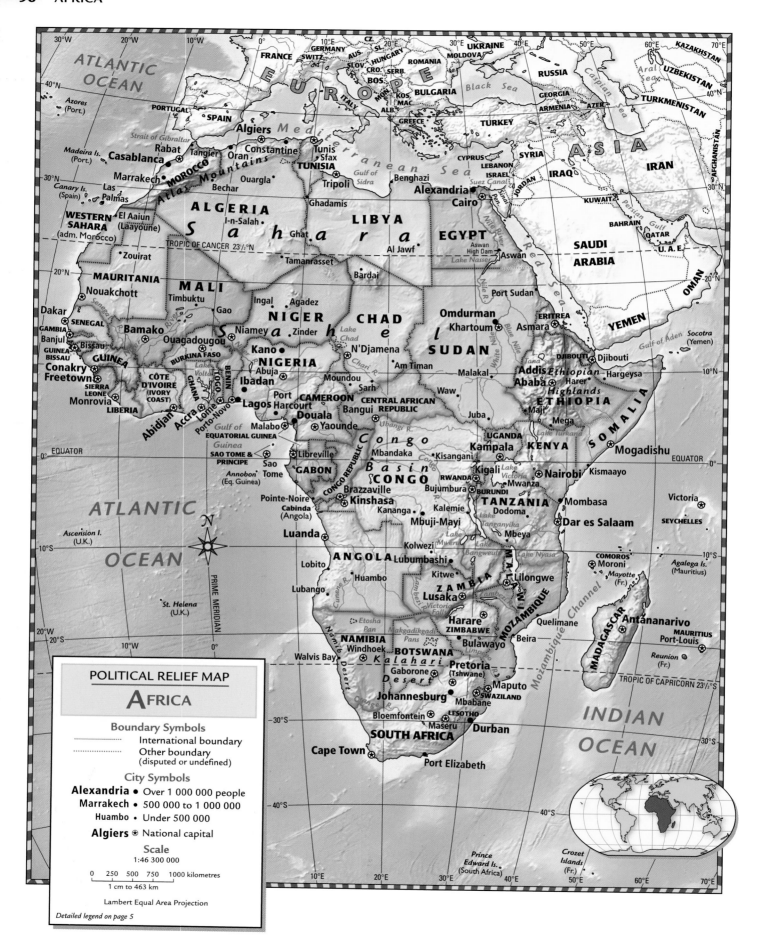

POLITICAL RELIEF MAP

AFRICA

Boundary Symbols
.... International boundary
.... Other boundary
(disputed or undefined)

City Symbols
Alexandria ● Over 1 000 000 people
Marrakech ● 500 000 to 1 000 000
Huambo ● Under 500 000

Algiers ⊛ National capital

Scale
1:46 300 000

0   250 500 750   1000 kilometres
1 cm to 463 km

Lambert Equal Area Projection

Detailed legend on page 5

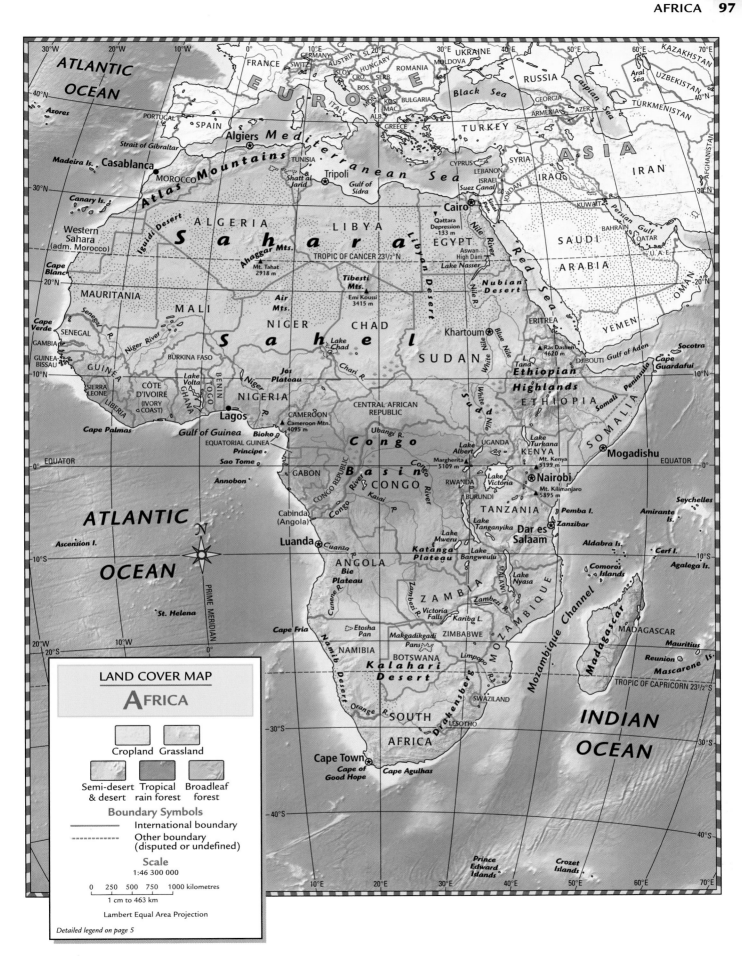

ATLANTIC OCEAN

Azores

Madeira Is.

Canary Is.

Western Sahara (adm. Morocco)

Cape Blanc

Cape Verde

GAMBIA

GUINEA-BISSAU

SIERRA LEONE

LIBERIA

Cape Palmas

Ascension I.

ATLANTIC OCEAN

St. Helena

EUROPE

FRANCE

PORTUGAL

SPAIN

Strait of Gibraltar

Casablanca

MOROCCO

Atlas Mountains

Algiers

TUNISIA

Mediterranean Sea

Tripoli

Gulf of Sidra

ALGERIA

LIBYA

Sahara

TROPIC OF CANCER 23½°N

Iguidi Desert

Mt. Tahat 2918 m

Ahaggar Mts.

MAURITANIA

MALI

Air Mts.

Tibesti Mts.

Emi Koussi 3415 m

NIGER

CHAD

Sahel

Senegal R.

Niger River

SENEGAL

BURKINA FASO

Lake Chad

Chari R.

GUINEA

CÔTE D'IVOIRE (IVORY COAST)

Lake Volta

BENIN

TOGO

GHANA

Jos Plateau

NIGERIA

Niger R.

Lagos

Gulf of Guinea

Bioko

CAMEROON

Cameroon Mtn. 4095 m

EQUATORIAL GUINEA

Principe

Sao Tome

Annobon

GERMANY

SWITZ.

CZ.

AUSTRIA

HUNGARY

SL.

SLOV

CRO

BOS

SERB.

MON.

MAC.

ALB.

ITALY

GREECE

ROMANIA

BULGARIA

MOLDOVA

UKRAINE

Black Sea

RUSSIA

GEORGIA

ARMENIA

AZER.

Caspian Sea

Aral Sea

KAZAKHSTAN

UZBEKISTAN

TÜRKMENISTAN

TURKEY

CYPRUS

SYRIA

LEBANON

ISRAEL

JORDAN

IRAQ

IRAN

AFGHANISTAN

Suez Canal

Cairo

Qattara Depression -133 m

EGYPT

Aswan High Dam

Lake Nasser

Nile River

Libyan Desert

Nubian Desert

Nile R.

Red Sea

SAUDI ARABIA

KUWAIT

BAHRAIN

QATAR

U.A.E.

OMAN

YEMEN

ASIA

Persian Gulf

Socotra

Cape Guardafui

Gulf of Aden

DJIBOUTI

Khartoum

SUDAN

ERITREA

Ras Dashen 4620 m

L. Tana

Ethiopian Highlands

ETHIOPIA

Somali Peninsula

SOMALIA

Mogadishu

CENTRAL AFRICAN REPUBLIC

Ubangi R.

Congo River

Congo Basin

Congo River

GABON

CONGO

CONGO REPUBLIC

Congo R.

Kasai R.

Cabinda (Angola)

Luanda

Cuanza R.

ANGOLA

Bie Plateau

Cunene R.

Lake Albert

Margherita 5109 m

UGANDA

RWANDA

BURUNDI

Lake Victoria

Lake Turkana

KENYA

Mt. Kenya 5199 m

Nairobi

Mt. Kilimanjaro 5895 m

TANZANIA

Lake Tanganyika

Lake Mweru

Katanga Plateau

Lake Bangweulu

Pemba I.

Zanzibar

Dar es Salaam

EQUATOR

Seychelles

Amirante Is.

Aldabra Is.

Cerf I.

Agalega Is.

Comoros Islands

ZAMBIA

MALAWI

Lake Nyasa

Zambezi R.

Victoria Falls

Kariba L.

Zambezi R.

ZIMBABWE

Cape Fria

Etosha Pan

Makgadikgadi Pans

NAMIBIA

BOTSWANA

Kalahari Desert

Namib Desert

Orange R.

Limpopo

MOZAMBIQUE

Mozambique Channel

MADAGASCAR

Mauritius

Reunion

Mascarene Is.

SWAZILAND

LESOTHO

SOUTH AFRICA

Drakensberg

Cape Town

Cape of Good Hope

Cape Agulhas

TROPIC OF CAPRICORN 23½°S

INDIAN OCEAN

Prince Edward Islands

Crozet Islands

PRIME MERIDIAN

N

30°W 20°W 10°W 0° 10°E 20°E 30°E 40°E 50°E 60°E 70°E

40°N 30°N 20°N 10°N EQUATOR 10°S 20°S 30°S 40°S

LAND COVER MAP
AFRICA

Cropland   Grassland

Semi-desert & desert   Tropical rain forest   Broadleaf forest

Boundary Symbols

———— International boundary

------------- Other boundary (disputed or undefined)

Scale
1:46 300 000

0 250 500 750 1000 kilometres

1 cm to 463 km

Lambert Equal Area Projection

Detailed legend on page 5

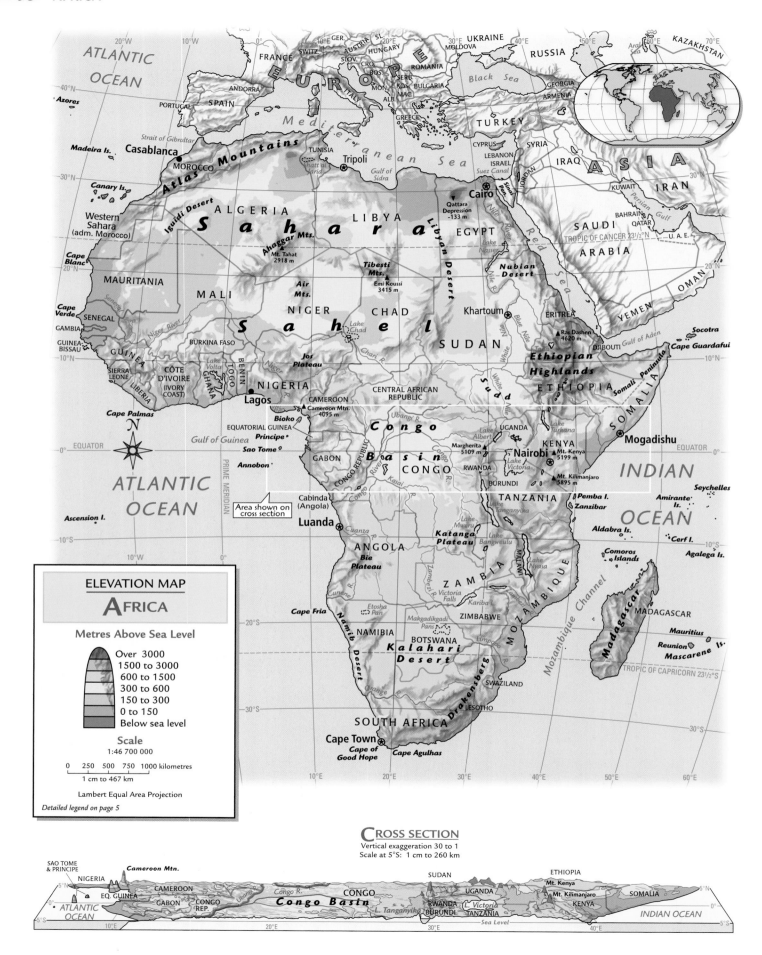

ATLANTIC OCEAN

Azores

Madeira Is.

Canary Is.

Western Sahara (adm. Morocco)

Cape Blanc

MAURITANIA

Cape Verde

SENEGAL

GAMBIA

GUINEA-BISSAU

SIERRA LEONE

LIBERIA

GUINEA

Cape Palmas

CÔTE D'IVOIRE (IVORY COAST)

GHANA

TOGO

BENIN

Casablanca
MOROCCO

Atlas Mountains

Strait of Gibraltar

PORTUGAL

SPAIN

ANDORRA

FRANCE

SWITZ.

Iguidi Desert

ALGERIA

Sahara

Ahaggar Mts.

Mt. Tahat 2918 m

MALI

Air Mts.

NIGER

Sahel

BURKINA FASO

Niger River

Lake Volta

NIGERIA

Lagos

Jos Plateau

Tibesti Mts.

Emi Koussi 3415 m

CHAD

Lake Chad

Chari R.

Saha

EUROPE

GER.
AUSTRIA
SL.
HUNGARY
SLOV.
CRO.
BOS.
MON.
SERB.
KOS.
MAC.
ALB.
ITALY
GREECE

Mediterranean Sea

TUNISIA

Chott el Jerid

Tripoli

Gulf of Sidra

LIBYA

Libyan Desert

Nubian Desert

EGYPT

SUDAN

ROMANIA
BULGARIA

Black Sea

UKRAINE
MOLDOVA

RUSSIA

GEORGIA
ARMENIA

TURKEY

CYPRUS
SYRIA
LEBANON
ISRAEL
Suez Canal
JORDAN
Sinai Pen.

Cairo

Qattara Depression -133 m

Nile River

Lake Nasser

TROPIC OF CANCER 23½°N

IRAQ

KUWAIT

SAUDI ARABIA

Red Sea

Khartoum

Blue Nile

White Nile

Ras Dashen 4620 m

ERITREA

DJIBOUTI

Gulf of Aden

ETHIOPIA

Ethiopian Highlands

KAZAKHSTAN

Aral Sea

ASIA

IRAN

BAHRAIN
QATAR
Persian Gulf
U.A.E.

YEMEN

OMAN

Socotra

Cape Guardafui

Somali Peninsula

CAMEROON

Cameroon Mtn. 4095 m

Bioko

EQUATORIAL GUINEA

Principe

Sao Tome

Annobon

GABON

CONGO REPUBLIC

Congo Basin

Congo River

Kasai

CONGO

Ubangi R.

CENTRAL AFRICAN REPUBLIC

Sudd

White Nile

UGANDA

Lake Albert

Lake Turkana

KENYA

Margherita 5109 m

RWANDA

BURUNDI

Nairobi

Mt. Kenya 5199 m

Lake Victoria

Mt. Kilimanjaro 5895 m

SOMALIA

Mogadishu

INDIAN OCEAN

EQUATOR

Seychelles

Amirante Is.

Area shown on cross section

Gulf of Guinea

PRIME MERIDIAN

EQUATOR

ATLANTIC OCEAN

Ascension I.

Cabinda (Angola)

Luanda

Cuanza

ANGOLA

Bie Plateau

Katanga Plateau

Lake Mweru

Lake Bangweulu

ZAMBIA

Zambezi R.

TANZANIA

Lake Tanganyika

Lake Nyasa

MALAWI

Pemba I.

Zanzibar

Mozambique Channel

Aldabra Is.

Cerf I.

Agalega Is.

Comoros Islands

MADAGASCAR

MADAGASCAR

Mauritius

Reunion

Mascarene Is.

Cape Fria

Namib Desert

NAMIBIA

Etosha Pan

Makgadikgadi Pans

BOTSWANA

Kalahari Desert

Victoria Falls

Kariba

ZIMBABWE

Limpopo

MOZAMBIQUE

SWAZILAND

Drakensberg

LESOTHO

SOUTH AFRICA

Cape Town

Cape of Good Hope

Cape Agulhas

Orange

TROPIC OF CAPRICORN 23½°S

ELEVATION MAP

AFRICA

Metres Above Sea Level

- Over 3000
- 1500 to 3000
- 600 to 1500
- 300 to 600
- 150 to 300
- 0 to 150
- Below sea level

Scale
1:46 700 000

0 250 500 750 1000 kilometres

1 cm to 467 km

Lambert Equal Area Projection

Detailed legend on page 5

CROSS SECTION

Vertical exaggeration 30 to 1
Scale at 5°S: 1 cm to 260 km

SAO TOME & PRINCIPE

Cameroon Mtn.

NIGERIA

ATLANTIC OCEAN

EQ. GUINEA

CAMEROON

GABON

CONGO REP.

Ubangi

Congo R.

CONGO

Congo Basin

L. Tanganyika

SUDAN

UGANDA

RWANDA

BURUNDI

Victoria

TANZANIA

ETHIOPIA

Mt. Kenya

Mt. Kilimanjaro

KENYA

SOMALIA

INDIAN OCEAN

Sea Level

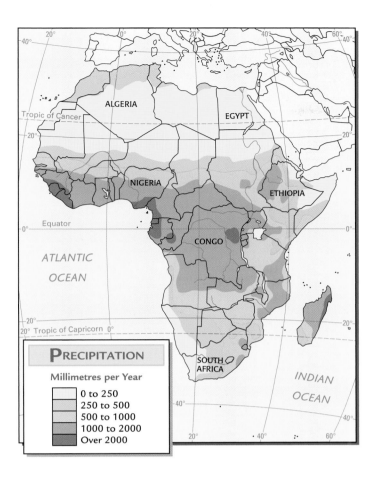

PRECIPITATION

Millimetres per Year

- 0 to 250
- 250 to 500
- 500 to 1000
- 1000 to 2000
- Over 2000

Niger is one of the world's poorest countries, with 60 percent of its population living on less than C$1.15 a day. Ninety percent of its labour force is involved in agriculture. Unsophisticated farming methods and cycles of drought, however, result in shortages of food. Here, a woman in Niger threshes millet by hand.

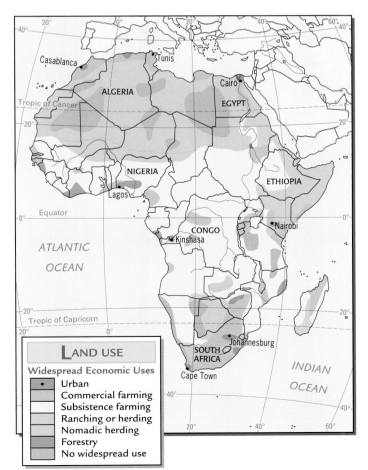

LAND USE

Widespread Economic Uses

- • Urban
- Commercial farming
- Subsistence farming
- Ranching or herding
- Nomadic herding
- Forestry
- No widespread use

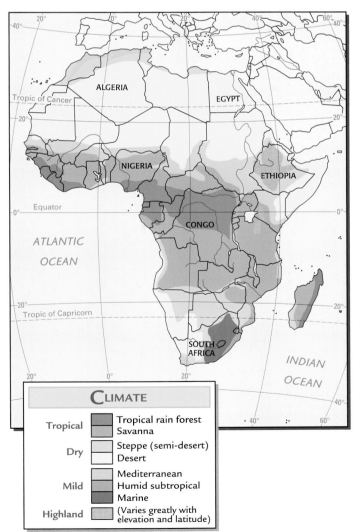

CLIMATE

Tropical		Tropical rain forest
		Savanna
Dry		Steppe (semi-desert)
		Desert
Mild		Mediterranean
		Humid subtropical
		Marine
Highland		(Varies greatly with elevation and latitude)

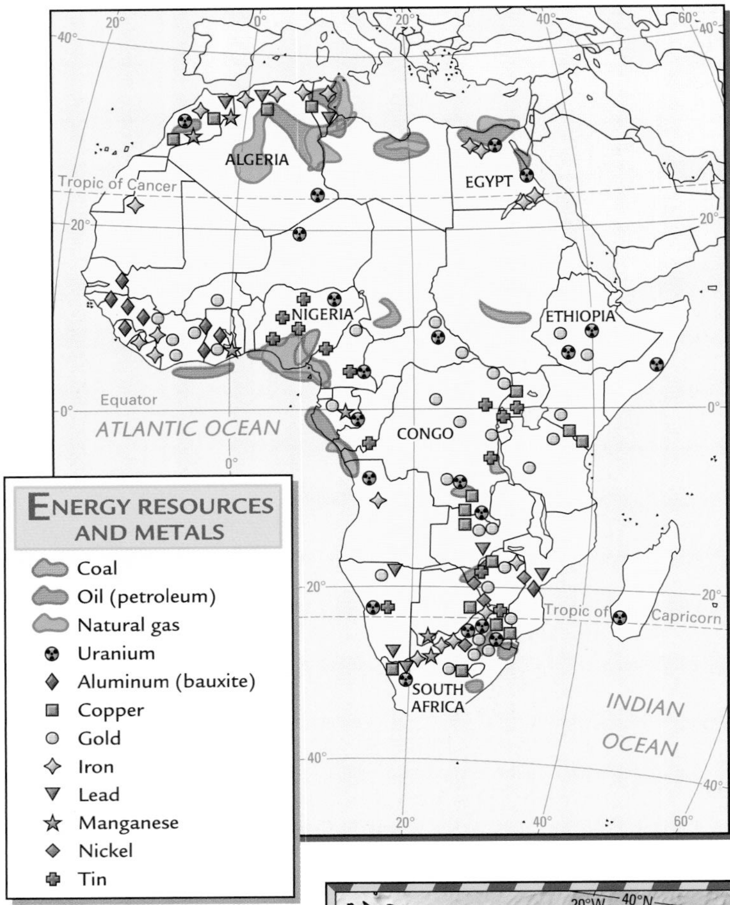

BALANCE OF TRADE

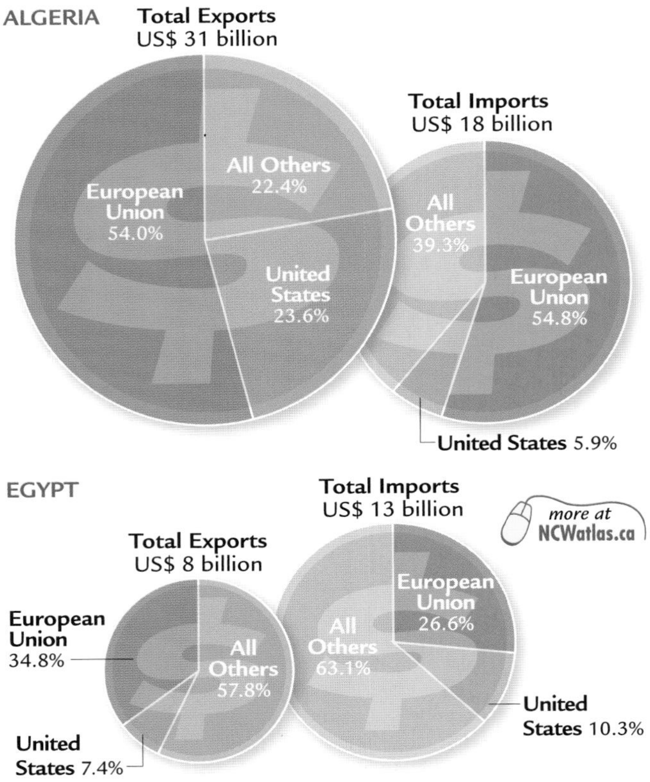

ALGERIA

Total Exports
US$ 31 billion

- European Union 54.0%
- All Others 22.4%
- United States 23.6%

Total Imports
US$ 18 billion

- All Others 39.3%
- European Union 54.8%
- United States 5.9%

EGYPT

Total Exports
US$ 8 billion

- European Union 34.8%
- All Others 57.8%
- United States 7.4%

Total Imports
US$ 13 billion

- All Others 63.1%
- European Union 26.6%
- United States 10.3%

more at
NCWatlas.ca

ENERGY RESOURCES AND METALS

- Coal
- Oil (petroleum)
- Natural gas
- Uranium
- Aluminum (bauxite)
- Copper
- Gold
- Iron
- Lead
- Manganese
- Nickel
- Tin

Map labels: ALGERIA, EGYPT, NIGERIA, ETHIOPIA, CONGO, SOUTH AFRICA, ATLANTIC OCEAN, INDIAN OCEAN, Tropic of Cancer, Equator, Tropic of Capricorn

Continues on page 117

POLITICAL RELIEF MAP
NORTHERN AFRICA

City Symbols

Casablanca ● Over 1 000 000 people
Benghazi ● 500 000 to 1 000 000
Qabis · Under 500 000
Cairo ⊗ National capital

Scale
1:24 500 000

0   150   300   450   600 kilometres

1 cm to 245 km

Lambert Equal Area Projection

Detailed legend on page 5

Map labels: Sao Jorge, Sao Miguel, Azores (Portugal), Santa Maria, Porto, Madrid, SPAIN, Barcelona, Corsica (France), Rome, Tyrrhenian Sea, Lisbon, PORTUGAL, Tagus R., Iberian Peninsula, Valencia, Balearic Is. (Spain), Sardinia (Italy), Mediterranean, ATLANTIC OCEAN, Madeira Is. (Portugal), Funchal, Strait of Gibraltar, Tangier, Ceuta (Spain), Tetouan, Gibraltar (U.K.), Melilla (Spain), Algiers, Bejaia, Annaba, Bizerte, Tunis, La Palma, Santa Cruz, Tenerife, Lanzarote, Fuerteventura, El Hierro, Gran Canaria, Las Palmas, Canary Is. (Spain), Rabat, Kenitra, Fez, Oujda, Oran, Tiaret, Constantine, Batna, Susah, Sfax, Casablanca, Khouribga, Meknes, Sidi-Bel-Abbes, Touggourt, TUNISIA, Tripoli, Safi, MOROCCO, Bouarfa, Mountains, Ouargla, Al Aziziya, Marrakech, Bechar, Gulf of Gabes, Agadir, Jebel Toubkal 4165 m, Zagora, Atlas, Grand Erg Occidental (desert), Grand Erg Oriental (desert), Ghadamis, Goulimine, Tan-Tan, ALGERIA, I-n-Salah, Sahara, Tindouf, Erg Iguidi (desert), Ghat, El Aaiun (Laayoune), Western Sahara (adm. by Morocco), Erg Chech (desert), Tanezrouft, Ahaggar Mts., Dakhla, TROPIC OF CANCER 23½°N, Zouirat, Mt. Tahat 2918 m, Tamanrasset, Nouadhibou, Cape Blanc, Atar, MAURITANIA, Azaouad, PRIME MERIDIAN, Arlit, Air Mts., Grand Erg de Bilma (desert), Nouakchott, El Djouf (desert), MALI, Agadez, NIGER, Rosso, Bogue, Ingal, Saint-Louis, Kaedi, Timbuktu, Gao, Dakar, Thies, SENEGAL, Niger River, Senegal R., Kayes, Mopti, Tahoua, Kaolack, Cape Verde

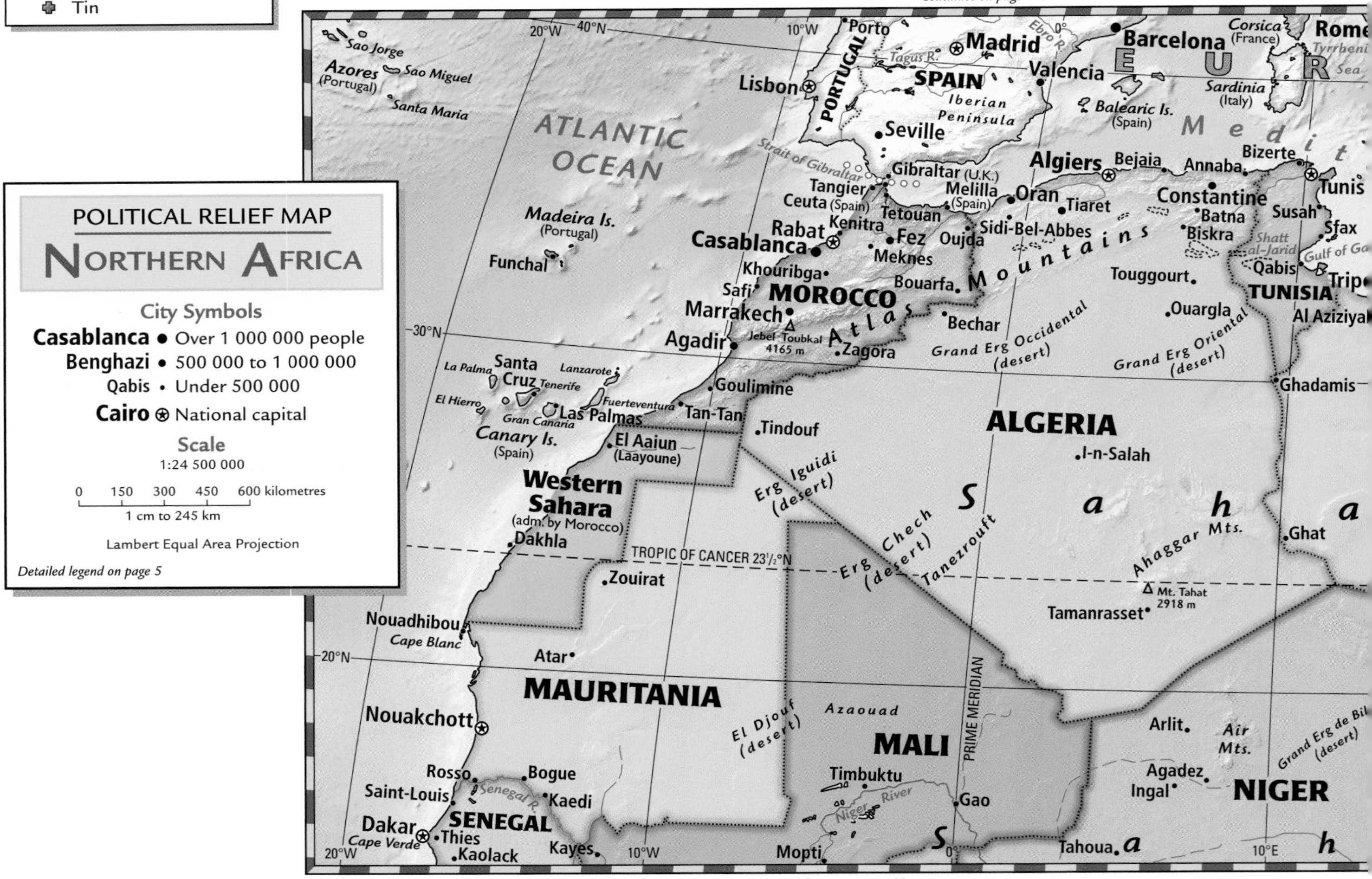

Continues on page 102

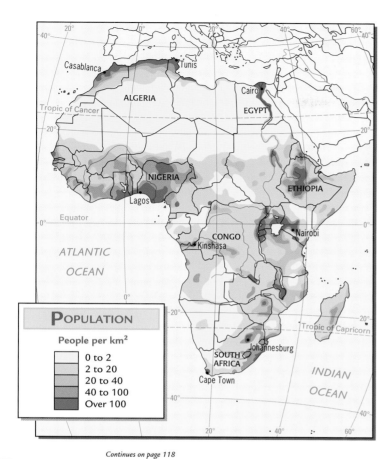

POPULATION

People per km²

- 0 to 2
- 2 to 20
- 20 to 40
- 40 to 100
- Over 100

Natural Population Growth
AFRICA

Ethiopia 2.4% — Births 39, Deaths 15

Niger 3.0% — Births 51, Deaths 21

South Africa -0.3% — Births 18, Deaths 21

World 1.1% — Births 20, Deaths 9

Births
Deaths

Annual Birth and Death Rates
(per 1000 people)

more at NCWatlas.ca

Continues on page 118

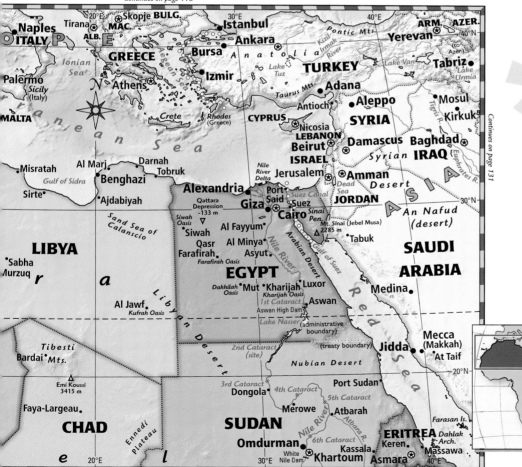

Continues on page 131

Continental Divide

Africa is divided both physically and culturally by the Sahara. Most Africans living north of the Sahara are Arab and Muslim. About 75 percent of all Africans live south of the Sahara. They are more diverse than northern Africans. They belong to 800 ethnic groups and follow Christianity, Islam, or traditional religions.

Continues on page 103

Continues on page 104

Continues on pages 100–101

Nouakchott ⊛

MAURITANIA

El Djouf (desert)

Azaouad

10°W

0°

Arlit

Air Mts.

10°E

Grand Erg de Bilma (desert)

Rosso
Saint-Louis
Bogue
Kaedi

Senegal R.

MALI

Timbuktu

Ingal

Agadez

⊛ Dakar
Thies **SENEGAL**
Kaolack

Kayes

Gao

Niger River

NIGER

Tahoua

Cape Verde
Banjul ⊛

GAMBIA

Gambia R.

Segou

Bani R.

⊛ Niamey

Maradi

Zinder

Diffa

CHAD

Ziguinchor
Bissau ⊛
GUINEA-BISSAU

Bamako ⊛

Faleme R.

Mopti

S   a   h   e   l

Sokoto

Katsina

Lake Chad

⊛ N'Djamena

Bijagos Is.

Boke

GUINEA

Kouroussa

BURKINA FASO

Ouagadougou ⊛

Koudougou

White Volta

Bawku

Kano

Zaria

Maiduguri

Maroua

10°N

Kindia
Dabola
Kankan

Sikasso

Bobo Dioulasso

Wa

Kaduna

Bauchi

Mandara Mts.

Conakry ⊛

Kissidougou

Korhogo

Black Volta

Tamale

BENIN

Djougou

Kainji Lake

Kainji Dam

NIGERIA

Jos Plateau

Abuja

Garoua

Gotel Mts.

10°N

SIERRA LEONE

Loma Mts.

Freetown ⊛
Bo

Nzerekore

Kenema

Man

CÔTE D'IVOIRE (IVORY COAST)

Bouake

Komoe R.

GHANA

Sokode

Parakou

Ogbomosho

TOGO

Porto-Novo

Iwo
Ilesha

Benue R.

Adamoua Plateau

Ngaoundere

Ilorin

Ibadan

Makurdi

Bouar

ATLANTIC OCEAN

Monrovia ⊛

Gbaranga

Daloa

Sassandra R.

Yamoussoukro

Kumasi

Obuasi

Lake Volta

Akosombo Dam

Ogbomosho

Benin City

Enugu

Onitsha

Bamenda

CAMEROON

Buchanan

LIBERIA

San Pedro

Abidjan

Cape Three Points

Accra ⊛

Tema

Lome ⊛

Cotonou

Lagos

Port Harcourt

Aba

Mt. Cameroon 4095 m △

Douala

Sanaga R.

Greenville

Cape Palmas

Sekondi-Takoradi

Bight of Benin

Niger River Delta

Bioko

⊛ **Yaounde**

10°E

N

Gulf   of   Guinea

10°W

0°

Continues on page 103

POLITICAL RELIEF MAP

WESTERN AFRICA

City Symbols

Lagos ● Over 1 000 000 people
Kumasi • 500 000 to 1 000 000
Parakou · Under 500 000
Freetown ⊛ National capital

Scale
1:20 300 000

0 100 200 300 400 500 kilometres

1 cm to 203 km

Lambert Equal Area Projection

Detailed legend on page 5

Forced Together

European countries divided Africa among themselves during the late 1800s, drawing arbitrary boundary lines that often put rival ethnic groups in the same country. These divisions have led to bloody conflicts that continue to disrupt Africa today. For example, more than 180 000 people in western Sudan have been killed since 2003 because of ethnic tensions.

more at NCWatlas.ca

ETHNIC COMPOSITION

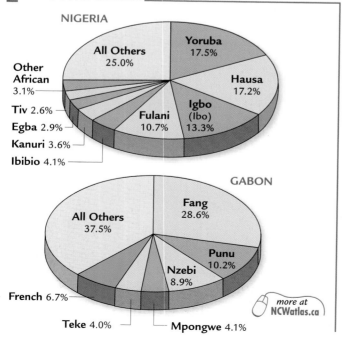

NIGERIA

- Yoruba 17.5%
- Hausa 17.2%
- Igbo (Ibo) 13.3%
- Fulani 10.7%
- All Others 25.0%
- Other African 3.1%
- Tiv 2.6%
- Egba 2.9%
- Kanuri 3.6%
- Ibibio 4.1%

GABON

- Fang 28.6%
- Punu 10.2%
- Nzebi 8.9%
- All Others 37.5%
- French 6.7%
- Teke 4.0%
- Mpongwe 4.1%

more at NCWatlas.ca

Education is important to economic development, yet 40 million African children—most of them girls—do not attend school. Here a Nigerian student completes a math assignment. Only 76 percent of all men and 61 percent of all women in Nigeria can read and write.

Hutu women return to their homes after civil war erupts in Congo. In 1996 more than 700 000 Congolese refugees fled to neighboring countries. About one-third of the world's refugees are African.

POLITICAL RELIEF MAP
CENTRAL AFRICA

City Symbols

Douala ● Over 1 000 000 people
Lubumbashi • 500 000 to 1 000 000
Bambari • Under 500 000
Brazzaville ⊛ National capital

Scale
1:17 900 000

0 100 200 300 400 kilometres
1 cm to 179 km
Lambert Equal Area Projection

Detailed legend on page 5

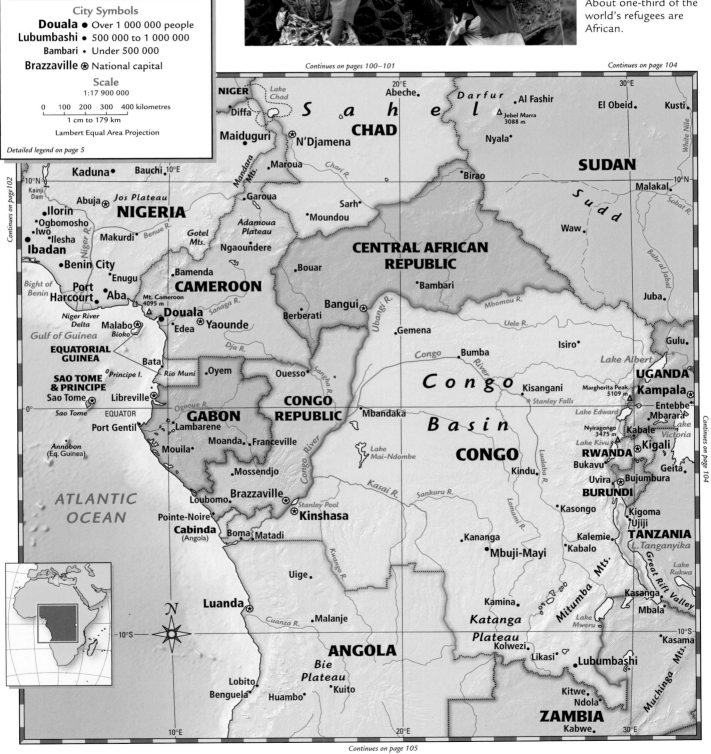

Continues on pages 100–101
Continues on page 104
Continues on page102
Continues on page 104
Continues on page 105

Continues on pages 100–101
Continues on page 131
Continues on page 103
Continues on page 105

30°E   40°E   50°E   20°N

LIBYA
Libyan Desert
Nubian Desert
SAUDI ARABIA
Rub Al Khali (Empty Quarter)
ASIA
OMAN
YEMEN

CHAD
Ennedi Plateau
3rd Cataract
Dongola
4th Cataract
Merowe
5th Cataract
Atbarah
Port Sudan
Red Sea
Farasan Is.
ERITREA
Keren
Dahlak Arch.
Massawa
Sanaa
Arabian Sea
Salalah
Socotra (Yemen)

Omdurman
Khartoum
White Nile Dam
Kassala
Asmara
Al Hudaydah
Taizz
Abd al Kuri (Yemen)

Sahel
SUDAN
Darfur
Al Fashir
△ Jebel Marra 3088 m
Wad Medani
Sennar Dam
Mekele
Ras Dashen 4620 m
Denakil Depression -116 m
Assab
Aden
Gulf of Aden
Cape Guardafui (Raas Caseyr)

El Obeid
Kusti
Sennar
Gonder
Lake Tana
Tisissat Falls
Lake Assal -156 m
DJIBOUTI
Djibouti
Berbera
Cape Hafun

Nyala
Bahir Dar
Ethiopian
Dese
Dire Dawa
Hargeysa
Somaliland
Burao
Somali Peninsula
10°N

Birao
Malakal
Sudd
Sobat R.
Addis Ababa
Nazret
Highlands
Jima
Harer
Nugaal Valley
Garoowe

CENTRAL AFRICAN REPUBLIC
Waw
Bahr al Jabal
ETHIOPIA
Awasa
Maji
Ogaden
Shebele R.

Mbomou R.
Juba
Lake Turkana
Mega
Moyale
Baidoa
Hobyo
SOMALIA

Uele R.
Bumba
Isiro
Lake Albert
Gulu
UGANDA
KENYA
Jubba R.
Merca
Jawhar
Mogadishu
EQUATOR

Congo
Kisangani
Stanley Falls
Margherita Peak 5109 m △
Lake Kyoga
Kampala
Jinja
Mt. Elgon △ 4321 m
Eldoret
Kisumu
Meru
△ Mt. Kenya 5199 m
Garissa
Kismaayo

Basin
Lake Edward
Entebbe
Mbarara
Nakuru
Nairobi
Machakos
0°

CONGO
Nyiragongo 3475 m
Lake Kivu
Kigali
RWANDA
Bukavu
Lake Victoria
Serengeti Plain
Mwanza
Mt. Kilimanjaro 5895 m
Malindi
INDIAN OCEAN

Kindu
Lualaba R.
Bujumbura
BURUNDI
Shinyanga
Arusha
Moshi
Mombasa

Kasongo
Sankuru R.
Kigoma
Ujiji
Tabora
Dodoma
Morogoro
Tanga
Pemba I.

Kananga
Lomami R.
Kalemie
Lake Tanganyika
Mwanza
TANZANIA
Zanzibar
Zanzibar I.

Mbuji-Mayi
Kabalo
Kamina
Mitumba Mts.
Lake Mweru
Mbala
Lake Rukwa
Mbeya
Great Rift Valley
Rufiji R.
Dar es Salaam
Mafia I.
SEYCHELLES
Aldabra Is.

Katanga Plateau
Kolwezi
Kasama
Kasama
ZAMBIA
Tunduru
Mtwara
10°S

Likasi
Muchinga Mts.
Mzuzu
Lake Nyasa (Lake Malawi)
MALAWI
MOZAMBIQUE
Moroni
COMOROS
Mayotte (France)
50°E

N

POLITICAL RELIEF MAP
EASTERN AFRICA

City Symbols
Omdurman ● Over 1 000 000 people
Mombasa ● 500 000 to 1 000 000
Zanzibar ● Under 500 000
Nairobi ⊛ National capital

Scale
1:19 900 000

0   100   200   300   400   500 kilometres

1 cm to 199 km

Lambert Equal Area Projection

Detailed legend on page 5

Both Rich and Poor

Nine out of ten of the world's poorest countries
are in Africa. Nearly half of the population
of sub-Saharan Africa survives on less than
C$ 1.15 a day. Although Africa is rich with
gold and oil, most mining companies are
foreign-owned and employ few Africans.

more at NCWatlas.ca

GREAT RIFT VALLEY

The Great Rift Valley stretches 7200 kilometres from Syria in western Asia to Mozambique in southern Africa. The valley is being formed along a fault zone that is becoming a divergent plate boundary (see pages 14–15). In places, the valley has stretched Africa by up to 100 kilometres. Lake Tanganyika and Lake Nyasa are just two of the many lakes formed by the rift.

Great Rift Valley

In a dry, mountainous region of northwestern Namibia, the Himba people maintain most of their traditional ways of life. These herders, once threatened by war and drought, now profit from ecotourism.

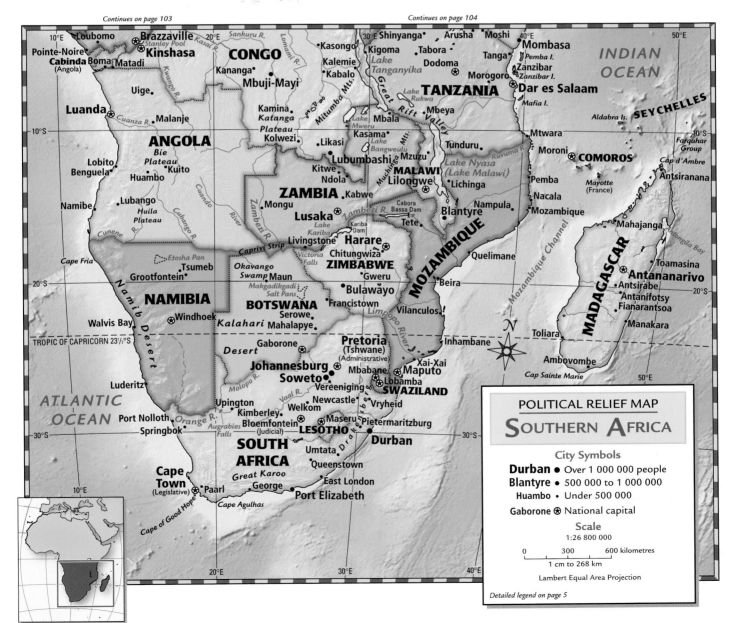

Continues on page 103
Continues on page 104

POLITICAL RELIEF MAP
SOUTHERN AFRICA

City Symbols

Durban ● Over 1 000 000 people
Blantyre ● 500 000 to 1 000 000
Huambo • Under 500 000

Gaborone ⊛ National capital

Scale
1:26 800 000

0 — 300 — 600 kilometres

1 cm to 268 km

Lambert Equal Area Projection

Detailed legend on page 5

POLITICAL RELIEF MAP
EUROPE

Boundary Symbols
.... International boundary
.... Other boundary
(disputed or undefined)
▣ Small country

City Symbols
Hamburg ● Over 1 000 000 people
Seville • 500 000 to 1 000 000
Orel • Under 500 000
Prague ⊗ National capital

Scale
1:17 400 000

0   100   200   300   400 kilometres
1 cm to 174 km
Bonne Projection

Detailed legend on page 5

40°W 60°W 30°W 20°W 10°W 70°N 0° 10°E

ARCTIC

Reykjavik
Surtsey I.
Iceland
ICELAND
ARCTIC CIRCLE 66½°N
PRIME MERIDIAN
Lofoten Is.

Norwegian Sea

Faroe Islands (Den.)

Trondheims Fiord
Trondheim
Scandinavian
NORWAY
SWEDEN
Peninsula
Lillehammer
Sogne Fiord
Bergen
Hardanger Fiord
Bokna Fiord
Stavanger
Oslo
Uppsala
L. Malaren
Stockholm
L. Vanern
L. Vattern
Norrkoping
Goteborg

Rockall (U.K.)

Shetland Islands (U.K.)

Orkney Islands (U.K.)

North Sea

Skagerrak
Arhus
DENMARK
Copenhagen
Malmo
Kattegat
Bornholm (Den.)
Baltic
Gdansk

British Isles
Glasgow
Edinburgh
Belfast
Great Britain
Ireland
Dublin
IRELAND
Liverpool
Irish Sea
UNITED KINGDOM
Leeds
Cork
Manchester
Cardiff
Birmingham
Bristol
London
Southampton
Thames
Amsterdam
The Hague
Rotterdam
IJsselmeer
NETHERLANDS
Essen
Elbe R.
Hamburg
Berlin
Oder R.
Poznan
GERMANY
North
POLA
Wroclaw

English Channel
Channel Is. (U.K.)
Le Havre
Strait of Dover
Lille
Brussels
BELGIUM
Bonn
Cologne
Leipzig
Krakow
Rhine R.
Seine
Paris
LUXEMBOURG
Luxembourg
Frankfurt
Prague
CZECH REPUBLIC
Loire R.
Orleans
Strasbourg
Elbe R.
Stuttgart
Danube
Vienna
SLOVAKIA
Nantes
FRANCE
Bratislava

ATLANTIC OCEAN

50°N

40°N

20°W

Celtic Sea

Bay of Biscay

Bordeaux

La Coruna
Porto
Douro R.
Cantabrian Mts.
Bilbao
Pyrenees
Toulouse
Limoges
Massif Central
Lyon
Geneva
Bern
SWITZERLAND
LIECH.
L. Geneva
Rhône
Munich
AUSTRIA
Graz
SLOVENIA
Ljubljana
Budapest
HUNGARY
Szeged
Carp
Alps
Turin
Milan
Po R.
Venice
Zagreb
CROATIA

PORTUGAL
Lisbon
Duero R.
Iberian Peninsula
SPAIN
Madrid
Tagus R.
Zaragoza
Ebro R.
ANDORRA
MONACO
Genoa
Marseille
Gulf of Lion
Bastia
Corsica (Fr.)
Florence
Tiber R.
Apennines
SAN MARINO
VATICAN CITY
Rome
ITALY
Adriatic Sea
Belgrade
BOSNIA
Sarajevo
SERBIA
MONTENEGRO
Podgorica
KOSOV
Pristina
Skopje
MAC
Tirana
ALBANIA

Seville
Guadiana R.
Guadalquivir
Valencia
Palma
Balearic Islands
Balearic Sea
Malaga
Strait of Gibraltar
Gibraltar (U.K.)
Ceuta (Sp.)
Melilla (Sp.)
Rabat
Sardinia (Italy)
Cagliari
Mediterranean
Naples
Tyrrhenian Sea
Palermo
Messina
Sicily
Ionian Islands
Bari
Gulf of Taranto
Ionian Sea
Peloponnes

MOROCCO
AFRICA
ALGERIA
Algiers
TUNISIA
Tunis
MALTA
Maltese Is.
Valletta

30°N

10°W 30°N 0° 10°E 20°E

OCEAN

20°E   30°E   40°E   50°E   60°E   70°N   70°E   80°E

TIC Hammerfest
• Vardo
Narvik   Novaya Zemlya   Barents Sea   Kolguyev I.
• Kiruna
L. Inari   • Murmansk
Lapland   Kola Pen.   Pechora R.

White Sea

Bothnia   Oulu   • Arkhangelsk   RUSSIA
FINLAND
Vaasa   Omega R.   Northern Dvina R.   • Syktyvkar
Lake Ladoga   Sukhona R.   Kamskoye Res.
Tampere   Lake Saimaa   Lake Onega   Yekaterinburg •
Turku Helsinki   Kirov •   Perm •   Ural Mountains
Gulf of Finland   • St. Petersburg   Izhevsk •   Chelyabinsk •
                                            Vyatka R.   Kama R.   60°N
Sea   Tallinn   Peipus   Rybinsk   Gorki   Kazan •
ESTONIA   • Pskov   Res.   Yaroslavl •   Res.   Volga River   70°E
                            Tver •   Nizhniy   Ufa •
Riga •   LATVIA   European   Plain   • Moscow   Novgorod   Kuybyshev
                                        Oka R.   Res.   50°N
LITHUANIA   Western Dvina   • Smolensk   Samara •
Neman R.   • Vilnius   • Tula
to Russia)   • Minsk   Penza •   Orenburg Ural River
E   BELARUS   • Orel   Oral •
                    Pripyat R.   • Bryansk   KAZAKHSTAN   ASIA
Warsaw •   • Kursk   Steppe   • Saratov   Aral Sea Syr Darya
ND   Bug R.   Chernobyl •   • Voronezh   Volgograd Res.
        Vistula R.   Kiev ✪   Ural River
• Lviv   Dniester R.   Kharkiv •   Donets R.   • Volgograd
        UKRAINE   Dnieper R.   Volga River   Astrakhan •   UZBEKISTAN
athian Mountains   Dnipropetrovsk •   • Donetsk   Don R.   • Rostov-na-Donu   Volga R. Delta   Amu Darya
uj-Napoca   MOLDOVA Chisinau •   Krasnodar
        Prut R.   • Odessa   Sea of Azov   Kerch   Caspian
ROMANIA   Mures R.   Crimean   • Novorossiysk   Caucasus Mountains   Sea   TURKMENISTAN
Transylvanian Alps   Pen. Yalta   40°N
Bucharest •   Danube River   Sevastopol •   Black Sea   GEORGIA   Groznyy •   Ashgabat •
                Constanta   Tbilisi •   Baku •   60°E
BULGARIA   Varna   ARMENIA AZERBAIJAN
• Sofia   Yerevan ✪
Balkan   Bosporus
• Plovdiv
ONIA   Peninsula   • Istanbul   Sea of Marmara   Ankara ✪   Lake Van   Lake Urmia   IRAN
Thessaloniki   Dardanelles
EECE   TURKEY   Lake Tuz   Tehran •
Athens ✪
Cyclades   Aegean Sea   SYRIA   IRAQ
Rhodes
Crete   CYPRUS Nicosia
(Greece)   Sea   Cyprus
                LEBANON   30°E   40°E   50°E

LAND COVER MAP

EUROPE

Cropland Grassland Tundra Glacier

Semi-desert Broadleaf Needleleaf
& desert   forest   forest

Boundary Symbols

International boundary

Other boundary
(disputed or undefined)

⊡ Small country

Scale
1:17 400 000

0 100 200 300 400 kilometres

1 cm to 174 km

Bonne Projection

Detailed legend on page 5

ARCTIC

ICELAND

Reykjavik
Surtsey I.°
Iceland
Hekla
1491 m

Lofoten
Is.

ARCTIC CIRCLE 66½°N

PRIME MERIDIAN

Norwegian
Sea

Trondheims Fiord

Faeroe
Islands

Scandinavian Peninsula

NORWAY

SWEDEN

Shetland
Islands

Sogne Fiord

Rockall

Hebrides

Orkney
Islands

Hardanger Fiord

Bokna Fiord

Skagerrak

Oslo

L. Malaren
L.
Vanern
L.
Vattern
Stockholm

Gotaland

British
Isles

Grampian Mts.

North
Sea

ATLANTIC

Ireland

IRELAND

Irish Sea

Great
Britain

Cambrian
Mts.

UNITED
KINGDOM

Jutland

Kattegat

DENMARK

Copenhagen

Baltic

Bornholm

Celtic

Sea

London
Thames

Frisian Is.

Ijsselmeer

Elbe R.

Berlin

Oder R.

Vistula R.

POL

OCEAN

English Channel

Channel Is.

Strait of Dover

NETHERLANDS

BELGIUM

Rhine

GERMANY

Northern

Seine
River

Paris Basin

Paris

LUXEMBOURG

Ore Mts.

CZECH REPUBLIC

Elbe R.

Carp

Loire
R.

FRANCE

Danube
River

Munich

SLOVAK

Cape Finisterre

Bay of
Biscay

Massif
Central

L. Geneva

SWITZERLAND

LIECH.

AUSTRIA

HUNGARY

Cantabrian Mts.

Pyrenees

Rhone

Mt. Blanc
4807 m

Alps

SLOVENIA

Drava R.

Great
Hungar

Douro R.

Iberian

ANDORRA

Po R.

CROATIA

Duero R.

Ebro R.

MONACO

Ligurian
Sea

SAN
MARINO

Dinaric

Lisbon

PORTUGAL

Madrid

SPAIN

Tagus R.

Gulf of
Lion

Corsica

Apennines

Tiber

BOSNIA

Adriatic Sea

SERBIA

Alps

Cape St. Vincent

Peninsula

Guadiana
R.

Balearic Sea

VATICAN CITY

Rome

MONTENEGRO

KOSOVO

Guadalquivir R.

Sardinia

ITALY

MACEDON

Strait of
Gibraltar

Gibraltar (U.K.)

Balearic Islands

Mt. Vesuvius
1277 m

ALBANIA

Mediterranean

Tyrrhenian
Sea

Pindus M

Algiers

MOROCCO

AFRICA

ALGERIA

TUNISIA

Tunis

Sicily

MALTA

Maltese Is.

Ionian
Sea

Gulf of
Taranto

Ionian
Islands

Peloponnes

OCEAN

North Cape

20°E   30°E   40°E   50°E   60°E   70°N   0   70°E   80°E

TIC

Barents Sea   Novaya Zemlya   Kolguyev I.

L. Inari

Lapland   Kanin Pen.   Pechora   Pechora Basin   Mt. Narodnaya 1895 m   Ob River   60°N

Kola Pen.

Gulf of Bothnia   White Sea   Arkhangelsk   Forest   U r a l s   M o u n t a i n s

FINLAND   Boreal   Northern Dvina R.   R U S S I A

Lule R.   Lake Region   Onega R.   Northern Dvina R.

L. Saimaa   Lake Onega   Sukhona R.   Kamskoye Res.

Åland Is.   Lake Ladoga   Kama Upland   Kama R.

Gulf of Finland   Vyatka R.

Sea   St. Petersburg   Rybinsk Res.   Kuybyshev Res.   70°E

ESTONIA   L. Peipus   Gorki Res.   Volga River

Riga   LATVIA   Volga R.   Upland

Western Dvina   Moscow   Oka R.

LITHUANIA   Central   Oka-Don   50°N

Neman R.   E u r o p e a n   P l a i n   Russian   Plain   Volga

(to Russia)   Upland   Kuybyshev Res.   Ural River   50°N

Warsaw   Pripyat Marshes   Volgograd Res.   KAZAKHSTAN   A S I A

Pripyat   S t e p p e s   Aral Sea   Syr Darya

ND   Bug R.   Dnieper   Kiev   Caspian Depression   Ural River

Vistula R.   Lowland   Donets R.   Volga River

UKRAINE   Dnieper R.   Don R.   Volga R. Delta   UZBEKISTAN   Amu Darya

Dniester R.   MOLDOVA

ian Mountains   Prut R.   Black Sea Lowland   Sea of Azov

ROMANIA   Odessa   Crimean Pen.   Caspian Depression

Transylvanian Alps   Black Sea   Volga R. Delta   TURKMENISTAN   60°E

Bucharest   C a s p i a n   S e a

Danube River   Caucasus   Mountains   Mt. Elbrus 5642 m   Baku   40°N

BULGARIA   Black Sea   GEORGIA

Balkan Mts.   AZERBAIJAN   Baku

alkan   ARMENIA

eninsula   Bosporus   Istanbul

t. Olympus 17 m   Sea of Marmara   T U R K E Y   Lake Van   Lake Urmia

REECE   Dardanelles

Euboea   Lake Tuz   Tehran

Cyclades   Aegean Sea   IRAN

Rhodes

Crete   S e a   IRAQ   SYRIA

30°E   CYPRUS   LEBANON   40°E   50°E

ELEVATION MAP

EUROPE

Metres Above Sea Level

Over 3000
1500 to 3000
600 to 1500
300 to 600
150 to 300
0 to 150
Below sea level

Scale
1:20 800 000

0   125   250   375   500 kilometres

1 cm to 208 km

Lambert Equal Area Projection

Detailed legend on page 5

Area shown on cross section

CROSS SECTION

Vertical exaggeration 40 to 1
Scale at 42°N: 1 cm to 184 km

ATLANTIC OCEAN   Cantabrian Mts.   SPAIN   Bay of Biscay   Pyrenees   Massif Central   Rhone R.   Alps   Corsica   ITALY   Apennines   BOSNIA-HERZEGOVINA   Dinaric Alps   CROATIA   MONTENEGRO   KOSOVO   SERBIA   Balkan Peninsula   ROMANIA   Danube R.   BULGARIA

Adriatic Sea   Mediterranean Sea   Sea Level

FRANCE   Alps   ITALY

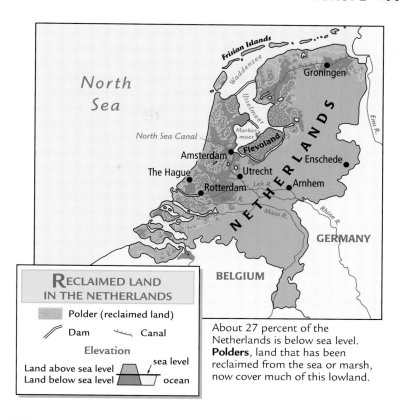

Map labels:
North Sea
Frisian Islands
Waddenzee
Groningen
IJsselmeer
North Sea Canal
Marker meer
Amsterdam
Flevoland
Enschede
The Hague
Utrecht
Arnhem
Rotterdam
Lek R.
Waal R.
Maas R.
Ems R.
Rhine R.
NETHERLANDS
BELGIUM
GERMANY

RECLAIMED LAND IN THE NETHERLANDS

Polder (reclaimed land)

Dam   Canal

Elevation

Land above sea level — sea level
Land below sea level — ocean

About 27 percent of the Netherlands is below sea level. **Polders**, land that has been reclaimed from the sea or marsh, now cover much of this lowland.

Life Beneath the Sea

For centuries the Dutch have reclaimed land from the North Sea. Dikes hold the sea back, while canals and pumps drain the water. Windmills once powered the pumps, but today they run on diesel and electricity. In 1986 the most recent Dutch province, Flevoland, was created entirely from reclaimed land.

In the central Swiss Alps, green Lauterbrunnen Valley sits 3353 metres below the summit of the mountain Jungfrau. Jungfrau has an elevation of 4158 metres and is snow-capped year-round.

Map labels (left map):
Novaya Zemlya
Kolguyev I.
Barents Sea
Kanin Pen.
Pechora Basin
Ural Mountains
Mt. Narodnaya 1895 m
Ob River
Kola Pen.
White Sea
Arkhangelsk
Plain
Northern Dvina R.
RUSSIA
Lake Onega
Sukhona R.
Vychegda R.
Kama Upland
Kamskoye Res.
Kama R.
Rybinsk Res.
Vetluga R.
Gorkiy Res.
Moscow
Oka R.
Volga River
Volga Upland
Kuybyshev Res.
Central Russian Upland
Oka-Don Plain
Don R.
Volgograd Res.
Steppes
KAZAKHSTAN
Volga R. Delta
Ural River
Caspian Depression
Donets R.
Dnieper R.
Lowland
Sea of Azov
Crimea Pen.
Black Sea
Caspian Sea
Caucasus Mountains
Mt. Elbrus 5642 m
GEORGIA
Baku
ARMENIA
AZERBAIJAN
Lake Van
Lake Urmia
Lake Tuz
ASIA
IRAN
SYRIA
IRAQ
CYPRUS

Caucasus Mountains

UKRAINE
Crimean Peninsula
RUSSIA
Mt. Elbrus
GEORGIA
Black Sea
Caspian Sea

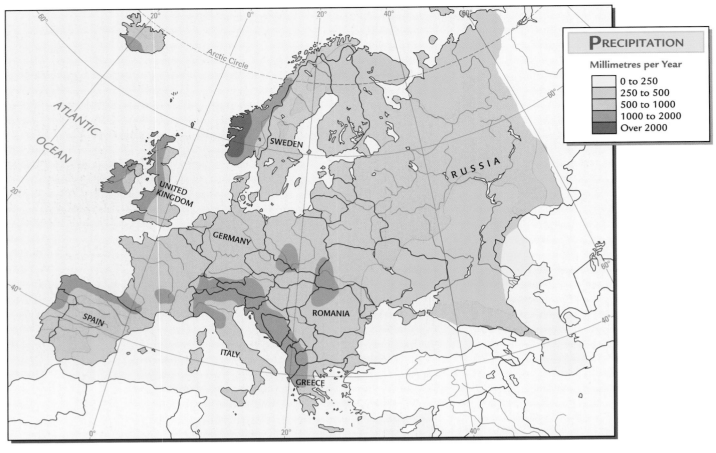

PRECIPITATION

Millimetres per Year

- 0 to 250
- 250 to 500
- 500 to 1000
- 1000 to 2000
- Over 2000

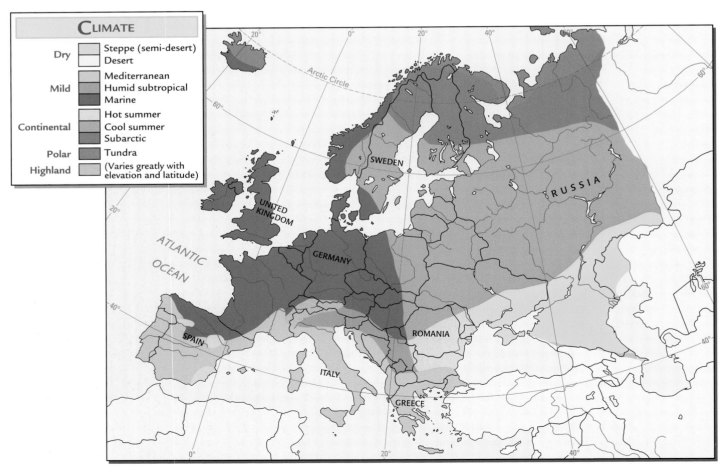

CLIMATE

Dry		Steppe (semi-desert)
		Desert
Mild		Mediterranean
		Humid subtropical
		Marine
Continental		Hot summer
		Cool summer
		Subarctic
Polar		Tundra
Highland		(Varies greatly with elevation and latitude)

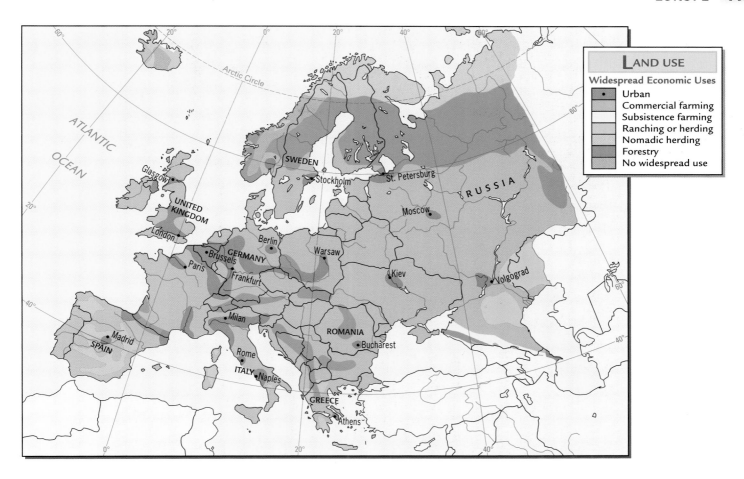

LAND USE

Widespread Economic Uses

- Urban
- Commercial farming
- Subsistence farming
- Ranching or herding
- Nomadic herding
- Forestry
- No widespread use

BALANCE OF TRADE
EUROPEAN UNION

Total Exports
US$ 1204 billion

Total Imports
US$ 1281 billion

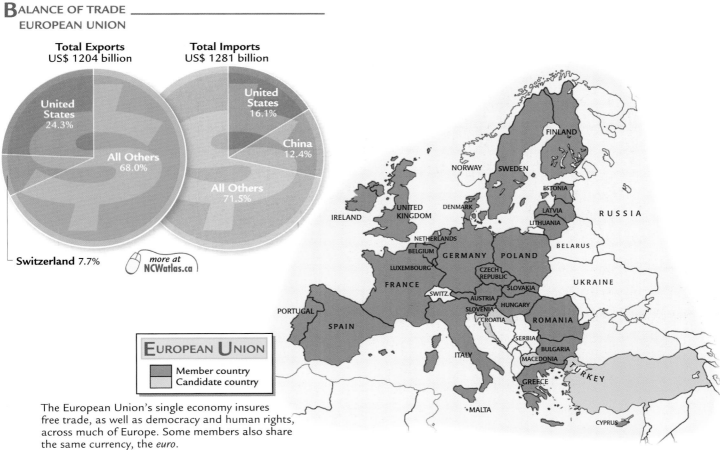

Total Exports:
- United States 24.3%
- All Others 68.0%
- Switzerland 7.7%

Total Imports:
- United States 16.1%
- China 12.4%
- All Others 71.5%

more at NCWatlas.ca

EUROPEAN UNION

- Member country
- Candidate country

The European Union's single economy insures free trade, as well as democracy and human rights, across much of Europe. Some members also share the same currency, the *euro*.

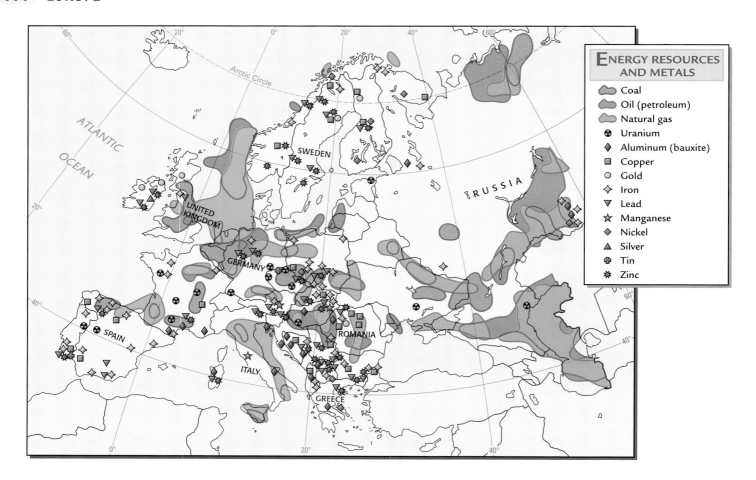

ENERGY RESOURCES AND METALS

- Coal
- Oil (petroleum)
- Natural gas
- ☢ Uranium
- ◆ Aluminum (bauxite)
- ■ Copper
- ○ Gold
- ◇ Iron
- ▽ Lead
- ★ Manganese
- ◆ Nickel
- ▲ Silver
- ✚ Tin
- ✳ Zinc

Geothermal power, energy from the earth's heat, can generate electricity with little pollution. This geothermal power plant in Iceland is located on a plate boundary, near a volcano. About half of Iceland's energy is geothermal.

SOURCES OF EUROPEAN ELECTRICITY

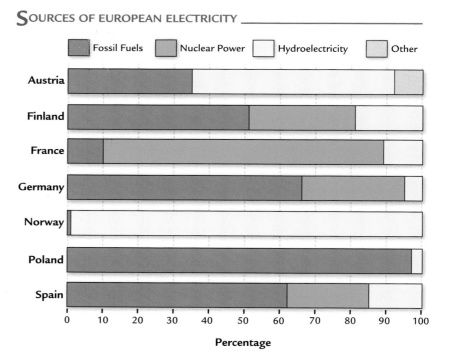

Legend: Fossil Fuels | Nuclear Power | Hydroelectricity | Other

Countries: Austria, Finland, France, Germany, Norway, Poland, Spain

Percentage (0 to 100)

Due to local resources and government priorities, European countries stress different methods of meeting their energy needs. Even so, most European countries make use of more than one energy source. Compare this with a similar graph on page 67.

Natural Population Growth Europe

Albania 1.0%
- Births: 15
- Deaths: 5

France 0.3%
- Births: 12
- Deaths: 9

Russia -0.5%
- Births: 10
- Deaths: 15

World 1.1%
- Births: 20
- Deaths: 9

Annual Birth and Death Rates
(per 1000 people)

more at NCWatlas.ca

Major Highways and Airports

Europe's highways and airports are concentrated in western Europe, where the population density and wealth are highest. Compare this map with similar maps on pages 59 and 79.

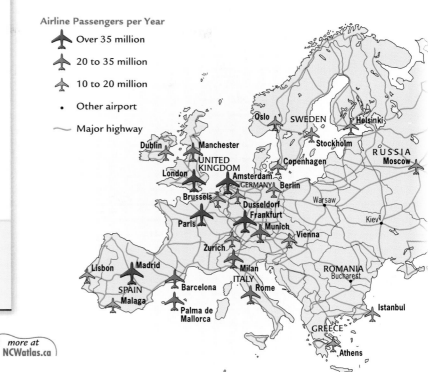

Airline Passengers per Year
- Over 35 million
- 20 to 35 million
- 10 to 20 million
- Other airport
- Major highway

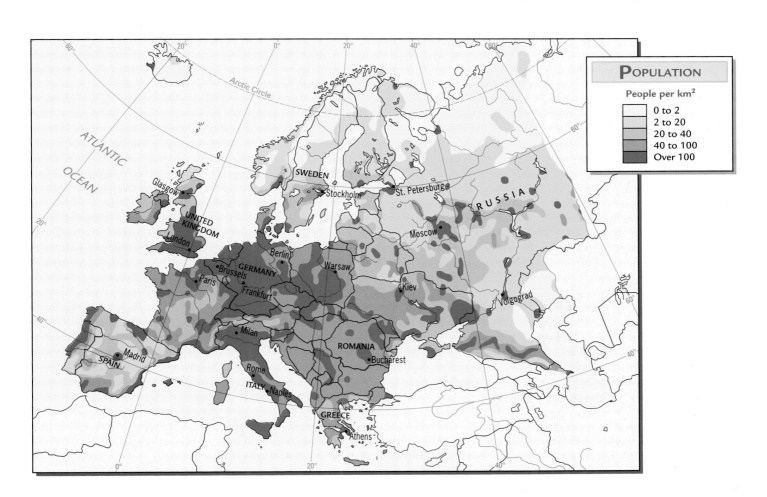

POPULATION

People per km²
- 0 to 2
- 2 to 20
- 20 to 40
- 40 to 100
- Over 100

Ireland, one of the British Isles, is divided between the country of Ireland and the land of Northern Ireland, which is part of the United Kingdom. These parade-goers are celebrating St. Patrick's Day in Belfast, Northern Ireland.

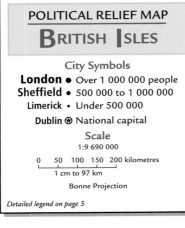

POLITICAL RELIEF MAP
BRITISH ISLES

City Symbols

London ● Over 1 000 000 people
Sheffield • 500 000 to 1 000 000
Limerick • Under 500 000
Dublin ⊛ National capital

Scale
1:9 690 000

0 50 100 150 200 kilometres

1 cm to 97 km

Bonne Projection

Detailed legend on page 5

Continues on page 117

The North Atlantic Drift is responsible for the mild climate of western and northern Europe. It relays the warm currents and winds of the Gulf Stream to the continent. Increasing amounts of cold meltwater from Greenland's ice cap, though, could block its eastward flow.

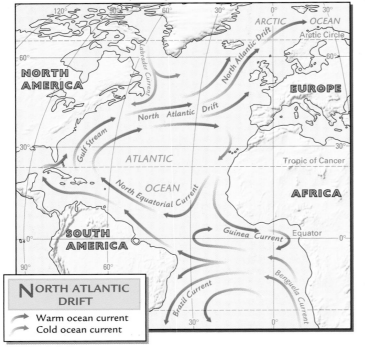

NORTH ATLANTIC DRIFT

→ Warm ocean current
→ Cold ocean current

CLIMOGRAPHS

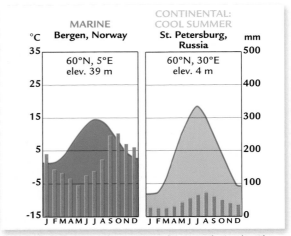

MARINE
Bergen, Norway
60°N, 5°E
elev. 39 m

CONTINENTAL: COOL SUMMER
St. Petersburg, Russia
60°N, 30°E
elev. 4 m

Bergen and St. Petersburg share the same latitude. The North Atlantic Drift, however, keeps Bergen, on the Atlantic, warmer overall than St. Petersburg, which is much farther from the ocean.

more at NCWatlas.ca

Ethnic Composition

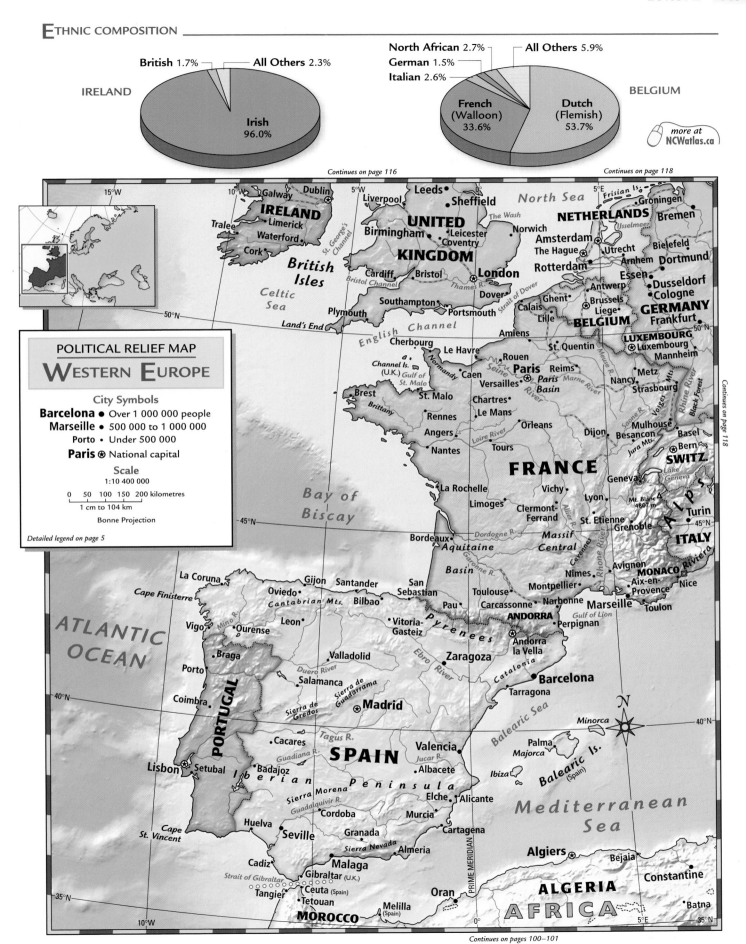

Continues on page 116

Continues on page 118

Continues on page 118

Continues on pages 100–101

Continues on pages 106–107

POLITICAL RELIEF MAP

CENTRAL EUROPE

City Symbols

Milan • Over 1 000 000 people
Bremen • 500 000 to 1 000 000
Salzburg • Under 500 000
Warsaw ⊗ National capital

Scale
1:10 900 000

0   75   150   225   300 kilometres

1 cm to 109 km

Bonne Projection

Detailed legend on page 5

North Sea

Skagerrak
Goteborg • Jonkoping
Alborg • Visby
SWEDEN
Gotland
Jutland • Randers • Arhus
Kattegat • Gotaland • Oland
DENMARK • Kalmar
Helsingborg
Esbjerg • Odense • Copenhagen • Lund • Malmo
Fyn • Sjaelland • Bornholm (Denmark)

EST.
LATVIA
Riga • W. Dvina R.
Liepaja
Siauliai • Daugavpils
Baltic Sea
Klaipeda
LITHUANIA
Neman R. • Kaunas
(to Russia) • Vilnius
Kaliningrad
BELARUS

Gdynia • Gdansk • Elblag
Szczecin • Olsztyn
Bydgoszcz • Torun • Bialystok
Northern European Plain
Wloclawek • Vistula R.
Poznan • POLAND • Warsaw ⊗
Warta R.
Kalisz • Lodz • Radom
Wroclaw • Lublin
Kielce • Ostrowiec • Bug R.
Czestochowa
Katowice • Rzeszow
Krakow

Frisian Is.
NETH. • Hamburg
IJsselmeer
Amsterdam • Bremen • Hannover • Brandenburg • Berlin • Potsdam
The Hague • Bielefeld • Braunschweig • Magdeburg • Elbe R.
Rotterdam • Munster • Halle • Leipzig • Dresden
Essen • Dortmund • Kassel • Erfurt • Chemitz • Ore Mts.
Aachen • Dusseldorf
Brussels • Bonn • Cologne
BELGIUM • Wiesbaden • GERMANY
LUXEMBOURG • Frankfurt • Prague
Luxembourg • Main R. • CZECH REPUBLIC
Mannheim • Bayreuth • Plzen • Bohemia • Ostrava
Metz • Nuremberg • Moravia
Strasbourg • Stuttgart • Bavaria • Brno
FRANCE • Vosges Mts. • Ulm • Augsburg • Danube R. • Linz
Black Forest • Munich
Saone R. • Rhine River • Salzburg • Vienna
Jura Mts. • Basel • Zurich • AUSTRIA
SWITZERLAND • LIECHTENSTEIN • Innsbruck
Bern • Lake Geneva • Bolzano • Klagenfurt • Graz
Geneva • ALPS • Trento • Ljubljana • Maribor
Grenoble • Mt. Blanc 4807 m • Lake Como • SLOVENIA
Milan • Brescia • Lake Garda • Trieste • Zagreb
Turin • Verona • Padua • Venice • Rijeka
Genoa • Po River • Modena • Ferrara • CROATIA
La Spezia • Bologna • Dinaric Alps
Nice • Ligurian Sea • Pisa • Rimini • Zadar
MONACO • Carrara • Florence • SAN MARINO • Banja Luka
Livorno • Ancona • BOSNIA-HERZEGOVINA
Bastia • Perugia • Split • Sarajevo
Corsica (France) • Elba (Italy) • Tiber R. • Mostar
Ajaccio • VATICAN CITY • Rome • Pescara • Adriatic Sea • Dubrovnik • MONTENEGRO
ITALY • Foggia • Podgorica • KOSOVO
Sardinia (Italy) • Mt. Vesuvius 1277 m • Bari • ALBANIA • MACEDONIA
Naples • Salerno • Brindisi • Durres • Tirana • Bitola
Cagliari • Taranto • Korce • Florina • Thessaloniki
Gulf of Taranto • Vlore • Katerini
Annaba • Tyrrhenian Sea • Cosenza • Mt. Olympus 2917 m • Ioannina • Larisa • Volos
Tunis • Lipari Is. • Catanzaro • Corfu • Agrinion • GREECE
ALGERIA • Palermo • Ionian Sea • Pindus Mts. • Khalkis
AFRICA • Messina • Reggio di Calabria • Patrai • Athens • Piraeus
Susah • Mt. Etna 3323 m • Catania • Ionian Is. • Peloponnesus
Pantelleria (Italy) • Sicily (Italy) • Strait of Messina • Kalamai
TUNISIA • Lampedusa (Italy) • MALTA • Valletta
Sfax • Mediterranean Sea • Crete (Greece) • Khania • Iraklion

UKRAINE
Miskolc • Satu Mare • Iasi • Chisinau
Debrecen • Oradea • Cluj-Napoca • MOL.
Gyor • SLOVAKIA • Kosice
Bratislava • Budapest • Targu Mures
HUNGARY • Great Hungarian Plain • Arad • ROMANIA
Lake Balaton • Szeged • Timisoara • Brasov • Galati
Pecs • Subotica • Transylvanian Alps • Ploiesti • Braila
Drava R. • Osijek • Novi Sad • Drobeta-Turnu Severin • Pitesti • Bucharest
Sava R. • SERBIA • Belgrade • Craiova • Oltul R. • Constanta
Kragujevac • Nis • Danube River • Ruse • Dobrich
Cacak • Balkan Mts. • Sofia • BULGARIA • Varna
Morava R. • Pristina • Stara Zagora • Sliven • Burgas
Tetovo • Skopje • Rhodope Mts. • Plovdiv • Black Sea
Serrai • Kavalla • Edirne • Bosporus • Istanbul
Maritsa R. • Thrace • Sea of Marmara • TURKEY • Bursa
Samothrace • Gokceada • Balikesir • ASIA
Limnos • Dardanelles • Aegean Sea • Lesbos • Manisa • Izmir
Northern Sporades • Euboea • Chios • Samos • Dodecanese
Cyclades • Rhodes (Greece) • Rhodes

Carpathian Mts. • Mures R. • Tisza R. • Prut R. • Balkan Peninsula

Continues on page 117
Continues on page 119
Continues on page 131

Continues on pages 120–121

Continues on page 118

Continues on page 131

ATLANTIC OCEAN

NORTH POLE

Polar Sea Ice

Norwegian Sea

ARCTIC CIRCLE 66½°N

Svalbard (Norway)

Severnaya Zemlya (Russia)

Franz Josef Land (Russia)

Barents Sea

Novaya Zemlya (Russia)

Kara Sea

IRELAND

UNITED KINGDOM

North Sea

NORWAY

SWEDEN

FINLAND

Baltic Sea

ARCTIC

ATLANTIC

Norilsk

PORTUGAL

SPAIN

MOROCCO

Strait of Gibraltar

Bay of Biscay

FRANCE

SWITZ.

BELGIUM

LUX.

NETH.

GERMANY

DEN.

EUROPE

CZ REP.

POLAND

ESTONIA

LATVIA

LITHUANIA

(Russia)

BELARUS

Moscow

Nizhniy Novgorod

RUSSIA

Yekaterinburg

Omsk

Chelyabinsk

Ural Mountains

Ob River

Siberia

Yenisey River

Krasnoyarsk

Lower Tunguska

ITALY

ALP.

MON.

MAC.

GREECE

AUS.

SLOV.

CRO.

HUNGARY

SLOVAKIA

BOS.

SERBIA

MOL.

ROMANIA

BULGARIA

UKRAINE

Kharkiv

Don R.

Volga R.

Volga

Steppes

Ural

Atyrau

KAZAKHSTAN

Astana

Qaraghandy

Aral

Aral Sea

Novosibirsk

Barnaul

Ob R.

Altai Mts.

Lake Zaysan

Mediterranean Sea

Istanbul

Izmir

Anatolia

Ankara

TURKEY

Nicosia

CYPRUS

Black Sea

Caucasus Mts.

GEORGIA

ARMENIA

AZERBAIJAN

Caspian Sea

Turan Lowland

Syr Darya

Lake Balkhash

Almaty

Urumqi

ALGERIA

TUNISIA

LIBYA

EGYPT

Cairo

Beirut

LEBANON

Jerusalem

ISRAEL

SYRIA

Damascus

Amman

JORDAN

Baghdad

IRAQ

Tabriz

Tigris R.

Zagros Mts.

Tehran

Mashhad

TURKMENISTAN

Ashgabat

UZBEKISTAN

Amu Darya

Tashkent

Bishkek

KYRGYZSTAN

TAJIKISTAN

Dushanbe

Pamirs

Shache

Tarim

Taklimakan Desert

Tien Shan

Nile River

Red Sea

SAUDI ARABIA

Mecca (Makkah)

Riyadh

Arabian Peninsula

KUWAIT

Kuwait

BAHRAIN

QATAR

Doha

IRAN

Isfahan

Shiraz

Herat

Kabul

AFGHANISTAN

Kandahar

Hindu Kush

Islamabad

PAKISTAN

Lahore

Delhi

New Delhi

Plateau of Tibet

Salween

Lhasa

NEPAL

Himalayas

CHAD

SUDAN

ERITREA

ETHIOPIA

DJIBOUTI

Sanaa

YEMEN

Aden

Gulf of Aden

UNITED ARAB EMIRATES

Abu Dhabi

Gulf of Oman

Bandar-e Abbas

OMAN

Muscat

Karachi

Indus R.

Hyderabad

Ahmadabad

Kanpur

Kathmandu

Thimphu

BHUTAN

Ganges R.

Brahmaputra

Dhaka

BANGLADESH

Narmada R.

Kolkata (Calcutta)

Nagpur

INDIA

Deccan Plateau

Mumbai (Bombay)

Hyderabad

Godavari

Bangalore

Chennai (Madras)

Andaman Is. (India)

Bay of Bengal

CONGO

UGANDA

KENYA

Lake Victoria

SOMALIA

Mogadishu

Socotra (Yemen)

Arabian Sea

Laccadive Is. (India)

Laccadive Sea

Colombo

SRI LANKA

Nicobar Is. (India)

AFRICA

TANZANIA

Dar es Salaam

SEYCHELLES

EQUATOR

Male

MALDIVES

INDIAN OCEAN

ZAMBIA

MALAWI

ZIMBABWE

MOZAMBIQUE

COMOROS

MADAGASCAR

Diego Garcia (U.K.)

TROPIC OF CANCER 23½°N

20°W 10°W 0° 10°E 20°E 30°E 40°E 50°E 60°E 70°E 80°E 90°E

50°N 40°N 30°N 20°N 10°N 0° 10°S

80°N 70°N 60°N

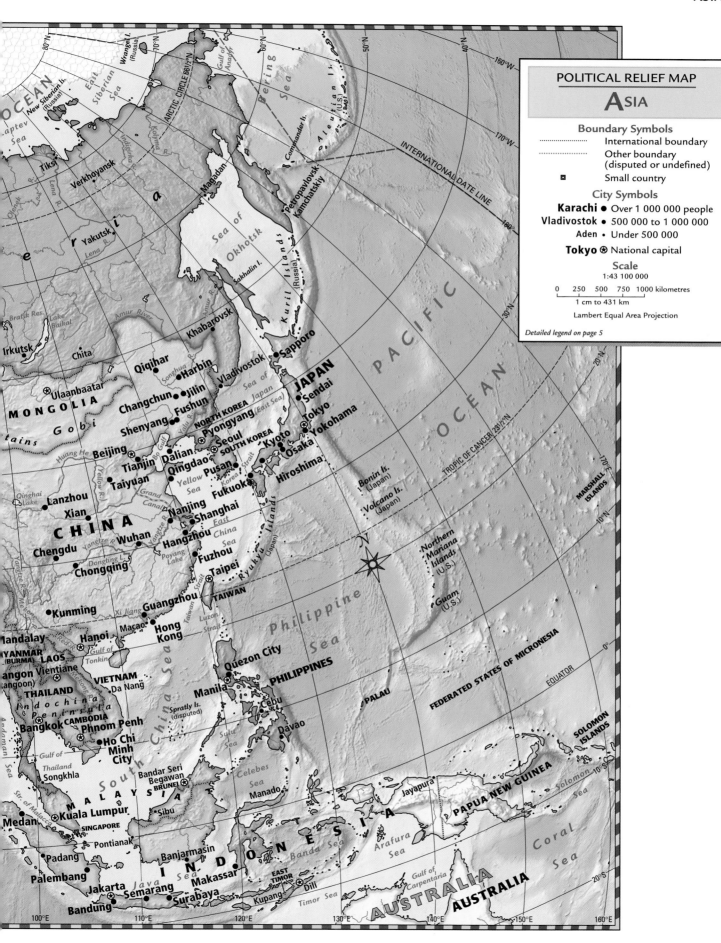

POLITICAL RELIEF MAP

ASIA

Boundary Symbols
.... International boundary
.... Other boundary
(disputed or undefined)
▣ Small country

City Symbols
Karachi ● Over 1 000 000 people
Vladivostok ● 500 000 to 1 000 000
Aden • Under 500 000

Tokyo ⊛ National capital

Scale
1:43 100 000

0 250 500 750 1000 kilometres

1 cm to 431 km

Lambert Equal Area Projection

Detailed legend on page 5

OCEAN

New Siberian Is.
(Russia)

Laptev
Sea

East
Siberian
Sea

Wrangel I.
(Russia)

Gulf of
Anadyr

Bering
Sea

ARCTIC CIRCLE 66½°N

Tiksi

Indigirka

Kolyma

Magadan

Commander Is.
(Russia)

INTERNATIONAL DATE LINE

Verkhoyansk

Lena

Yakutsk

Olenek

r i a

Sea of
Okhotsk

Petropavlovsk-
Kamchatskiy

Kamchatka

Bratsk Res.

Lake
Baikal

Amur River

Khabarovsk

Sakhalin I.

Kuril Islands
(Russia)

PACIFIC

Irkutsk

Chita

Qiqihar

Songhua

Harbin

Vladivostok

Sapporo

Sea of
Japan
(East Sea)

JAPAN

Ulaanbaatar

MONGOLIA

Gobi

Changchun

Jilin

Fushun

Sendai

Shenyang

Pyongyang

NORTH KOREA

Tokyo

OCEAN

tains

Beijing

Huang He
(Yellow R.)

Dalian

Bo Gulf

Seoul

Kyoto

Osaka

Yokohama

TROPIC OF CANCER 23½°N

MARSHALL
ISLANDS

Qinghai
Lake

Tianjin

Qingdao

SOUTH KOREA

Pusan

Korea Strait

Fukuoka

Hiroshima

Taiyuan

Yellow
Sea

Bonin Is.
(Japan)

Lanzhou

Grand

Nanjing

Shanghai

Volcano Is.
(Japan)

Xian

CHINA

Canal

Hangzhou

East
China
Sea

Chengdu

Yangtze R.

Wuhan

Dongting L.

Poyang
Lake

Fuzhou

Northern
Mariana
Islands
(U.S.)

Chongqing

Taipei

Ryukyu Islands (Japan)

Guam
(U.S.)

Kunming

Xi Jiang

Guangzhou

TAIWAN

Taiwan Strait

Philippine

Mandalay

Red R.

Hanoi

Macao

Hong
Kong

Luzon
Strait

Sea

MYANMAR
(BURMA)

LAOS

Gulf of
Tonkin

Quezon City

FEDERATED STATES OF MICRONESIA

angon
(angoon)

Vientiane

VIETNAM

Da Nang

Manila

PHILIPPINES

EQUATOR

THAILAND

Indochina
peninsula

Cebu

PALAU

Bangkok

CAMBODIA

Phnom Penh

Spratly Is.
(disputed)

Davao

SOLOMON
ISLANDS

Ho Chi
Minh
City

Sulu
Sea

Andaman
Sea

Gulf of
Thailand

Songkhla

Bandar Seri
Begawan

BRUNEI

Celebes
Sea

Manado

Jayapura

PAPUA NEW GUINEA

Solomon
Sea

Str. of Malacca

Medan

MALAYSIA

Kuala Lumpur

Sibu

SINGAPORE

Coral

Padang

Pontianak

I N D O N E S I A

Banda Sea

Arafura
Sea

Gulf of
Carpentaria

AUSTRALIA

Sea

Palembang

Java

Banjarmasin

Makassar

EAST
TIMOR

Jakarta

Semarang

Surabaya

Kupang

Dili

Timor Sea

AUSTRALIA

Bandung

100°E   110°E   120°E   130°E   140°E   150°E   160°E

ATLANTIC OCEAN

NORTH POLE

Polar Sea Ice

ARCTIC

Norwegian Sea

Svalbard

Franz Josef Land

Severnaya Zemlya

Barents Sea

Novaya Zemlya

Taymyr Peninsula

North Cape

Kolguyev I.

Kara Sea

Gydan Pen.

Taymyr Pen.

Central Siberian Plateau

IRELAND

UNITED KINGDOM

North Sea

N O R W A Y

SWEDEN

FINLAND

Ob River

Lower Tunguska

PORTUGAL

SPAIN

Bay of Biscay

FRANCE

BELGIUM

NETH.

LUX.

GERMANY

DENM.

Baltic Sea

ESTONIA

LATVIA

LITHUANIA

(to Russia)

West Siberian Plain

S i b e r

Yenisey River

MOROCCO

Strait of Gibraltar

ALGERIA

Mediterranean

ITALY

SWITZ.

AUS.

SLO.

CZ. REP.

POLAND

BELARUS

UKRAINE

Boreal

ALGERIA

TUNISIA

Adriatic Sea

CRO.

BOS.

SERBIA

HUNGARY

SLOVAKIA

ROMANIA

MOL.

Don R.

Volga R.

Ural

KAZAKHSTAN

Novosibirsk

Ob R.

Sayan Mts.

MON.

KOS.

ALB.

MAC.

BULGARIA

Volga

Volga R.

Ural R.

Kazakh Uplands

Irtysh

Lake Zaysan

Altai Mts.

GREECE

Aegean Sea

Black Sea

Caucasus Mts.

Caspian Depression

Aral Sea

Lake Balkhash

Dzungarian Basin

LIBYA

EUROPE

Steppes

Ural Mountains

RUSSIA

Anatolia

TURKEY

Ankara

GEORGIA

ARMENIA

AZERBAIJAN

Caspian Sea

Turan Lowland

Syr Darya

Tashkent

Almaty

KYRGYZSTAN

Tien Shan

Altai Mts.

CYPRUS

LEBANON

SYRIA

Euphrates R.

Tigris R.

Elburz Mts.

Tehran

TURKMENISTAN

UZBEKISTAN

Kara Kum Desert

Amu Darya

TAJIKISTAN

Tarim R.

Taklimakan Desert

Kunlun Mountains

EGYPT

TROPIC OF CANCER 23 1/2°N

ISRAEL

Jerusalem

JORDAN

Sinai Pen.

IRAQ

Zagros Mts.

IRAN

Plateau of Iran

AFGHANISTAN

Hindu Kush

Pamirs

Mt. Godwin Austen (K2) 8611 m

Plateau of Tibet

Salween

Nile River

Red Sea

An Nafud

SAUDI ARABIA

KUWAIT

Persian Gulf

BAHRAIN

QATAR

PAKISTAN

Indus R.

Great Indian Desert

Mt. Everest 8850 m

NEPAL

BHUTAN

Himalayas

Ganges Plain

Brahmaputra

CHAD

SUDAN

Mecca (Makkah)

Arabian Peninsula

Empty Quarter

UNITED ARAB EMIRATES

Gulf of Oman

Karachi

INDIA

Ganges R.

Irrawaddy

YEMEN

OMAN

Narmada R.

Kolkata (Calcutta)

BANGLADESH

ERITREA

AFRICA

DJIBOUTI

Gulf of Aden

Mumbai (Bombay)

Godavari

Western Ghats

Deccan Plateau

Eastern Ghats

Bay of Bengal

CONGO

UGANDA

ETHIOPIA

Socotra

Arabian Sea

Andaman Islands

KENYA

SOMALIA

Laccadive Islands

Laccadive Sea

Sri Lanka

SRI LANKA

Nicobar Islands

Lake Victoria

Maldive Islands

TANZANIA

EQUATOR

INDIAN

Amirante Isles

Seychelles

OCEAN

ZAMBIA

MALAWI

Comoros Is.

Diego Garcia

ZIMBABWE

MOZAMBIQUE

MADAGASCAR

20°W

10°W

0°

10°E

20°E

30°E

40°E

50°E

60°E

70°E

80°E

90°E

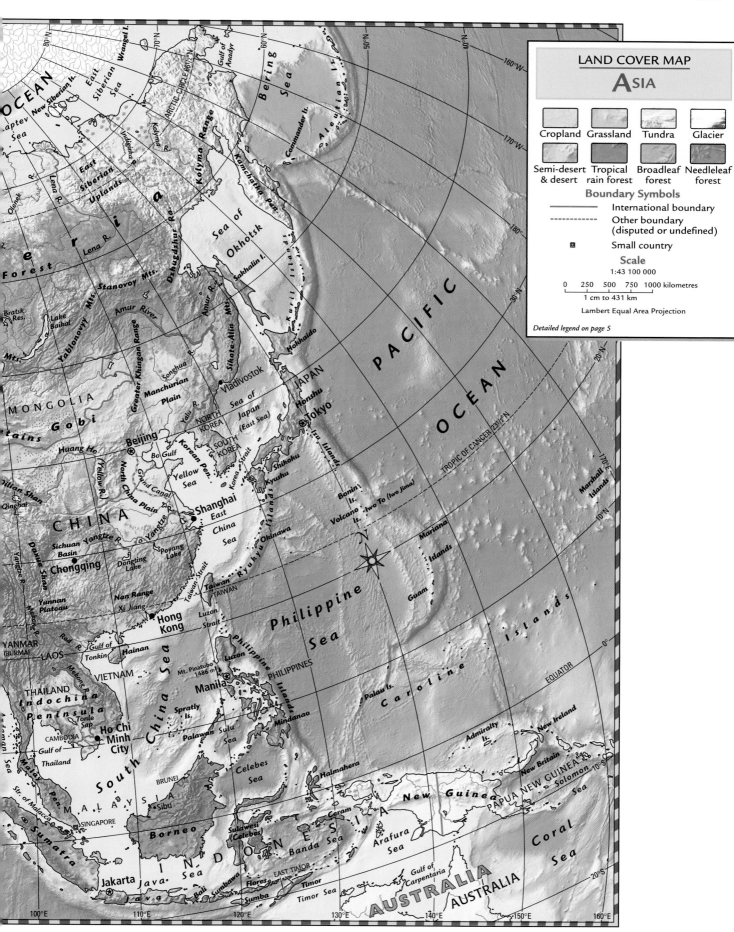

LAND COVER MAP
ASIA

Cropland Grassland Tundra Glacier

Semi-desert Tropical Broadleaf Needleleaf
& desert rain forest forest forest

Boundary Symbols

International boundary

Other boundary
(disputed or undefined)

Small country

Scale
1:43 100 000

0   250   500   750   1000 kilometres

1 cm to 431 km

Lambert Equal Area Projection

Detailed legend on page 5

OCEAN

Laptev
Sea

New Siberian Is.

East
Siberian
Sea

Wrangel I.

Gulf of
Anadyr

Bering
Sea

Commander Is.

Aleutian Is.

ARCTIC CIRCLE 66½°N

Kolyma R.

Indigirka R.

Kolyma Range

Dzhugdzhur Ra.

Kamchatka Pen.

Sea of
Okhotsk

Sakhalin I.

Kuril Islands

Hokkaido

S   i   b   e   r   i   a

Forest

Olenek R.

Lena R.

East
Siberian
Uplands

Bratsk
Res.

Lake
Baikal

Stanovoy Mts.

Amur River

Amur R.

Sikhote-Alin

Mts.

Yablonovyy Mts.

Greater Khingan Range

Songhua R.

Manchurian
Plain

Vladivostok

Yalu R.

Sea of
Japan
(East Sea)

JAPAN

Honshu

Tokyo

PACIFIC

OCEAN

TROPIC OF CANCER 23½°N

Marshall
Islands

MONGOLIA

Gobi

tains

Beijing

Huang He
(Yellow R.)

Bo Gulf

Korean Pen.

NORTH
KOREA

SOUTH
KOREA

Korea Strait

Shikoku

Kyushu

Izu Islands

Bonin
Is.

Iwo To (Iwo Jima)

Volcano
Is.

Mariana

Islands

Jilian Shan

Qinghai
L.

North China Plain

Grand Canal

Yellow
Sea

CHINA

Shanghai

East
China
Sea

Okinawa

Ryukyu Islands

Guam

Caroline   Islands

Sichuan
Basin

Yangtze R.

Dabie Shan

Yangtze R.

Chongqing

Yangtze R.

Dongting
Lake

Poyang
Lake

Nan Range

Yunnan
Plateau

Xi Jiang

Hong
Kong

Taiwan Strait

Taiwan

TAIWAN

Luzon
Strait

Philippine

Sea

N

MYANMAR
(BURMA)

LAOS

Red R.

Mekong R.

Gulf of
Tonkin

Hainan

VIETNAM

Mt. Pinatubo
1486 m

Luzon

PHILIPPINES

Manila

Philippine Islands

THAILAND

Indochina

Peninsula

Tonle
Sap

CAMBODIA

Ho Chi
Minh
City

Gulf of
Thailand

South   China   Sea

Spratly
Is.

Palawan

Sulu
Sea

Mindanao

Palau Is.

Caroline   Islands

EQUATOR

Admiralty
Is.

New Ireland

Andaman
Sea

Malay Pen.

MALAYSIA

Sibu

BRUNEI

Celebes
Sea

Halmahera

New Britain

New   Guinea

PAPUA NEW GUINEA

Solomon
Sea

Str. of Malacca

Sumatra

SINGAPORE

Borneo

INDONESIA

Sulawesi
(Celebes)

Banda Sea

Ceram

Arafura
Sea

AUSTRALIA

Coral

Sea

Jakarta

Java
Sea

Java

Bali

Sumbawa

Flores

Sumba

Timor

EAST TIMOR

Timor Sea

Gulf of
Carpentaria

AUSTRALIA

AUSTRALIA

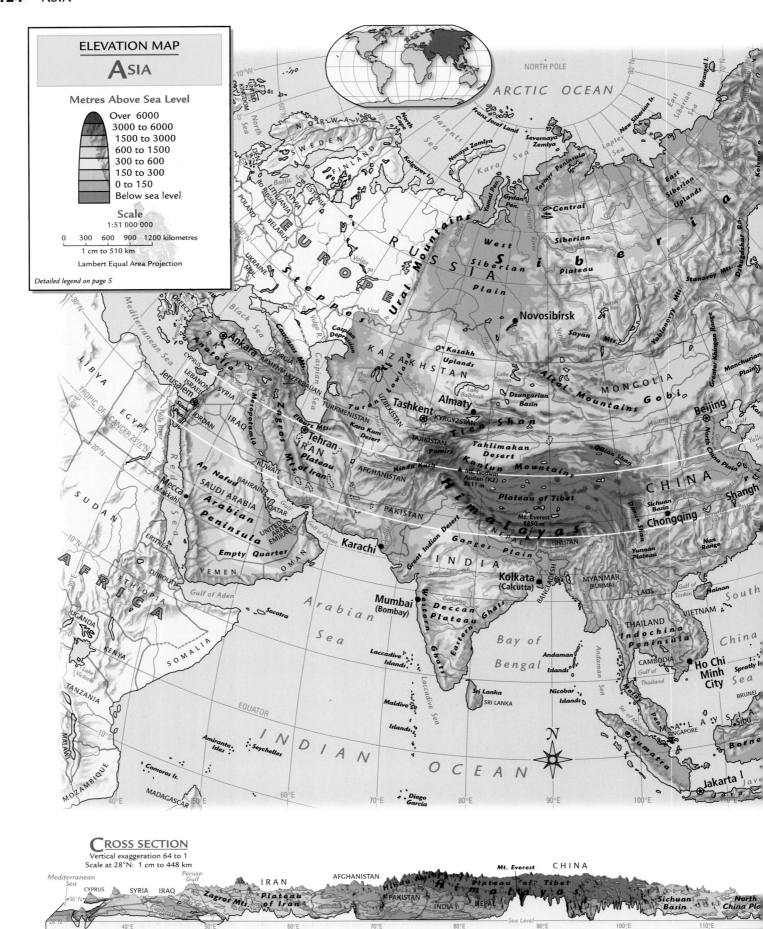

ELEVATION MAP
ASIA

Metres Above Sea Level

Over 6000
3000 to 6000
1500 to 3000
600 to 1500
300 to 600
150 to 300
0 to 150
Below sea level

Scale
1:51 000 000

| 0 | 300 | 600 | 900 | 1200 kilometres |

1 cm to 510 km

Lambert Equal Area Projection

Detailed legend on page 5

NORTH POLE

ARCTIC OCEAN

EUROPE

NORWAY
SWEDEN
FINLAND
UNITED KINGDOM
North Sea
Baltic Sea
ESTONIA
LATVIA
LITHUANIA
POLAND
BELARUS
UKRAINE
MOL.
GREECE
CYPRUS
Mediterranean Sea

Barents Sea
Novaya Zemlya
Kara Sea
Laptev Sea
East Siberian Sea
New Siberian Is.
Wrangel I.
Franz Josef Land
Severnaya Zemlya
Kolguyev I.
North Cape
Tamal Pen.
Gydan Pen.
Taymyr Peninsula
Central Siberian Plateau
East Siberian Uplands
Stanovoy Mts.
Dzhugdzhur R.
Kolyma R.
Lena R.

R U S S I A
Ural Mountains
Steppes
West Siberian Plain
S i b e r i a
Novosibirsk
Sayan Mts.
Yablonovyy Range
Amur River
Greater Khingan Range

Volga R.
Don
Ural R.
Caspian Depression
Caspian Sea
Caucasus Mts.
GEORGIA
ARMENIA AZERBAIJAN
Black Sea
TURKEY
Ankara
Anatolia
SYRIA
LEBANON
ISRAEL
Jerusalem
Sinai Pen.
JORDAN
IRAQ
Mesopotamia
Tigris R.
Euphrates R.

KAZAKHSTAN
Kazakh Uplands
Lake Balkhash
Aral Sea
UZBEKISTAN
Tashkent
TURKMENISTAN
Kara Kum Desert
Kyzyl Kum Desert
Turan Lowland
Syr Darya
Amu Darya
KYRGYZSTAN
Almaty
Lake Zaysan
Dzungarian Basin
Altai Mountains
MONGOLIA
Gobi
Manchurian Pl.
Beijing
North China Plain
Bo Gulf
Yellow
Huang He

Elburz Mts.
Tehran
IRAN
Plateau of Iran
Zagros Mts.
AFGHANISTAN
Hindu Kush
Pamirs
TAJIKISTAN
Tien Shan
Taklimakan Desert
Kunlun Mountains
Qilian Shan
CHINA
Sichuan Basin
Chongqing
Shangh
Yangtze R.
Poyang Lake
Pianma Lake

KUWAIT
BAHRAIN
QATAR
UNITED ARAB EMIRATES
Persian Gulf
Gulf of Oman
An Nafud
SAUDI ARABIA
Arabian Peninsula
Mecca (Makkah)
Empty Quarter
YEMEN
OMAN

Mt. Godwin Austen (K2) 8611 m
Plateau of Tibet
Mt. Everest 8850 m
H i m a l a y a s
NEPAL
BHUTAN
Ganges Plain
Ganges R.
Brahmaputra
Great Indian Desert
PAKISTAN
Karachi
INDIA
Kolkata (Calcutta)
BANGLADESH
Narmada
Godavari
Deccan Plateau
Western Ghats
Eastern Ghats
Mumbai (Bombay)
Yunnan Plateau
Nan Range
MYANMAR (BURMA)
LAOS
Gulf of Tonkin
Hainan

LIBYA
EGYPT
Nile River
TROPIC OF CANCER 23½°N
Red Sea
SUDAN
ERITREA
DJIBOUTI
Gulf of Aden
Socotra
ETHIOPIA
AFRICA
UGANDA
KENYA
Lake Victoria
SOMALIA
TANZANIA
MALAWI
MOZAMBIQUE
MADAGASCAR

Arabian Sea
Laccadive Islands
Laccadive Sea
Maldive Islands
Sri Lanka
SRI LANKA
Nicobar Islands
Andaman Islands
Bay of Bengal
Andaman Sea
THAILAND
Indochina Peninsula
Tonle Sap
CAMBODIA
VIETNAM
Ho Chi Minh City
Gulf of Thailand
BRUNEI
Spratly Is.
South China Sea
China
Malay Pen.
SINGAPORE
Sibu
M A L A Y S I A
Sumatra
Borneo
Jakarta
Java

EQUATOR
Amirante Isles
Seychelles
Comoros Is.
Diego Garcia
INDIAN OCEAN
N

CROSS SECTION

Vertical exaggeration 64 to 1
Scale at 28°N: 1 cm to 448 km

Mediterranean Sea
CYPRUS
SYRIA IRAQ
Zagros Mts.
Euphrates R.
Persian Gulf
IRAN
Plateau of Iran
AFGHANISTAN
PAKISTAN
Hindu Kush
INDIA
NEPAL
Mt. Everest
H i m a l a y a s
Plateau of Tibet
CHINA
Sea Level
Sichuan Basin
North China Pl.

40°E   50°E   60°E   70°E   80°E   90°E   100°E   110°E
36°N
28°N

The Himalayas are the highest mountain range in the world. At an elevation of about 3400 metres, this village in Nepal is surrounded by many of the world's highest peaks.

Plate movement and the Himalayas

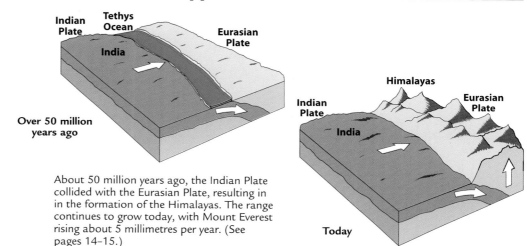

Indian Plate · **Tethys Ocean** · **Eurasian Plate**

India

Over 50 million years ago

Himalayas

Indian Plate · **India** · **Eurasian Plate**

Today

About 50 million years ago, the Indian Plate collided with the Eurasian Plate, resulting in in the formation of the Himalayas. The range continues to grow today, with Mount Everest rising about 5 millimetres per year. (See pages 14–15.)

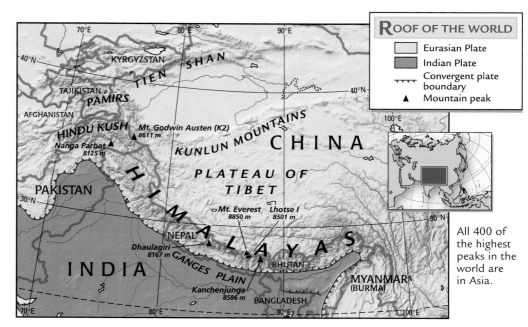

Roof of the world

- ☐ Eurasian Plate
- ▨ Indian Plate
- ⌄ Convergent plate boundary
- ▲ Mountain peak

KYRGYZSTAN · TIEN SHAN · CHINA
TAJIKISTAN · PAMIRS
AFGHANISTAN · HINDU KUSH · Mt. Godwin Austen (K2) 8611 m · KUNLUN MOUNTAINS
Nanga Parbat ▲ 8125 m
PLATEAU OF TIBET
PAKISTAN · HIMALAYAS
Mt. Everest 8850 m · Lhotse I 8501 m
NEPAL
Dhaulagiri 8167 m · GANGES PLAIN · BHUTAN
INDIA
Kanchenjunga 8586 m · BANGLADESH · MYANMAR (BURMA)

All 400 of the highest peaks in the world are in Asia.

SOUTH KOREA · JAPAN
East China Sea · PACIFIC OCEAN

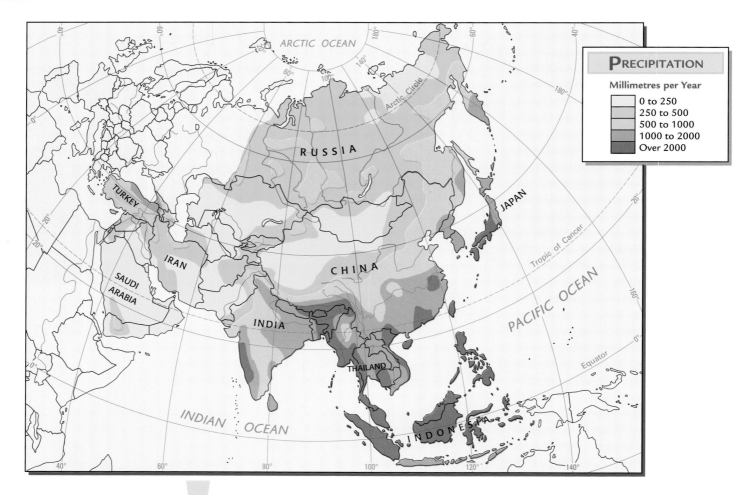

The Dry Continent

More than half of Asia receives 500 millimetres of precipitation or less per year. Asian deserts include the An Nafud and Empty Quarter on the Arabian Peninsula, as well as the Kara Kum Desert, Great Indian Desert, Taklimakan Desert, and Gobi. Even Siberia's tundra has been called the "cold desert."

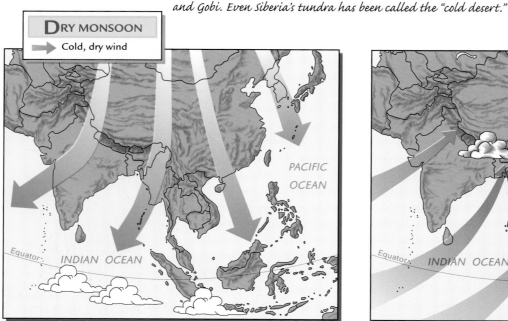

The climate of southeastern Asia and India is greatly influenced by large-scale seasonal wind systems called **monsoons**. In winter, dry winds generated over the cold surface of the land blow toward the warmer oceans and keep clouds away.

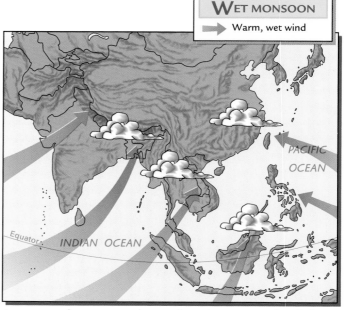

In summer, the monsoon changes from dry to wet as the winds reverse direction. Cooler air over the oceans rushes toward warm land, bringing massive amounts of moisture that produce rain. The region's growing season occurs with the wet monsoon.

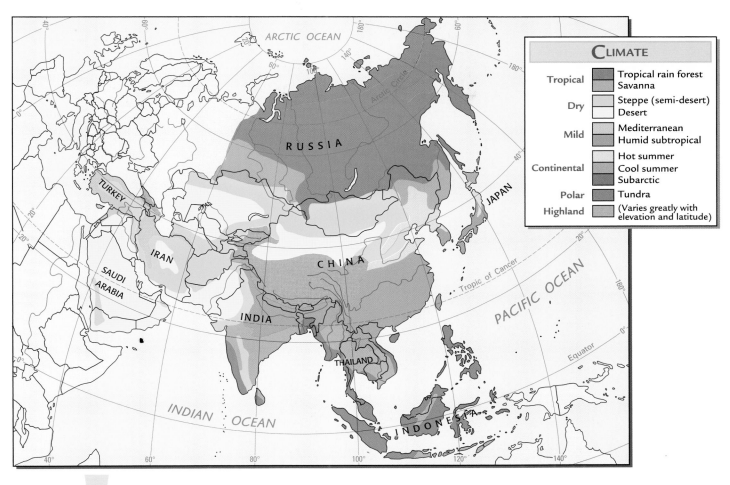

si-brrr-ia

In Russia, snow and ice cover Siberia for half the year, and the temperature can drop as low as -68°C. Verkhoyansk, a town in northeastern Siberia near the Arctic Circle, is the world's coldest continuously inhabited settlement. Without a nearby ocean to moderate its climate, Verkhoyansk can have annual high and low temperatures 80°C apart.

During the wet monsoons, intense rainfall can flood city streets, as it has here in India. In July of 2005, 940 millimetres of rain fell on Mumbai in just 24 hours.

CLIMOGRAPHS

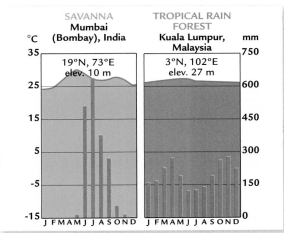

While Mumbai and Kuala Lumpur each receive over 2000 millimetres of precipitation per year, their rain patterns are very different. Kuala Lumpur receives significant amounts of rain each month, while Mumbai receives most of its rain during the summer monsoon.

more at
NCWatlas.ca

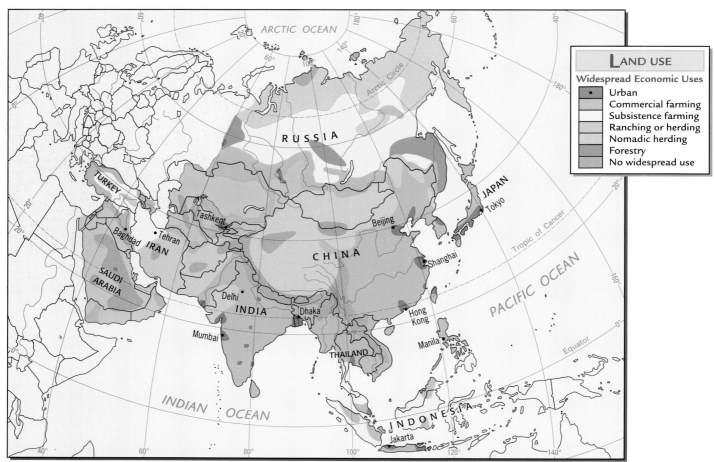

LAND USE

Widespread Economic Uses

- Urban
- Commercial farming
- Subsistence farming
- Ranching or herding
- Nomadic herding
- Forestry
- No widespread use

LEADING OIL EXPORTERS

The 13 member countries of the Organization of Petroleum Exporting Countries (OPEC) produce about 40 percent of the world's oil. OPEC exercises considerable influence over the world's oil prices by agreeing as a group to limit oil production.

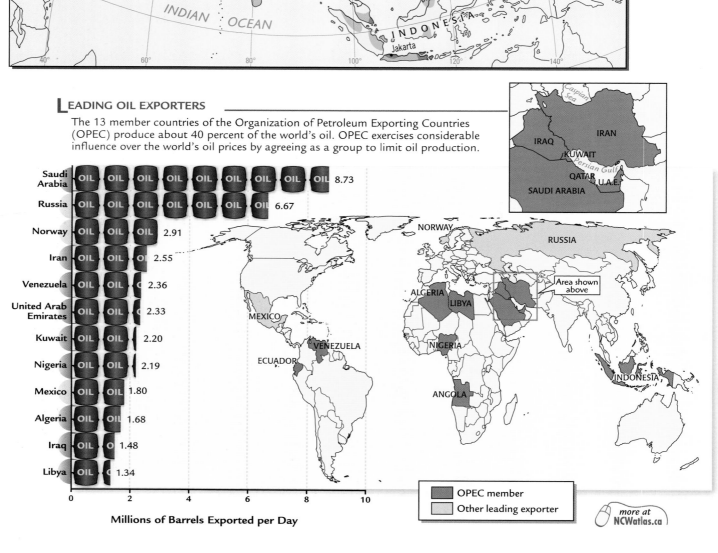

Country	Millions of Barrels Exported per Day
Saudi Arabia	8.73
Russia	6.67
Norway	2.91
Iran	2.55
Venezuela	2.36
United Arab Emirates	2.33
Kuwait	2.20
Nigeria	2.19
Mexico	1.80
Algeria	1.68
Iraq	1.48
Libya	1.34

Millions of Barrels Exported per Day

- OPEC member
- Other leading exporter

more at NCWatlas.ca

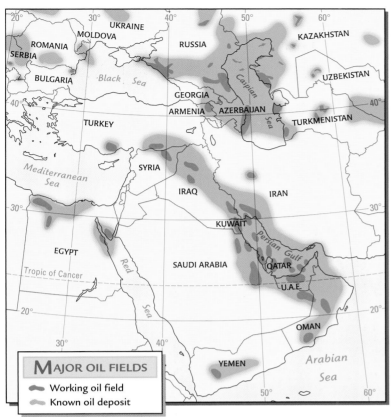

MAJOR OIL FIELDS

- Working oil field
- Known oil deposit

BALANCE OF TRADE
SAUDI ARABIA

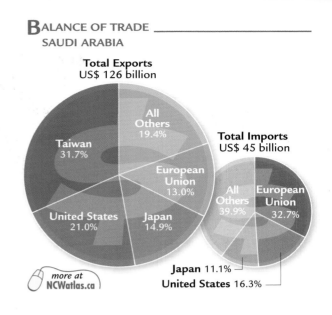

Total Exports
US$ 126 billion

- Taiwan 31.7%
- All Others 19.4%
- European Union 13.0%
- United States 21.0%
- Japan 14.9%

Total Imports
US$ 45 billion

- All Others 39.9%
- European Union 32.7%
- Japan 11.1%
- United States 16.3%

more at
NCWatlas.ca

Over half of the world's proven oil reserves are located in southwestern Asia. As global oil resources continue to be depleted, southwestern Asia is becoming increasingly important for meeting the world's energy needs.

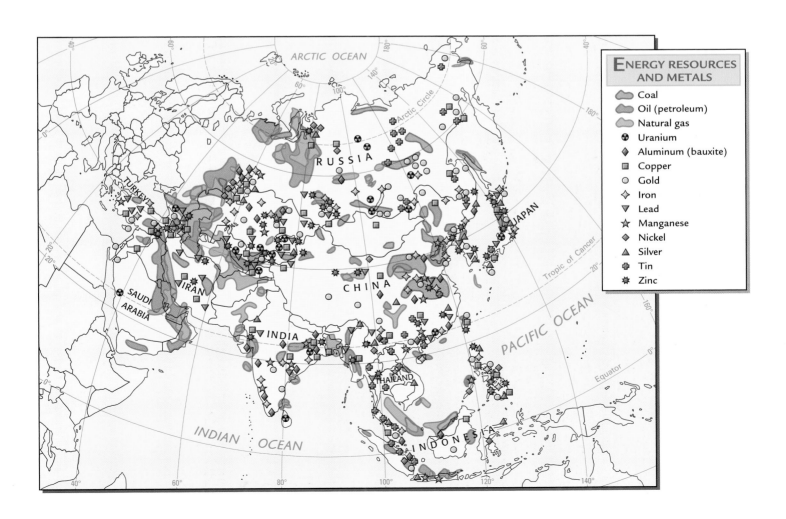

ENERGY RESOURCES AND METALS

- Coal
- Oil (petroleum)
- Natural gas
- ⊕ Uranium
- ◆ Aluminum (bauxite)
- ■ Copper
- ○ Gold
- ◇ Iron
- ▽ Lead
- ★ Manganese
- ◆ Nickel
- △ Silver
- ✛ Tin
- ✺ Zinc

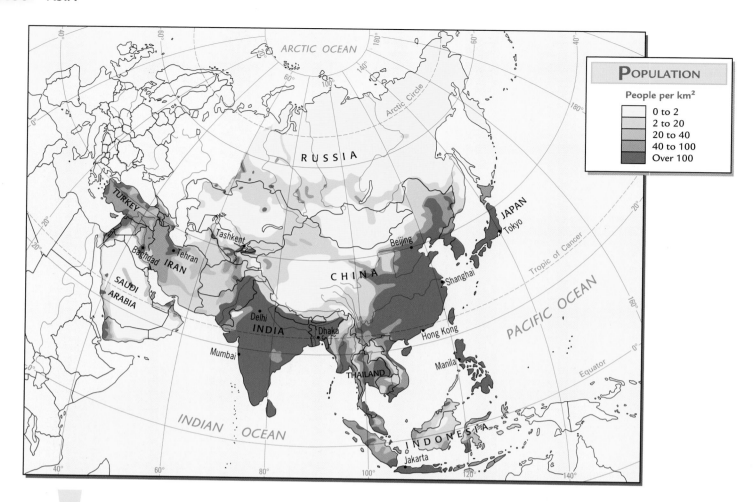

POPULATION
People per km²

	0 to 2
	2 to 20
	20 to 40
	40 to 100
	Over 100

Say It in Mandarin

Ni hao is a Mandarin greeting spoken by over 850 million people in China, Taiwan, and other countries. Mandarin, one of the most spoken languages in the world, is a Sino-Tibetan language. (See page 37.)

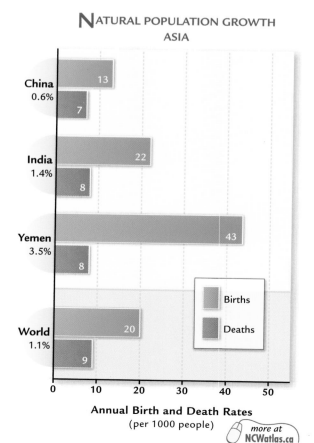

more at
NCWatlas.ca

NATURAL POPULATION GROWTH
ASIA

China
0.6%
- Births: 13
- Deaths: 7

India
1.4%
- Births: 22
- Deaths: 8

Yemen
3.5%
- Births: 43
- Deaths: 8

World
1.1%
- Births: 20
- Deaths: 9

Legend:
Births
Deaths

Annual Birth and Death Rates
(per 1000 people)

With a population of over 14 million people, Shanghai is the largest city in China. These shoppers in crowded Shanghai are enjoying the week-long Lunar New Year holiday.

more at
NCWatlas.ca

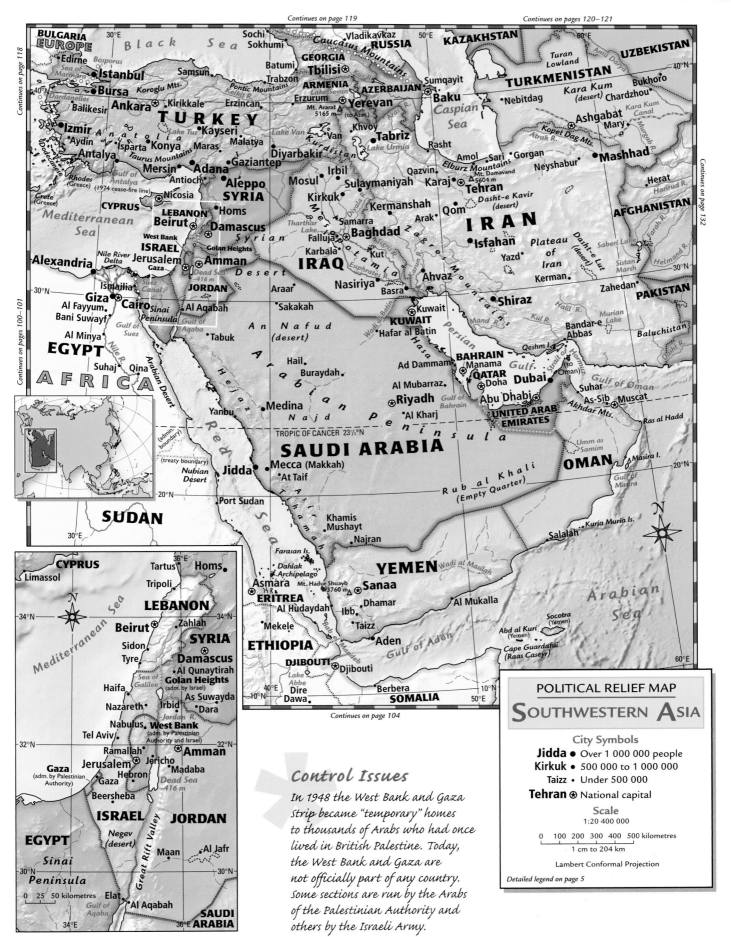

Continues on page 119   Continues on pages 120–121

Continues on page 118

Continues on pages 100–101

Continues on page 132

Continues on page 104

Control Issues

In 1948 the West Bank and Gaza Strip became "temporary" homes to thousands of Arabs who had once lived in British Palestine. Today, the West Bank and Gaza are not officially part of any country. Some sections are run by the Arabs of the Palestinian Authority and others by the Israeli Army.

POLITICAL RELIEF MAP
SOUTHWESTERN ASIA

City Symbols

Jidda ● Over 1 000 000 people
Kirkuk ● 500 000 to 1 000 000
Taizz • Under 500 000

Tehran ⊛ National capital

Scale
1:20 400 000

0 100 200 300 400 500 kilometres
1 cm to 204 km

Lambert Conformal Projection

Detailed legend on page 5

Teenagers in India celebrate Bhai Tika with music and dancing. Bhai Tika is a Hindu festival that honors brothers and sisters. It is part of Diwali, a festival of lights usually held in October or November.

Uniquely Indian

The Indian subcontinent is separated from the rest of Asia by the Himalayas. While the subcontinent was not completely cut off from the rest of the continent, it did develop its own unique culture. The subcontinent includes Pakistan, India, Nepal, Bhutan, Bangladesh, and Sri Lanka.

Continues on pages 120–121

POLITICAL RELIEF MAP

SOUTHERN ASIA

City Symbols

Mumbai ● Over 3 000 000 people
Rawalpindi ● 1 000 000 to 3 000 000
Khulna • Under 1 000 000

Dhaka ⊛ National capital

Scale
1:22 200 000

| 0 | 150 | 300 | 450 | 600 kilometres |

1 cm to 222 km

Lambert Equal Area Projection

Detailed legend on page 5

Continues on page 131

Continues on page 134

Continues on page 133

Continues on page 134

POLITICAL RELIEF MAP
SOUTHEASTERN ASIA

City Symbols
Guangzhou ● Over 3 000 000 people
Medan ● 1 000 000 to 3 000 000
Ipoh • Under 1 000 000
Bangkok ⊗ National capital

Scale
1:21 100 000

0 100 200 300 400 500 kilometres

1 cm to 211 km

Lambert Equal Area Projection

Detailed legend on page 5

Nanchang

Himalayas
BHUTAN
Brahmaputra R.
Guwahati
INDIA
Myitkyina
Imphal
Chittagong
Panzhihua
Guiyang
Yunnan Plateau
Kunming
CHINA
Namtu
Mandalay
Dien Bien Phu
Chindwin R.
Irrawaddy R.
Mekong R.
Yangtze
Hongshui R.
Wuzhou
Guangzhou
Shantou
TROPIC OF CANCER 23½°N
Black R.
Red R.
Xi Jiang
Nanning
Macao
Hong Kong
MYANMAR (BURMA)
Nay Pyi Taw
Thayetmyo
Myanaung
20°N
Louangphrabang
Hanoi
Haiphong
Nam Dinh
Haikou
20°N
LAOS
Chiang Rai
Vientiane (Viangchan)
Gulf of Tonkin
Hainan
Yangon (Rangoon)
Pegu
Chiang Mai
Salween R.
Ping R.
Mekong R.
Vinh
Bassein
Pagoda Point
Mouths of the Irrawaddy
Moulmein
THAILAND
Udon Thani
Khon Kaen
Chi R.
Mun R.
Savannakhet
Hue
Da Nang
Annamite Mts.
VIETNAM
Paracel Is. (disputed)
120°E
Escarpada Point
Luzon
Gulf of Martaban
Andaman Is. (India)
Thon Buri
Nakhon Ratchasima
Bangkok
Chao Phraya
Tonle Sap
CAMBODIA
Kratie
Khone Falls
Plateau of Kontum
Qui Nhon
Mt. Pinatubo 1486 m
Quezon City
Manila
Philippine Sea
Port Blair
Andaman Sea
Mergui Archipelago
Phnom Penh
Bien Hoa
Nha Trang
Mindoro
South China Sea
PHILIPPINES
Samar
10°N
Isthmus of Kra
Long Xuyen
Ho Chi Minh City
Can Tho
Mouths of the Mekong
Con Son Is.
Panay
Iloilo
Bacolod
Cebu
10°N
Nicobar Is. (India)
Surat Thani
Gulf of Thailand
Point Bai Bung
Spratly Is. (disputed)
Puerto Princesa
Palawan
Negros
Butuan
Banda Aceh
Songkhla
Malay Peninsula
Kuala Terengganu
Natuna Besar Is. (Indonesia)
Balabac Strait
Kinabalu 4101 m
Kota Kinabalu
Sandakan
Pagadian
Mindanao
Davao
General Santos
Sulu Sea
George Town
Ipoh
MALAYSIA
M
Kuantan
Bandar Seri Begawan
BRUNEI
Celebes Sea
Molucca Sea
INDONESIA
Medan
Pematangsiantar
Kelang
Kuala Lumpur
Putrajaya
Strait of Malacca
Serasun Strait
Sibu
Sarawak
Tarakan
Pekanbaru
Johor Baharu
SINGAPORE
Sumatra
Nias
Simeulue
Kuching
Rajang R.
Kapuas R.
Kayan R.
Borneo
Strait of Makassar
Sulawesi (Celebes)
Manado
Molucca Sea
INDIAN OCEAN
0° EQUATOR
100°E
110°E
120°E

Continues on page 132

100°E
110°E

Scale at Equator
1:31 800 000

0 250 km

1 cm to 318 km

Miller Projection

Banda Aceh
Ipoh
Kuala Lumpur
Natuna Besar Is. (Indonesia)
Kota Kinabalu
Bandar Seri Begawan
Sandakan
PHILIPPINES
Talaud Is. (Indonesia)
130°E
140°E
Medan
Strait of Malacca
MALAYSIA
BRUNEI
Tarakan
Celebes Sea
Morotai I.
Simeulue I.
Nias
Pekanbaru
SINGAPORE
EQUATOR
Sibu
Kuching
Borneo
Manado
Halmahera
Waigeo I.
0°
0°
Batu Is.
Padang
Jambi
Sumatra
Bangka
Pontianak
Samarinda
Balikpapan
Palu
Sula Is.
Molucca Sea
Sorong
Manokwari
Biak I.
Mentawai Is.
Belitung
Karimata Strait
Buru I.
Ceram Sea
Fakfak
Jayapura
Dempo 3159 m
Palembang
INDONESIA
Banjarmasin
Sulawesi (Celebes)
Ambon
Ceram
Jaya Peak 5030 m
New Guinea
PAPUA NEW GUINEA
Enggano I.
Greater Sunda Is.
Java Sea
Makassar
Flores Sea
Banda Sea
Aru Is.
Jakarta
Sunda Strait
Semarang
Java
Surabaya
Mt. Tambora 2850 m
Wetar
Moa
Tanimbar Is.
Dolak I.
INDIAN OCEAN
Bandung
Slamet 3428 m
Malang
Semeru 3676 m
Bali
Lombok
Sumbawa
Sumba
Flores
Lesser Sunda Is.
Dili
EAST TIMOR
Kupang
Timor
Timor Sea
Arafura Sea
Merauke
Christmas I. (Australia)
10°S
10°S
100°E
110°E
120°E
130°E
140°E

Continues on pages 136–137

Continues on page 143

Balance of Trade
CHINA

Total Exports
US$ 593 billion

- United States 21.1%
- All Others 31.4%
- European Union 18.1%
- Hong Kong, China 17.0%
- Japan 12.4%

Total Imports
US$ 561 billion

- Japan 16.8%
- All Others 48.1%
- European Union 12.5%
- Taiwan 11.5%
- South Korea 11.1%

more at NCWatlas.ca

Top Asian GDPs

Country	GDP (US$ millions)
China	$8 158 000
Japan	$3 867 000
India	$3 678 000
South Korea	$983 300
Indonesia	$899 000

GDP (US$ millions)

Many of the world's largest economies are located in Asia. Some—such as South Korea and Japan—are **mature** with high standards of living and moderate growth, while others—such as India and China—are **emerging** with moderate to low standards of living and high growth.

more at NCWatlas.ca

POLITICAL RELIEF MAP
EASTERN ASIA
CHINA, MONGOLIA, and TAIWAN

City Symbols

Shenyang ● Over 3 000 000 people
Kaohsiung ● 1 000 000 to 3 000 000
Uliastay · Under 1 000 000
Beijing ⊛ National capital

Scale
1:30 700 000

0   200   400   600   800 kilometres

1 cm to 307 km

Lambert Equal Area Projection

Detailed legend on page 5

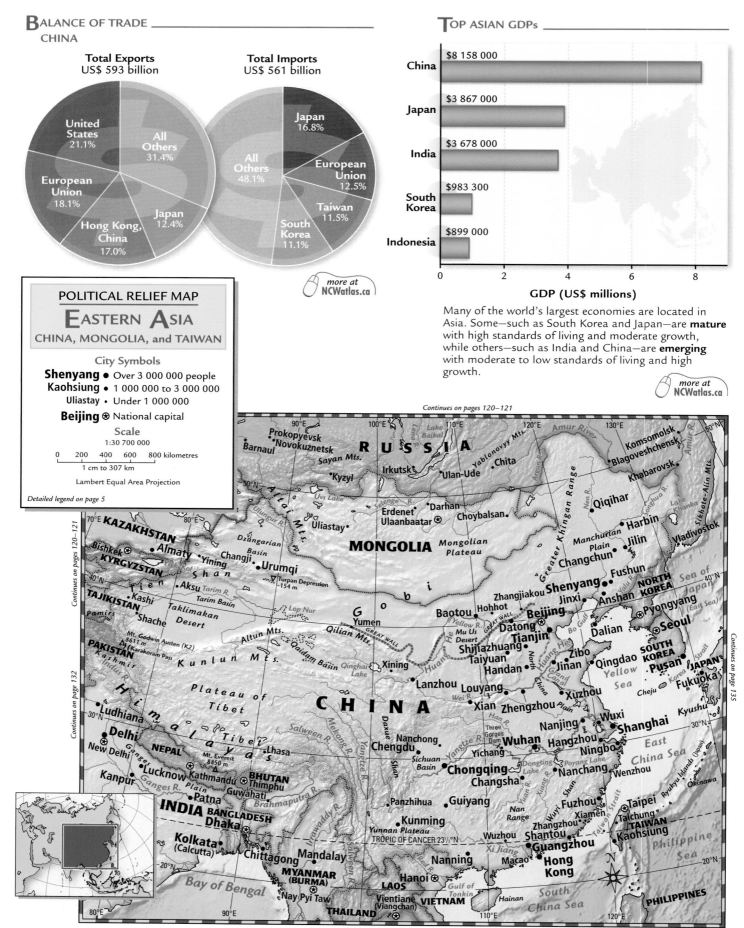

Continues on pages 120–121
Continues on pages 120–121
Continues on page 132
Continues on page 135
Continues on page 133

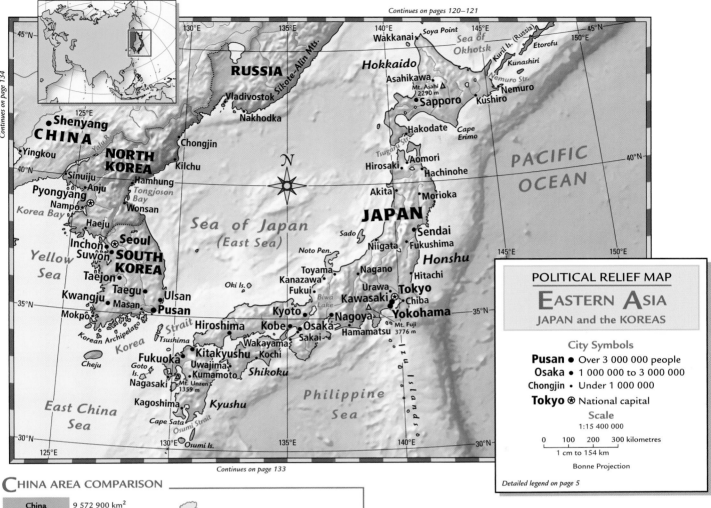

Continues on page 134
Continues on pages 120–121
Continues on page 133

POLITICAL RELIEF MAP

EASTERN ASIA

JAPAN and the KOREAS

City Symbols

Pusan ● Over 3 000 000 people
Osaka ● 1 000 000 to 3 000 000
Chongjin • Under 1 000 000

Tokyo ⊗ National capital

Scale
1:15 400 000

| 0 | 100 | 200 | 300 kilometres |

1 cm to 154 km

Bonne Projection

Detailed legend on page 5

CHINA AREA COMPARISON

| China | 9 572 900 km² |
| Canada | 9 984 670 km² |

ETHNIC COMPOSITION
SOUTH KOREA

Japanese 2.0%   All Others 0.3%

Korean 97.7%

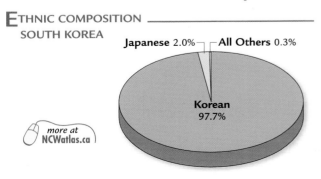

more at
NCWatlas.ca

The Japanese have one of the world's highest levels of personal income. These teenagers in Tokyo stop by a mall on the way home from school.

ASIA

CHINA
Chengdu
Chongqing
Nanjing
Wuhan
Shanghai
Changsha
Nanchang
Fuzhou
Nanning
Guangzhou
Macao
Hong Kong
Taipei
TAIWAN
Kaohsiung
Hanoi
LAOS
Vientiane (Viangchan)
THAILAND
Da Nang
VIETNAM
CAMBODIA
Phnom Penh
Ho Chi Minh City
Kuala Lumpur
MALAYSIA
SINGAPORE
EQUATOR
Baguio
Quezon City
Manila
Cebu
PHILIPPINES
Mindanao
Davao
Kota Kinabalu
Sandakan
Bandar Seri Begawan
BRUNEI
Sibu
Manado
Palu
Sulawesi (Celebes)
Makassar
Pontianak
Samarinda
Banjarmasin
Borneo
Palembang
INDONESIA
Jakarta
Bandung
Semarang
Surabaya
Malang
Java
Bali
Lombok
Sumbawa
Sumba
Kupang
Dili
EAST TIMOR
Ambon
Sorong
Jayapura
Wewak
Madang
Merauke

JAPAN
East China Sea
Okinawa
Ryukyu Islands (Japan)
TROPIC OF CANCER 23½°N
Nampo Islands
Bonin Islands (Japan)
Volcano Islands (Japan)
Iwo To (Iwo Jima)
Daito Islands (Japan)
Minami Tori Shima (Japan)
Philippine Sea
Luzon Strait
Babuyan Is.
Luzon
Palawan
Hainan
Xi Jiang
Yangtze R.
Mekong R.
Sumatra
Bangka
Belitung
Christmas I. (Australia)
Java Sea
Celebes Sea
Sulu Sea
Molucca Sea
Ceram Sea
Banda Sea
Flores Sea
Timor Sea
Halmahera
Ceram
Buru I.
Tanimbar Is.
Aru Is.
Dolak I.
Flores
Timor

PACIFIC OCEAN
Okino Tori Shima (Japan)
Farallon de Pajaros
Asuncion I.
Maug Is.
Pagan I.
Agrihan I.
Alamagan I.
Guguan I.
Farallon de Medinilla
Anatahan I.
Saipan I.
Tinian I.
Rota I.
Chalan Kanoa
Northern Mariana Islands (U.S.)
Guam (U.S.)
Agana
FEDERATED STATES OF MICRONESIA
Ulithi Atoll
Yap Is.
Ngulu Atoll
Sorol Atoll
Namonuito Atoll
Hall Islands
Oroluk Atoll
Pohnpei Islands
Palikir
Ifalik Atoll
Pulusuk Atoll
Chuuk (Truk) Islands
Mortlock Islands
Ngatik Atoll
Kosrae I.
Kapingamarangi Atoll
Caroline Islands
PALAU
Babelthuap
Koror
Melekeok
Sonsorol Is.
Wake (U.S.)
MARSHALL ISLANDS
Taongi Atoll
Bikini Atoll
Enewetak Atoll
Ujelang Atoll
Kwajalein Atoll
Majuro
Majuro Atoll
Jaluit Atoll
Ratak Chain
Ralik Chain
Gilbert
Banaba
Yaren District (unofficial)
NAURU
Ninigo Group
Admiralty Is.
St. Matthias Group
Lyra Reef
Manus I.
New Hanover
New Ireland
Bismarck Archipelago
Buka I.
Rabaul
New Britain
Arawa
Bougainville
Solomon Sea
Ontong Java Atoll
Santa Isabel
SOLOMON ISLANDS
Choiseul I.
New Georgia Group
Honiara
Malaita I.
Reef Islands
Duff Islands
Santa Cruz Islands
Nendo I.
Vanikolo Is.
Woodlark I.
Guadalcanal
San Cristobal
Rennell I.
Indispensable Reefs
Louisiade Archipelago
Torres Islands
Banks Islands
Espiritu Santo
Maewo I.
Pentecost I.
Ambrym I.
VANUATU
Malakula I.
Epi I.
Port-Vila
Efate I.
Erromanga
New Hebrides
Chesterfield Isles
Belep Is.
Ouvea Atoll
New Caledonia
Noumea
Lifou I.
Mare I.
New Caledonia (France)
Loyalty Is.
Isle of Pines
Tanna I.
Anatom
Walpole I.

PAPUA NEW GUINEA
New Guinea
Lae
Port Moresby
Gulf of Papua
Bismarck Sea
Torres Strait
Cape York
New Georgia
Fergusson I.

INDIAN OCEAN
Browse I.
Kuri Bay
Broome
Eighty Mile Beach
Great Sandy Desert
Port Hedland
North West Cape
Geraldton
Fitzroy R.
Fortescue R.
Gibson Desert
Great Victoria Desert
Perth
Mandurah
Bunbury
Cape Leeuwin
Albany
Kalgoorlie
Woomera
Whyalla
Great Australian Bight

Darwin
Katherine
Gulf of Carpentaria
Groote Eylandt
Wellesley Is.
Mitchell R.
Cairns
Great Barrier Reef
Townsville
Mackay
Rockhampton
Bundaberg
Toowoomba
Brisbane
Gold Coast
Coffs Harbor
Tamworth
Newcastle
Gosford
Sydney
Canberra
AUSTRALIA
Plateau
Western
Macdonnell Ranges
Alice Springs
Central Lowlands
Great Artesian Basin
Great Dividing Range
Lake Eyre -16 m
Lake Argyle
Murray R.
Darling R.
Spencer Gulf
Mildura
Albury
Australian Alps
Adelaide
Kangaroo I.
Ballarat
Geelong
Melbourne
Bass Strait
Tasmania
Launceston
Hobart
TROPIC OF CAPRICORN 23½°S

Coral Sea
Arafura Sea
Gulf of Carpentaria
Tasman Sea
Norfolk I. (Australia)
Lord Howe I. (Australia)

INDIAN OCEAN
NEW ZEALAND
South Island
Milford Sound
Duned
Southern A

South China Sea

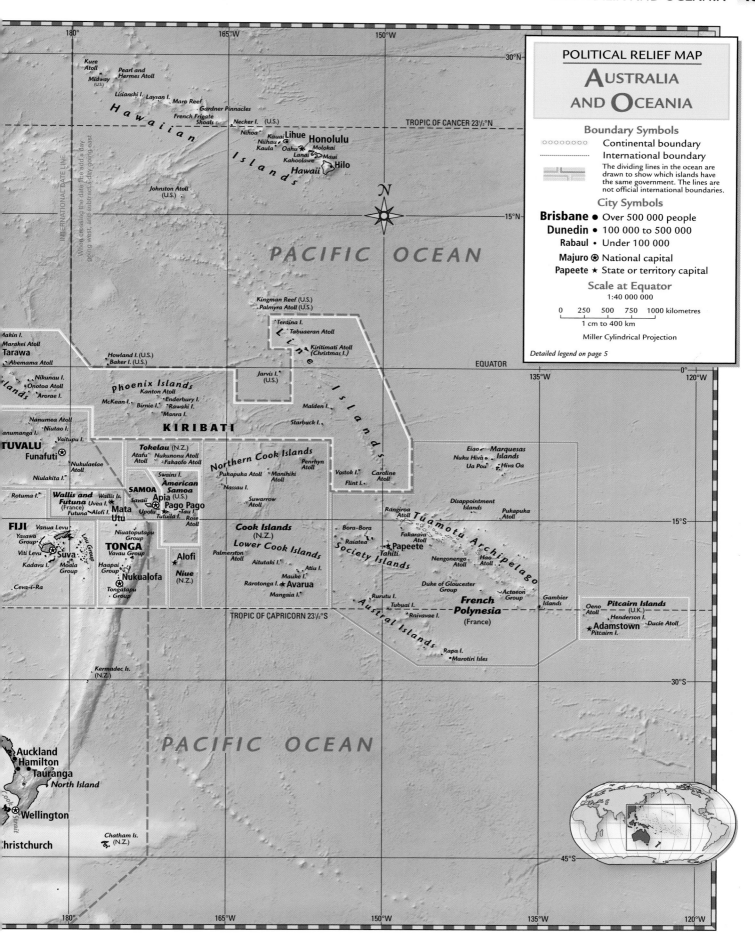

180°   165°W   150°W   30°N

Kure Atoll
Pearl and Hermes Atoll
Midway (U.S.)
Lisianski I. *Laysan I.*
Maro Reef
Gardner Pinnacles
French Frigate Shoals
Necker I. (U.S.)   TROPIC OF CANCER 23½°N
Nihoa *Kauai* **Lihue** **Honolulu**
Niihau *Oahu* *Molokai*
Kaula *Lanai* *Maui*
Kahoolawe **Hilo**
Hawaii

H a w a i i a n   I s l a n d s

Johnston Atoll (U.S.)

N

PACIFIC OCEAN   15°N

Kingman Reef (U.S.)
Palmyra Atoll (U.S.)
Teraina I.
Tabuaeran Atoll
Kiritimati Atoll (Christmas I.)

INTERNATIONAL DATE LINE
When crossing the date line add a day going west, and subtract a day going east

Makin I.
Marakei Atoll
Tarawa
Abemama Atoll
Howland I. (U.S.)
Baker I. (U.S.)
Jarvis I. (U.S.)

Nikunau I.
Onotoa Atoll
Arorae I.

Phoenix Islands
Kanton Atoll
McKean I. *Enderbury I.*
Birnie I. *Rawaki I.*
Manra I.

Malden I.

Starbuck I.

Nanumea Atoll
Niutao I.
anumanga I. *Vaitupu I.*
TUVALU **Funafuti** ⊗
Nukulaelae Atoll
Niulakita I.

KIRIBATI

Tokelau (N.Z.)
Atafu *Nukunonu Atoll*
Atoll *Fakaofo Atoll*

Northern Cook Islands
Pukapuka Atoll *Manihiki Atoll*
Nassau I. *Penrhyn Atoll*

Vostok I. *Caroline Atoll*
Flint I.

Eiao *Marquesas*
Nuku Hiva *Islands*
Ua Pou *Hiva Oa*

Rotuma I.
Wallis and *Wallis Is.*
Futuna *Uvea I.* ★
(France) *Futuna* *Alofi I.*
SAMOA *Swains I.*
Savaii **American**
Upolu **Samoa**
Apia *(U.S.)*
⊗ **Pago Pago**
Tutuila I. *Tau I.*
Rose Atoll

Suwarrow Atoll

Rangiroa Atoll
Disappointment Islands
Pukapuka Atoll

FIJI *Vanua Levu*
Yasawa Group
Viti Levu ⊗ **Suva** *Moala Group*
Kadavu I.
Ceva-i-Ra

Lau Group

TONGA
Niuatoputapu Group
Vavau Group
Haapai Group
Tongatapu Group
★ **Nukualofa**

Alofi ★

Niue (N.Z.)

Cook Islands (N.Z.)
Lower Cook Islands
Palmerston Atoll
Aitutaki I. *Mauke I.*
Atiu I.
Rarotonga I. ★ **Avarua**
Mangaia I.

Bora-Bora
Raiatea *Fakarava Atoll*
Society Islands *Tahiti* ★ **Papeete**
Nengonengo Atoll *Hao Atoll*

Tuamotu Archipelago

Duke of Gloucester Group *Actaeon Group*

Gambier Islands

Rurutu I.
Tubuai I.
Raivavae I.
Austral Islands
French Polynesia (France)

Oeno Atoll **Pitcairn Islands** (U.K.)
Henderson I.
★ **Adamstown** *Ducie Atoll*
Pitcairn I.

EQUATOR   135°W   0°   120°W

TROPIC OF CAPRICORN 23½°S   15°S

Kermadec Is. (N.Z.)

PACIFIC OCEAN   30°S

⊗ **Auckland**
Hamilton
Tauranga
North Island

⊗ **Wellington**

Cook Strait

Christchurch

Chatham Is. (N.Z.)   45°S

180°   165°W   150°W   135°W   120°W

POLITICAL RELIEF MAP
AUSTRALIA
AND **O**CEANIA

Boundary Symbols
○○○○○○○○ Continental boundary
.... International boundary

The dividing lines in the ocean are drawn to show which islands have the same government. The lines are not official international boundaries.

City Symbols
Brisbane ● Over 500 000 people
Dunedin ● 100 000 to 500 000
Rabaul • Under 100 000
Majuro ⊗ National capital
Papeete ★ State or territory capital

Scale at Equator
1:40 000 000

0 250 500 750 1000 kilometres
1 cm to 400 km

Miller Cylindrical Projection

Detailed legend on page 5

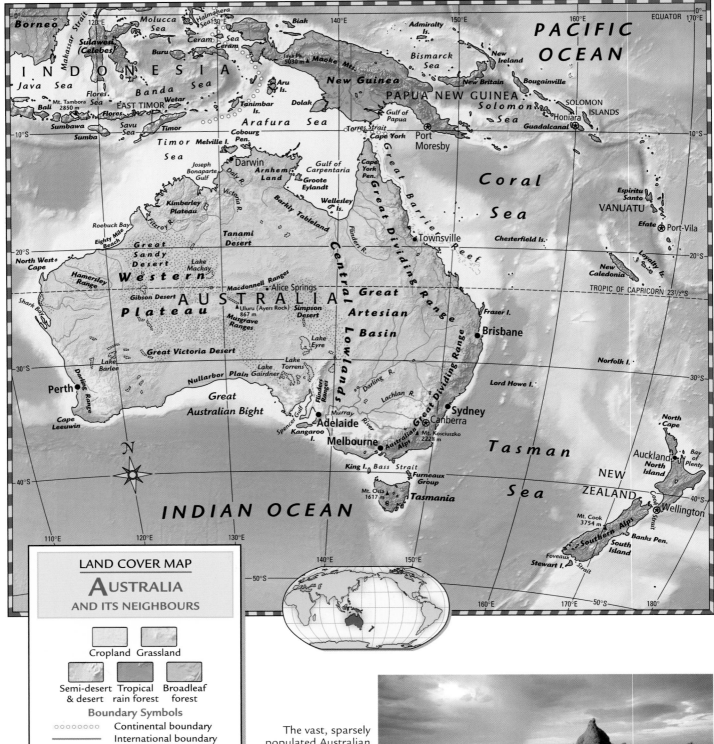

PACIFIC OCEAN

Borneo
Makassar Strait
Molucca Sea
Halmahera Sea
Biak
Admiralty Is.
Ceram Sea
Sulawesi (Celebes)
Buru
Java Pk. 5030 m
Maoke Mts.
Bismarck Sea
New Ireland
SOLOMON ISLANDS
I N D O N E S I A
New Guinea
New Britain
Bougainville
Java Sea
Banda Sea
Aru Is.
PAPUA NEW GUINEA
Solomon Sea
Honiara
Flores
Mt. Tambora 2850 m
EAST TIMOR
Wetar
Tanimbar Is.
Dolak
Gulf of Papua
Guadalcanal
Bali
Flores
Savu Sea
Timor
Arafura Sea
Torres Strait
Sumbawa
Sumba
Cobourg Pen.
Cape York
Port Moresby
Timor Sea
Melville I.
Coral
Joseph Bonaparte Gulf
Darwin
Arnhem Land
Gulf of Carpentaria
Cape York Pen.
Sea
VANUATU
Daly R.
Groote Eylandt
Espiritu Santo
Kimberley Plateau
Victoria R.
Wellesley Is.
Efate
Port-Vila
Roebuck Bay
Fitzroy R.
Barkly Tableland
Townsville
Chesterfield Is.
Eighty Mile Beach
Tanami Desert
Flinders R.
TROPIC OF CAPRICORN 23½°S
North West Cape
Great Sandy Desert
Lake Mackay
Great Dividing Range
New Caledonia
Loyalty Is.
Hamersley Range
Western
Macdonnell Ranges
Alice Springs
Great
Shark Bay
Gibson Desert
A U S T R A L I A
Uluru (Ayers Rock) 867 m
Simpson Desert
Artesian
Fraser I.
Plateau
Musgrave Ranges
Lake Eyre
Basin
Brisbane
Great Victoria Desert
Lowlands
Norfolk I.
Lake Barlee
Lake Torrens
Lake Gairdner
Darling R.
Lachlan R.
Lord Howe I.
Perth
Darling Range
Nullarbor Plain
Flinders Ranges
Central
Great Dividing Range
Sydney
Canberra
North Cape
Cape Leeuwin
Great Australian Bight
Spencer Gulf
Kangaroo I.
Adelaide
Murray River
Australian Alps
Mt. Kosciuszko 2228 m
Tasman
Auckland
Bay of Plenty
Melbourne
NEW
North Island
King I.
Bass Strait
Furneaux Group
Sea
ZEALAND
Mt. Ossa 1617 m
Tasmania
Wellington
INDIAN OCEAN
Mt. Cook 3754 m
Southern Alps
Banks Pen.
South Island
Foveaux Strait
Stewart I.
Cook Strait

0°
120°E
130°E
140°E
150°E
160°E
EQUATOR
170°E
10°S
20°S
30°S
40°S
50°S
110°E
120°E
130°E
140°E
150°E
160°E
170°E
50°S
180°

The vast, sparsely populated Australian **outback** covers about 80 percent of the continent. It consists mostly of large deserts and is known for its unusual wildlife. Here, an enormous termite mound in the Tanami Desert in north-central Australia dominates the landscape.

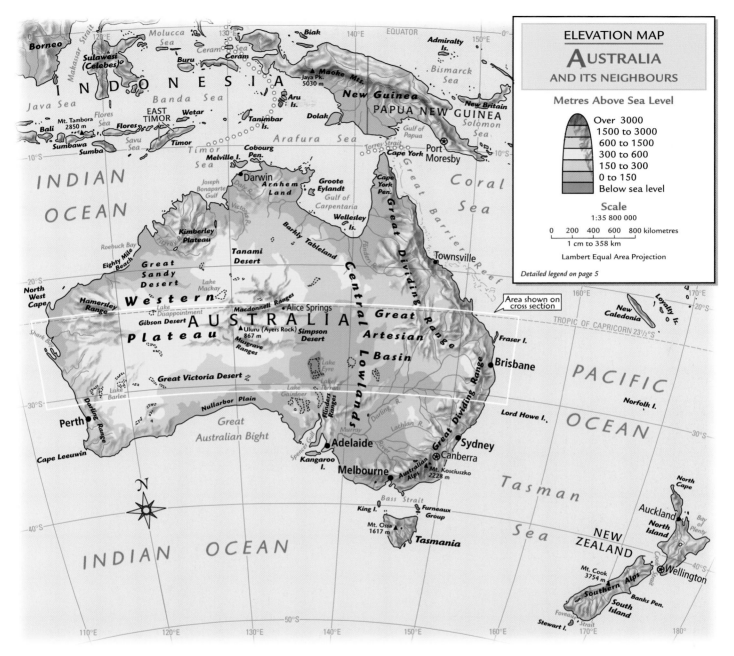

ELEVATION MAP

AUSTRALIA
AND ITS NEIGHBOURS

Metres Above Sea Level

Over 3000
1500 to 3000
600 to 1500
300 to 600
150 to 300
0 to 150
Below sea level

Scale
1:35 800 000

0   200   400   600   800 kilometres

1 cm to 358 km

Lambert Equal Area Projection

Detailed legend on page 5

Area shown on cross section

CROSS SECTION
Vertical exaggeration 78 to 1
Scale at 24°S: 1 cm to 298 km

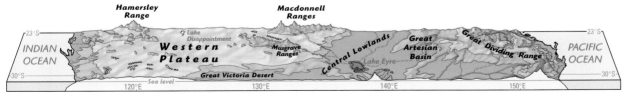

Drawing Lines

Alfred Russel Wallace, a British naturalist, discovered that animals in Indonesia are divided into two groups of species. He drew a line that runs through the Maskassar Strait and matches the geological history of the region. Species to the west of the **Wallace Line** are related to the animals of Asia, while those east of the line are relatives of Australian animals.

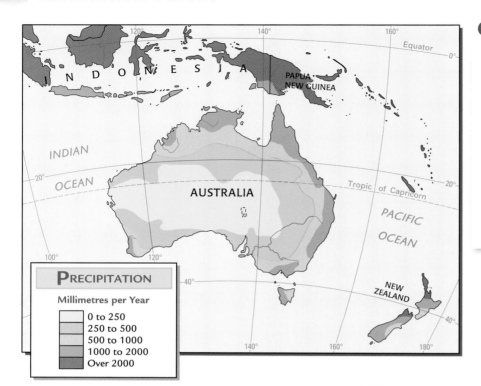

PRECIPITATION

Millimetres per Year

- 0 to 250
- 250 to 500
- 500 to 1000
- 1000 to 2000
- Over 2000

CLIMOGRAPHS

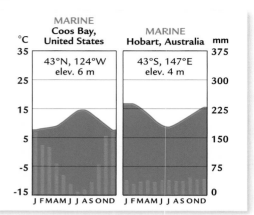

There is a six-month difference in seasons between Coos Bay and Hobart. This is because the Southern Hemisphere experiences winter when the Northern Hemisphere has summer. (For more information, see page 19.)

more at NCWatlas.ca

Tropical rain forests, such as this one in Papua New Guinea, exist only in regions that have high temperatures and high precipitation year-round. Tropical rain forests are the most biologically diverse ecosystems in the world. (For more information, see pages 26 and 92.)

Stations Down Under

In Australia and New Zealand, large cattle or sheep ranches are called **stations**. Cattle stations are usually much larger than sheep stations. Anna Creek in South Australia, Australia's largest cattle station, covers about 30 100 square kilometres and is about the size of Vancouver Island.

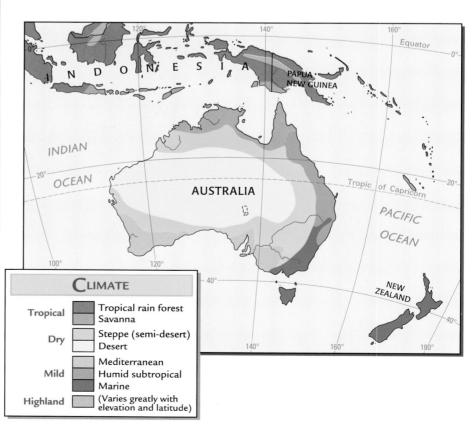

CLIMATE

Tropical		Tropical rain forest
		Savanna
Dry		Steppe (semi-desert)
		Desert
Mild		Mediterranean
		Humid subtropical
		Marine
Highland		(Varies greatly with elevation and latitude)

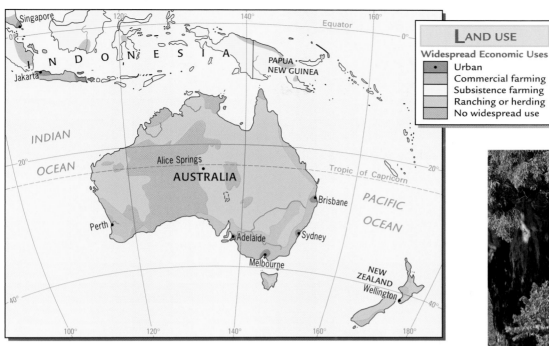

LAND USE

Widespread Economic Uses
- Urban
- Commercial farming
- Subsistence farming
- Ranching or herding
- No widespread use

BALANCE OF TRADE
AUSTRALIA

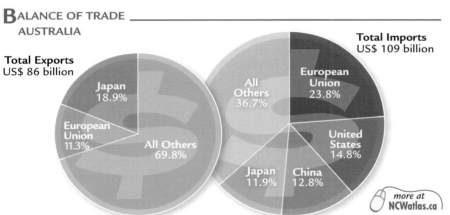

Total Exports
US$ 86 billion

Japan 18.9%
European Union 11.3%
All Others 69.8%

Total Imports
US$ 109 billion

European Union 23.8%
All Others 36.7%
United States 14.8%
Japan 11.9%
China 12.8%

more at NCWatlas.ca

Winemaking is a rapidly growing industry in Australia. The Barossa Valley, northeast of Adelaide in South Australia, produces more than 20 percent of the wine in the country.

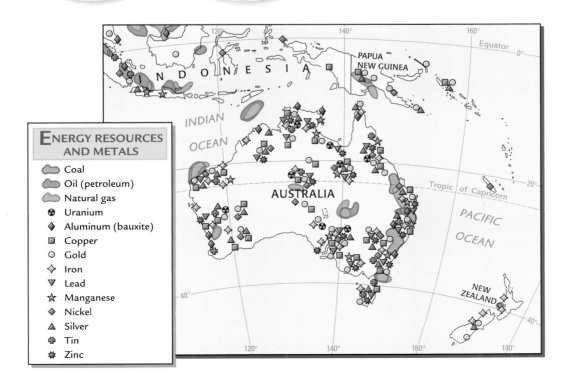

ENERGY RESOURCES AND METALS

- Coal
- Oil (petroleum)
- Natural gas
- Uranium
- Aluminum (bauxite)
- Copper
- Gold
- Iron
- Lead
- Manganese
- Nickel
- Silver
- Tin
- Zinc

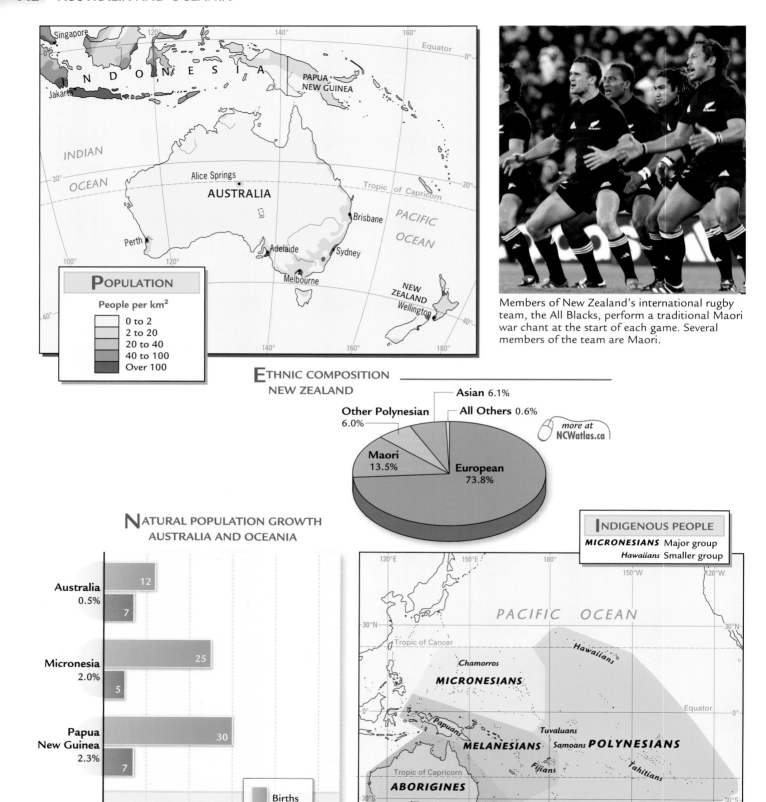

POPULATION

People per km²

- 0 to 2
- 2 to 20
- 20 to 40
- 40 to 100
- Over 100

Members of New Zealand's international rugby team, the All Blacks, perform a traditional Maori war chant at the start of each game. Several members of the team are Maori.

ETHNIC COMPOSITION
NEW ZEALAND

- Asian 6.1%
- All Others 0.6%
- Other Polynesian 6.0%
- Maori 13.5%
- European 73.8%

more at NCWatlas.ca

NATURAL POPULATION GROWTH
AUSTRALIA AND OCEANIA

Australia 0.5% — Births 12, Deaths 7

Micronesia 2.0% — Births 25, Deaths 5

Papua New Guinea 2.3% — Births 30, Deaths 7

World 1.1% — Births 20, Deaths 9

Births
Deaths

0 10 20 30 40 50

more at NCWatlas.ca

Annual Birth and Death Rates
(per 1000 people)

INDIGENOUS PEOPLE

MICRONESIANS Major group
Hawaiians Smaller group

PACIFIC OCEAN

Hawaiians

Chamorros

MICRONESIANS

Papuans

Tuvaluans

MELANESIANS   Samoans   POLYNESIANS

Fijians

Tahitians

ABORIGINES

Maori

Australian Aborigines have the oldest continuous culture on Earth. They arrived in Australia at least 50 000 years ago. Papuans occupied New Guinea about 40 000 years ago. However, some distant islands in Oceania were occupied much later. For example, Hawaii was first settled 2000 years ago.

Continues on page 133

Australia Map

Sumba · Savu Sea · Timor · Timor Sea
INDONESIA · Kupang
120°E · Ashmore Is. · Cartier I. · Melville I. · Bathurst I. · Cobourg Pen. · Arafura Sea
Arnhem Land · Darwin · 130°E · 140°E · Torres Strait · Cape York · Port Moresby
PAPUA NEW GUINEA · 150°E

INDIAN OCEAN
Browse I. · Joseph Bonaparte Gulf · Daly R. · Katherine · Groote Eylandt · Gulf of Carpentaria · Cape York Pen. · Coral Sea
Kuri Bay · Adele I. · Kimberley Plateau · Lake Argyle · Wyndham · Victoria R. · Wellesley Is. · Mitchell R. · Cooktown · Coral Sea Is. Territory (Australia)
Broome · Derby · Fitzroy R. · Barkly Tableland · Flinders R. · Cairns
Eighty Mile Beach · Great · Tanami Desert · Tennant Creek · Townsville · Bowen
20°S · Karratha · Port Hedland · Sandy Desert · NORTHERN TERRITORY · Mount Isa · 20°S · Mackay
Barrow I. · North West Cape · Hamersley Range · Lake Mackay · Macdonnell Ranges · Alice Springs · QUEENSLAND · Emerald · Rockhampton · Gladstone
TROPIC OF CAPRICORN 23½°S · Gibson Desert · Uluru (Ayers Rock) △ 867 m · Great Artesian Basin · Bundaberg · Fraser I. · Maryborough
Shark Bay · Carnarvon · Plateau · Simpson Desert · Roma · Toowoomba · Brisbane
WESTERN AUSTRALIA · Musgrave Ranges · Great Victoria Desert · SOUTH AUSTRALIA · Lake Eyre -16 m · Gold Coast · Lismore · Coffs Harbour
Geraldton · Lake Barlee · Kalgoorlie · Lake Gairdner · Lake Torrens · Woomera · Broken Hill · Darling R. · Tamworth · Port Macquarie · Lord Howe Island
30°S · Perth · Merredin · Nullarbor Plain · Port Augusta · Flinders Ranges · NEW SOUTH WALES · Newcastle · Gosford
Fremantle · Mandurah · Bunbury · Esperance · Great Australian Bight · Salisbury · Whyalla · Mildura · Lachlan R. · Orange · Sydney · Tasman Sea
110°E · Cape Leeuwin · Albany · Port Lincoln · Adelaide · Murray R. · Wagga Wagga · Albury · Great Dividing Range · Wollongong · Canberra
Spencer Gulf · Kangaroo Island · VICTORIA · Ballarat · Australian Alps · AUSTRALIAN CAPITAL TERRITORY
Mount Gambier · Geelong · Melbourne · Mt. Kosciuszko 2228 m
King I. · Bass Strait · Furneaux Group
INDIAN OCEAN · Devonport · Launceston · 40°S
130°E · 140°E · Mt. Ossa 1617 m △ TASMANIA · Hobart · 150°E · 160°E
Tasmania

POLITICAL RELIEF MAP
Australia

Boundary Symbols
.... State or territory boundary

City Symbols
Sydney ● Over 500 000 people
Mackay ● 100 000 to 500 000
Bunbury • Under 100 000
Canberra ⊛ National capital
Perth ★ State or territory capital

Scale
1:33 600 000

0   200   400   600   800 kilometres
1 cm to 336 km

Lambert Equal Area Projection

Detailed legend on page 5

POLITICAL RELIEF MAP
New Zealand

City Symbols
Auckland ● Over 100 000 people
Westport • Under 100 000
Wellington ⊛ National capital

Scale
1:19 000 000

0   100   200   300   400 kilometres
1 cm to 190 km

Miller Projection

Detailed legend on page 5

Students learn to surf on Manly Beach in Sydney. Water sports such as surfing are popular in Australia, where most people live near the ocean. Surfing originated in Hawaii, in northeastern Oceania, before the fifteenth century.

New Zealand Map

Three Kings Is. · North Cape · 175°E · 180°
35°S · Whangarei · 35°S
Auckland · Bay of Plenty
Manukau · Tauranga
Hamilton · Rotorua · Gisborne
North Island · Napier
New Plymouth · Lake Taupo · Hastings
Tasman Sea · Palmerston North · 40°S
40°S · Nelson · Cook Strait
Westport · Blenheim · Wellington
Greymouth
South Island · Mt. Cook (Aorangi) 3754 m · Christchurch · PACIFIC OCEAN
Milford Sound · Southern Alps · Timaru · 45°S
45°S · Oamaru
Gore · Dunedin
Foveaux Strait · Invercargill
Stewart I. · Bounty Is. (N.Z.)
The Snares
165°E · 170°E · 175°E · 180°

CLIMOGRAPHS

Antarctica's average elevation is 2300 metres, while most of the Arctic is at or near sea level. Antarctica is much colder due to its higher elevation. The world's coldest recorded temperature, -89.2°C, was measured at Vostok.

more at
NCWatlas.ca

TUNDRA
Alert Station, Canada

83°N, 62°W
elev. 63 m

ICE CAP
Vostok Research Station, Antarctica

78°S, 107°E
elev. 3500 m

°C
5
-10
-25
-40
-55
-70

J F M A M J J A S O N D   J F M A M J J A S O N D

Calving is the fracturing of large pieces of ice off the edge of a glacier as it reaches the sea. These chunks become icebergs. This Antarctic glacier is calving into Paradise Bay on the Antarctic Peninsula.

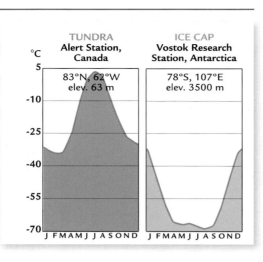

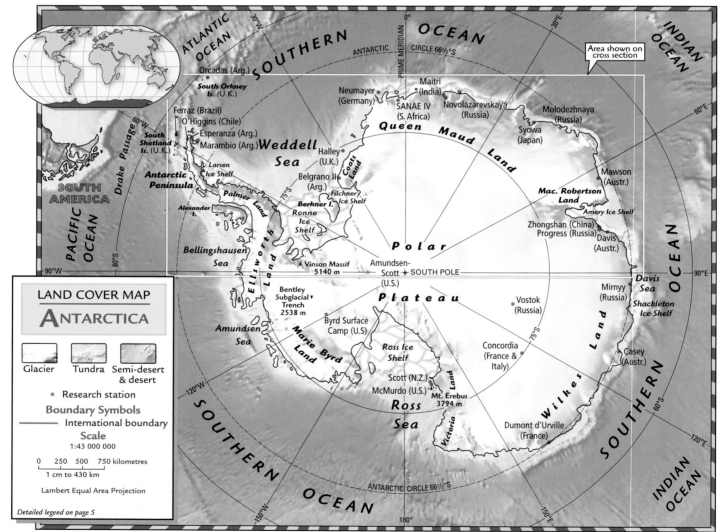

LAND COVER MAP

ANTARCTICA

Glacier   Tundra   Semi-desert & desert

• Research station

Boundary Symbols
—— International boundary

Scale
1:43 000 000

0   250   500   750 kilometres
1 cm to 430 km

Lambert Equal Area Projection

Detailed legend on page 5

CROSS SECTION

Vertical exaggeration 37 to 1
Scale at 90°E/W: 1 cm to 437 km

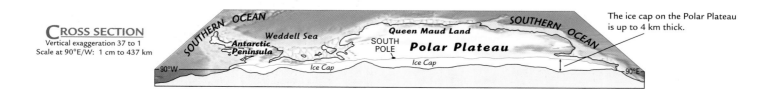

The ice cap on the Polar Plateau is up to 4 km thick.

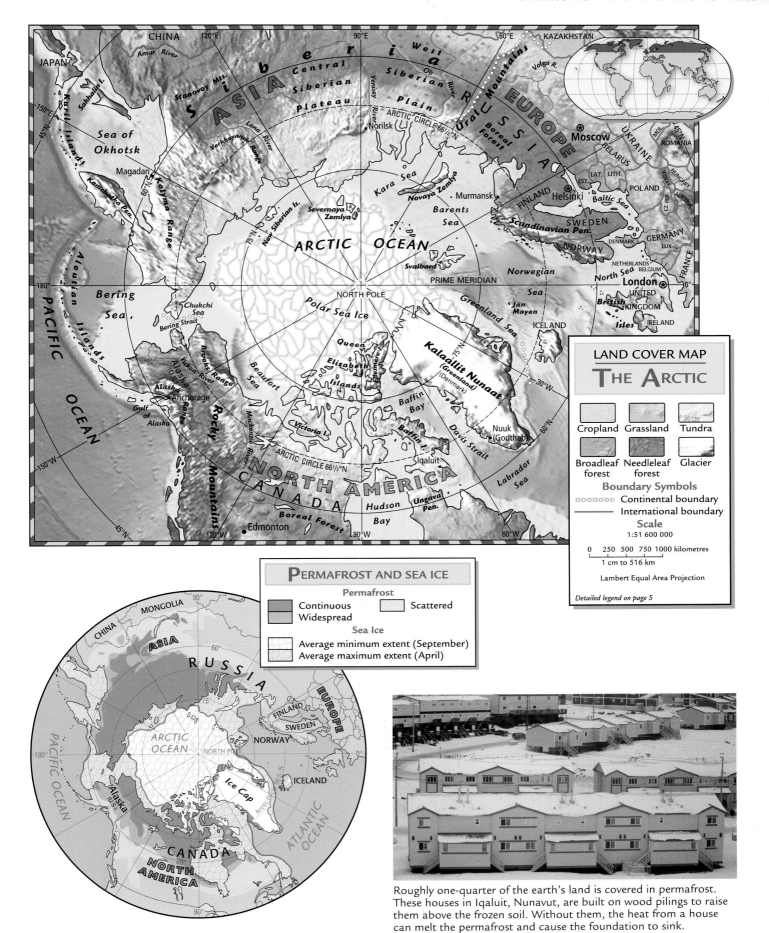

LAND COVER MAP
THE ARCTIC

Cropland   Grassland   Tundra

Broadleaf   Needleleaf   Glacier
forest   forest

Boundary Symbols

○○○○○○○   Continental boundary
───────   International boundary

Scale
1:51 600 000

0   250 500 750 1000 kilometres
1 cm to 516 km

Lambert Equal Area Projection

Detailed legend on page 5

PERMAFROST AND SEA ICE

Permafrost

Continuous
Widespread   Scattered

Sea Ice

Average minimum extent (September)
Average maximum extent (April)

Roughly one-quarter of the earth's land is covered in permafrost. These houses in Iqaluit, Nunavut, are built on wood pilings to raise them above the frozen soil. Without them, the heat from a house can melt the permafrost and cause the foundation to sink.

UNDERSTANDING MAP PROJECTIONS

Because the earth is a nearly perfect sphere, a globe is its only true model. It accurately shows the earth's shape, size, and direction. No flat map can do the same.

▶ Map projections are the means by which the curved surface of a globe is transferred onto the flat surface of a map.

▶ There are hundreds of map projections. They are often classified by their properties.

▶ **Conformal** projections show true shapes, but distort sizes.

▶ **Equal-area** projections show all areas in their true relative sizes, but distort shapes.

▶ **Compromise** projections allow some size distortions in order to portray shapes more accurately.

▶ Map legends often identify the projection used for the map.

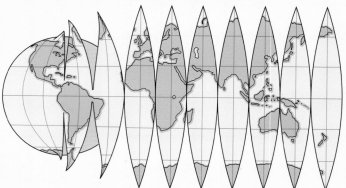

A map of a round object would be like a peeled and flattened orange peel if cartographers could not transform the information from the segments to make them fit together.

SHAPE AND SIZE

This **Mercator** view of Kalaallit Nunaat (Greenland) shows its **shape** fairly accurately. Mercator is a conformal projection.

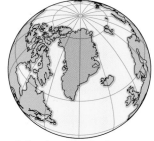

The **globe** view of Kalaallit Nunaat (Greenland) accurately shows both size and shape. Compare it with the Mercator on the left and the Eckert IV on the right.

This **Eckert IV** view of Kalaallit Nunaat (Greenland) accurately shows its **size**. Eckert IV is an equal-area projection.

DIRECTION

Follow the longitude grid lines (meridians) to find true north on a map.

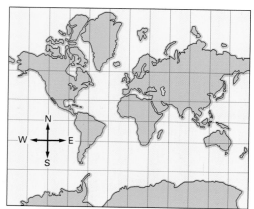

On **cylindrical** projections, such as the **Mercator**, both the parallels and meridians are straight lines. The North Pole is all along the top edge of the map.

On **pseudocylindrical** projections, such as the Robinson, the parallels are straight, but the meridians are curved. On world maps, the North Pole is along the top edge of the map.

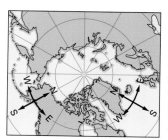

On **azimuthal** projections the parallels are circular lines and the meridians are straight. On this **orthographic** map, the North Pole is in the exact centre of the map.

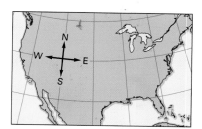

On **conic** projections, such as the **Albers Equal-Area**, parallels are curved, but the meridians are straight. The North Pole, if it appeared, would be in the top centre of the map.

SOME MAP PROJECTIONS USED IN THE *ATLAS OF CANADA AND THE WORLD*

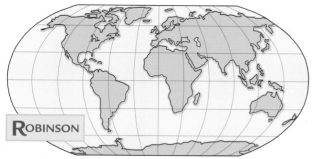

ROBINSON

Properties: Pseudocylindrical, compromise
Shape: Some shape distortion, especially near poles
Size: Minor area distortions
Direction: True along all parallels and Prime Meridian
Scale: Accurate at 38°N and 38°S
Examples: World Political Relief, Land Cover, and Elevation maps, pages 6–11

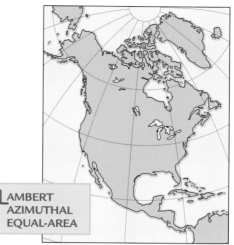

LAMBERT AZIMUTHAL EQUAL-AREA

Properties: Azimuthal, equal-area
Shape: Relatively little distortion
Size: True relative size
Direction: True only for the centre point
Scale: Accurate at centre point
Examples: North America, South America, Africa, Asia maps, pages 38, 88, 96, 120–121

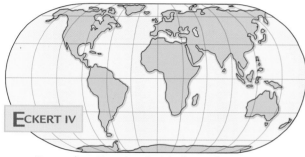

ECKERT IV

Properties: Pseudocylindrical, equal-area
Shape: Relatively minor distortions near Equator and poles
Size: True relative size
Direction: True along all parallels and Prime Meridian
Scale: Accurate at 40°N and 40°S
Examples: World thematic maps, pages 14–19, 22–37

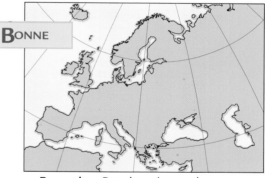

BONNE

Properties: Pseudoconic, equal-area
Shape: Fairly accurate shapes at mid-latitudes
Size: True relative size
Direction: True at centre meridian
Scale: Accurate along centre meridian
Examples: Europe map, pages 106–107

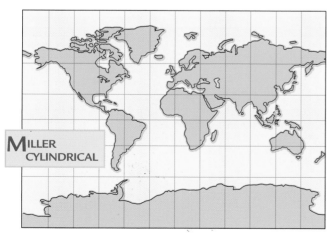

MILLER CYLINDRICAL

Properties: Cylindrical, compromise
Shape: Not as accurate Mercator
Size: Fairly accurate at mid-latitudes
Direction: Only true at the Equator
Scale: Accurate only at the Equator
Examples: Australia and Oceania, Time Zones maps, pages 136–137, 155

ALBERS EQUAL-AREA

Properties: Conic, equal-area
Shape: Good for regions that extend further east-west than north-south
Size: True relative size
Direction: True on both standard parallels
Scale: Accurate along the standard parallels
Examples: United States, Central America and Caribbean Sea, pages 72–73, 80–81

COUNTRY TABLES

COUNTRY, Dependency Official Name (if different)	CAPITAL(S) (Island location)	PRINCIPAL LANGUAGES OFFICIAL and other languages	AREA km²	POPULATION	POPULATION DENSITY per km²	NATURAL POP. GROWTH % gain	LIFE EXPECTANCY Male	Female
AFRICA (For country locations, see page 96.)								
ALGERIA People's Democratic Republic of Algeria	Algiers	ARABIC, French, Berber	2 381 741	32 930 091	13.8	1.3	71.7	74.9
ANGOLA Republic of Angola	Luanda	PORTUGUESE, Ovimbundu (Umbundu), Mbundu, Kongo	1 246 700	12 127 071	9.7	2.1	37.5	39.8
BENIN Republic of Benin	Porto-Novo, Cotonou	FRENCH, Fon, Yoruba (Nago), Adja	112 622	7 862 944	69.8	2.7	51.9	54.2
BOTSWANA Republic of Botswana	Gaborone	ENGLISH, Tswana	582 356	1 639 833	2.8	-0.6	33.9	33.6
BURKINA FASO	Ouagadougou	FRENCH, Moore (Mossi), Fula (Fulani)	267 950	13 902 972	51.9	3.0	47.3	50.4
BURUNDI Republic of Burundi	Bujumbura	RUNDI, FRENCH, Hutu	27 816	8 090 068	290.8	2.9	50.1	51.6
CAMEROON Republic of Cameroon	Yaounde	ENGLISH, FRENCH, Fang, Bamileke, Duala, Fula (Fulani), Tikar	475 442	17 340 702	36.5	2.1	51.0	51.3
CAPE VERDE Republic of Cape Verde	Praia (on Santiago)	Portuguese, Crioulo (Portuguese Creole)	4 033	420 979	104.4	1.9	67.4	74.2
CENTRAL AFRICAN REPUBLIC	Bangui	SANGO, FRENCH, Gbaya (Baya), Banda	622 436	4 303 356	6.9	1.6	43.5	43.6
CHAD Republic of Chad	N'Djamena	FRENCH, ARABIC, Sara, Mayo-Kebbi	1 284 000	9 944 201	7.7	2.9	45.9	49.2
COMOROS Union of the Comoros	Moroni (on Grande Comore)	COMORIAN, FRENCH, ARABIC	1 862	690 948	371.1	2.9	60.0	64.7
CONGO Democratic Republic of Congo	Kinshasa	FRENCH, ENGLISH, Lingala, Swahili, Kongo, Luba	2 344 858	62 660 551	26.7	3.1	50.0	52.9
CONGO REPUBLIC Republic of Congo	Brazzaville	FRENCH, Monokutuba, Lingala, Kongo	342 000	3 702 314	10.8	3.0	51.7	54.0
CÔTE D'IVOIRE (Ivory Coast) Republic of Côte d'Ivoire	Abidjan, Yamoussoukro	FRENCH, Akan, Gur, Malinke, Kru	320 803	17 654 843	55.0	2.1	46.2	51.5
DJIBOUTI Republic of Djibouti	Djibouti	FRENCH, ARABIC, Somali, Afar	23 200	486 530	21.0	2.1	41.9	44.5
EGYPT Arab Republic of Egypt	Cairo	ARABIC	997 739	78 887 007	79.1	1.8	68.8	73.9
EQUATORIAL GUINEA Republic of Equatorial Guinea	Malabo	SPANISH, FRENCH, Fang	28 051	540 109	19.3	2.1	48.0	51.1
ERITREA State of Eritrea	Asmara	Tigrinya, Tigre	121 100	4 786 994	39.5	2.5	57.4	60.7
ETHIOPIA Federal Democratic Republic of Ethiopia	Addis Ababa	Oromo (Oromifa), Amharic	1 127 127	74 777 981	66.3	2.4	47.9	50.2
GABON Gabonese Republic	Libreville	FRENCH, Fang	267 667	1 424 906	5.3	2.4	53.2	55.8
GAMBIA Republic of The Gambia	Banjul	ENGLISH, Malinke, Fula (Fulani), Wolof	10 689	1 641 564	153.6	2.7	52.3	56.0
GHANA Republic of Ghana	Accra	ENGLISH, Hausa, Akan	238 533	22 409 572	93.9	2.1	58.1	59.7
GUINEA Republic of Guinea	Conakry	FRENCH, Fula (Fulani), Malinke, Susu	245 836	9 690 222	39.4	2.6	48.3	50.7
GUINEA-BISSAU Republic of Guinea-Bissau	Bissau	PORTUGUESE, Crioulo (Portuguese Creole), Balante, Fula (Fulani)	36 125	1 442 029	39.9	2.1	45.1	48.8
KENYA Republic of Kenya	Nairobi	SWAHILI, ENGLISH, Kikuyu, Luhya, Luo	582 646	34 707 817	59.6	2.5	49.8	48.1
LESOTHO Kingdom of Lesotho	Maseru	SOTHO, ENGLISH, Zulu	30 355	2 022 331	66.6	-0.4	35.6	33.2
LIBERIA Republic of Liberia	Monrovia	ENGLISH, Krio (English Creole), Kpelle, Bassa	99 067	3 042 004	30.7	2.2	38.0	41.4
LIBYA Socialist People's Libyan Arab Jamahiriya	Tripoli	ARABIC, Berber	1 759 540	5 900 754	3.4	2.3	74.5	79.0
MADAGASCAR Republic of Madagascar	Antananarivo	Malagasy, French	587 041	18 595 469	31.7	3.0	54.9	59.8

COUNTRY, Dependency: all independent countries, as well as selected dependencies; includes both conventional and official forms of country names. **CAPITALS:** all national capitals, with island location when applicable. **PRINCIPAL LANGUAGE(S):** all official languages, as well as primary languages spoken by a substantial proportion of the population. **POPULATION DENSITY:** computed as population divided by area; given per square kilometer. **NATURAL POP. GROWTH:** annual population increase; does not include population change due to immigration or emigration. **LIFE EXPECTANCY:** average length of life in years at birth; given for males and females.

COUNTRY, Dependency Official Name (if different)	CAPITAL(S) (Island location)	PRINCIPAL LANGUAGES OFFICIAL and other languages	AREA km²	POPULATION	POPULATION DENSITY per km²	NATURAL POP. GROWTH % gain	LIFE EXPECTANCY Male	Female
MALAWI *Republic of Malawi*	Lilongwe	ENGLISH, Chewa, Lomwe, Yao	118 484	13 013 926	109.8	2.4	41.9	41.5
MALI *Republic of Mali*	Bamako	FRENCH, Bambara	1 248 574	11 716 829	9.4	3.3	47.1	51.0
MAURITANIA *Islamic Republic of Mauritania*	Nouakchott	ARABIC, Hassaniya Arabic	1 030 700	3 177 388	3.1	2.9	50.9	55.4
MAURITIUS *Republic of Mauritius*	Port Louis	ENGLISH, French, Creole, Bhojpuri	2 040	1 240 827	608.2	0.9	68.7	76.7
MOROCCO *Kingdom of Morocco*	Rabat	ARABIC, French, Berber	456 550	33 241 259	72.8	1.7	68.6	73.4
MOZAMBIQUE *Republic of Mozambique*	Maputo	PORTUGUESE, Makua	812 379	19 686 505	24.2	1.5	39.5	40.1
NAMIBIA *Republic of Namibia*	Windhoek	ENGLISH, Ovambo, Nama, Kavango, Afrikaans	825 118	2 044 147	6.4	0.7	44.5	42.3
NIGER *Republic of Niger*	Niamey	FRENCH, Hausa, Songhai, Zerma	1 189 546	12 525 094	10.5	3.0	43.8	43.7
NIGERIA *Federal Republic of Nigeria*	Abuja	ENGLISH, Hausa, Yoruba, Igbo (Ibo), Fula (Fulani)	923 768	131 859 731	142.7	2.3	46.5	47.7
RWANDA *Republic of Rwanda*	Kigali	RWANDA, FRENCH, ENGLISH	26 338	8 648 248	328.4	2.4	46.3	48.4
SAO TOME AND PRINCIPE *Democratic Republic of Sao Tome and Principe*	Sao Tome	PORTUGUESE, Crioulo (Portuguese Creole)	1 001	193 413	193.2	3.4	65.7	69.0
SENEGAL *Republic of Senegal*	Dakar	FRENCH, Wolof, Fula (Fulani)-Tukulor	196 722	11 987 121	60.9	2.4	57.7	60.9
SEYCHELLES *Republic of Seychelles*	Victoria (on Mahe)	French, English, Seselwa (French Creole)	455	81 541	179.2	1.0	66.7	77.6
SIERRA LEONE *Republic of Sierra Leone*	Freetown	ENGLISH, Krio (English Creole), Mende, Temne	71 740	6 005 250	83.7	2.3	38.1	42.5
SOMALIA	Mogadishu	SOMALI, ARABIC	637 000	8 863 338	13.9	2.9	46.7	50.3
SOUTH AFRICA *Republic of South Africa*	Pretoria (Tshawane), Cape Town, Bloemfontein (Mangaung)	ZULU, XHOSA, AFRIKAANS, SOTHO, TSWANA, ENGLISH, TSONGA, VENDA, SWASI, NDEBELE	1 219 090	44 187 637	36.2	-0.3	43.3	42.2
SUDAN *Republic of the Sudan*	Khartoum, Omdurman	ARABIC, Dinka, Nubian languages, Beja, Nuer	2 503 890	41 236 378	16.5	2.6	57.7	60.2
SWAZILAND *Kingdom of Swaziland*	Mbabane, Lobamba, Lozitha, Ludzidzini	SWAZI, ENGLISH	17 364	1 136 334	65.4	-0.1	32.1	33.2
TANZANIA *United Republic of Tanzania*	Dar es Salaam, Dodoma	SWAHILI, ENGLISH, Nyamwesi (Sukuma)	942 799	37 445 392	39.7	2.1	44.9	46.4
TOGO *Togolese Republic*	Lome	FRENCH, Ewe, Kabre	56 785	5 548 702	97.7	2.7	55.4	59.5
TUNISIA *Republic of Tunisia*	Tunis	ARABIC, French	163 610	10 175 014	62.2	1.0	73.4	77.0
UGANDA *Republic of Uganda*	Kampala	ENGLISH, Swahili, Ganda (Luganda)	241 038	28 195 754	117.0	3.5	51.7	53.7
Western Sahara (adm. Morocco) *Sahrawi Arab Democratic Republic*	El Aauin (Laayoune)	Arabic	266 000	273 008	1.0	no data	no data	no data
ZAMBIA *Republic of Zambia*	Lusaka	ENGLISH, Bemba, Nyanja, Tonga	752 612	11 502 010	15.3	2.1	39.8	40.3
ZIMBABWE *Republic of Zimbabwe*	Harare	ENGLISH, Shona, Ndebele	390 757	12 236 805	31.3	0.6	40.4	38.2

ASIA   (For country locations, see pages 120–121.)

COUNTRY, Dependency Official Name (if different)	CAPITAL(S) (Island location)	PRINCIPAL LANGUAGES OFFICIAL and other languages	AREA km²	POPULATION	POPULATION DENSITY per km²	NATURAL POP. GROWTH % gain	LIFE EXPECTANCY Male	Female
AFGHANISTAN *Islamic Republic of Afghanistan*	Kabul	PASHTO, DARI (Persian), Tajik, Hazara, Uzbek	645 807	31 056 997	48.1	2.6	43.2	43.5
ARMENIA *Republic of Armenia*	Yerevan	ARMENIAN	29 743	2 976 372	100.1	0.4	68.3	76.0
AZERBAIJAN *Republic of Azerbaijan*	Baku	AZERBAIJANI (Azeri)	86 600	7 961 619	91.9	1.1	59.8	68.1
BAHRAIN *Kingdom of Bahrain*	Manama	ARABIC	718	698 585	973.0	1.4	72.0	77.0
BANGLADESH *People's Republic of Bangladesh*	Dhaka	BANGLA (Bengali)	147 570	147 365 352	998.6	2.2	62.5	62.5
BHUTAN *Kingdom of Bhutan*	Thimphu	DZONGKHA, Nepali (Hindi)	38 394	2 279 723	59.4	2.1	55.0	54.5
BRUNEI *State of Brunei, Abode of Peace*	Bandar Seri Begawan	MALAY, English, Chinese	5 765	379 444	65.8	1.6	72.6	77.6
CAMBODIA *Kingdom of Cambodia*	Phnom Penh	KHMER	181 035	13 881 427	76.7	1.8	57.4	61.3

COUNTRY, Dependency Official Name (if different)	CAPITAL(S) (Island location)	PRINCIPAL LANGUAGES OFFICIAL and other languages	AREA km²	POPULATION	POPULATION DENSITY per km²	NATURAL POP. GROWTH % gain	LIFE EXPECTANCY Male	Female
CHINA People's Republic of China	Beijing	MANDARIN, Chinese (Han), Wu, Cantonese (Yue)	9 572 900	1 313 973 713	137.3	0.6	70.9	74.5
CYPRUS Republic of Cyprus	Nicosia	GREEK, TURKISH	5 896	784 301	133.0	0.5	75.4	80.3
EAST TIMOR Democratic Republic of Timor-Leste	Dili	Tetum (Tetun), Portuguese	14 604	1 062 777	72.8	2.1	64.0	68.7
GEORGIA	Tbilisi	GEORGIAN, Russian, Armenian	70 152	4 661 473	66.4	0.1	72.8	79.9
INDIA Republic of India	New Delhi	HINDI, ENGLISH, Bangla (Bengali), Telugu, Marathi, Tamil, Urdu, Gujarati	3 166 414	1 095 351 995	345.9	1.4	63.9	65.6
INDONESIA Republic of Indonesia	Jakarta (on Java)	INDONESIAN (Malay), Javanese, Sundanese	1 890 754	245 452 739	129.8	1.4	67.4	72.5
IRAN Islamic Republic of Iran	Tehran	FARSI (Persian), Azerbaijani (Azeri)	1 629 807	68 688 433	42.1	1.1	68.9	71.7
IRAQ Republic of Iraq	Baghdad	ARABIC, Kurdish	434 128	26 783 383	61.7	2.7	67.8	70.3
ISRAEL State of Israel	Jerusalem	HEBREW, ARABIC	21 671	6 352 117	293.1	1.2	77.3	81.7
JAPAN	Tokyo (on Honshu)	JAPANESE	377 873	127 463 611	337.3	0.1	78.0	84.7
JORDAN Hashemite Kingdom of Jordan	Amman	ARABIC	89 342	5 906 760	66.1	1.9	75.9	81.1
KAZAKHSTAN Republic of Kazakhstan	Astana	KAZAKH, Russian	2 724 900	15 233 244	5.6	0.6	61.6	72.5
KUWAIT State of Kuwait	Kuwait	ARABIC	17 818	2 418 393	135.7	1.9	76.1	78.3
KYRGYZSTAN Kyrgyz Republic	Bishkek	KYRGYZ, RUSSIAN, Uzbek	199 945	5 213 898	26.1	1.5	64.5	72.7
LAOS Lao People's Democratic Republic	Vientiane (Viangchan)	LAO-LUM (Lao), Lao-Theung	236 800	6 368 481	26.9	2.4	53.5	57.6
LEBANON Lebanese Republic	Beirut	ARABIC, French	10 400	3 874 050	372.5	1.3	70.4	75.5
MALAYSIA	Kuala Lumpur, Putrajaya	MALAY, English	329 847	24 385 858	73.9	1.8	69.8	75.4
MALDIVES Republic of Maldives	Male (on Male)	DIVEHI (Maldivian)	298	359 008	1 204.7	2.8	63.1	65.8
MONGOLIA	Ulaanbaatar	KHALKHA (Mongolian)	1 564 160	2 832 224	1.8	1.4	62.6	67.3
MYANMAR (Burma) Union of Myanmar	Yangon (Rangoon), Nay Pyi Taw	BURMESE	676 577	47 382 633	70.0	0.8	58.1	64.0
NEPAL Kingdom of Nepal	Kathmandu	NEPALI, English	147 181	28 287 147	192.2	2.2	60.4	59.9
NORTH KOREA Democratic People's Republic of Korea	Pyongyang	KOREAN	122 762	23 113 019	188.3	0.9	68.9	74.5
OMAN Sultanate of Oman	Muscat	ARABIC	309 500	3 102 229	10.0	3.3	71.1	75.7
PAKISTAN Islamic Republic of Pakistan	Islamabad	URDU, Punjabi, Pashto, Sindhi, English, Saraiki	796 096	165 803 560	208.3	2.2	62.4	64.4
PHILIPPINES Republic of the Philippines	Manila, (on Luzon)	PILIPINO, ENGLISH, Cebuano	316 294	89 468 677	282.9	2.0	67.3	73.2
QATAR State of Qatar	Doha	ARABIC	11 427	885 359	77.5	1.1	71.4	76.6
SAUDI ARABIA Kingdom of Saudi Arabia	Riyadh	ARABIC	2 149 690	27 019 731	12.6	2.7	73.7	77.8
SINGAPORE Republic of Singapore	Singapore	MANDARIN, ENGLISH, MALAY, TAMIL, Chinese	697	4 492 150	6 445.0	0.5	79.1	84.5
SOUTH KOREA Republic of Korea	Seoul	KOREAN	99 900	48 846 823	489.0	0.4	73.6	80.8
SRI LANKA Democratic Socialist Republic of Sri Lanka	Colombo, Sri Jayewardenepura Kotte	SINHALA, TAMIL	65 610	20 222 240	308.2	0.9	70.8	76.1
SYRIA Syrian Arab Republic	Damascus	ARABIC	185 180	18 881 361	102.0	2.3	69.0	71.7
TAIWAN Republic of China on Taiwan	Taipei	MANDARIN, Min, Hakka	36 179	23 036 087	636.7	0.6	74.7	80.5
TAJIKISTAN Republic of Tajikistan	Dushanbe	TAJIK, Uzbek	143 100	7 320 815	51.2	2.4	62.0	68.0
THAILAND Kingdom of Thailand	Bangkok	THAI (Siamese), Lao, Chinese	513 120	64 631 595	126.0	0.7	70.0	74.7
TURKEY Republic of Turkey	Ankara	TURKISH, Kurdish	774 815	70 413 958	90.9	1.1	70.2	75.2
TURKMENISTAN	Ashgabat	TURKMEN	488 100	5 042 920	10.3	1.9	58.4	65.4
UNITED ARAB EMIRATES	Abu Dhabi	ARABIC	83 600	2 602 713	31.1	1.5	72.9	78.1

COUNTRY, Dependency Official Name (if different)	CAPITAL(S) (Island location)	PRINCIPAL LANGUAGES OFFICIAL and other languages	AREA km²	POPULATION	POPULATION DENSITY per km²	NATURAL POP. GROWTH % gain	LIFE EXPECTANCY Male	Female
UZBEKISTAN *Republic of Uzbekistan*	Tashkent (Toshkent)	UZBEK	447 400	27 307 134	61.0	1.8	61.2	68.1
VIETNAM *Socialist Republic of Vietnam*	Hanoi	VIETNAMESE	332 501	84 402 966	253.8	1.1	68.1	73.9
YEMEN *Republic of Yemen*	Sanaa	ARABIC	555 000	21 456 188	38.7	3.5	60.2	64.1

AUSTRALIA AND OCEANIA (For country locations, see pages 136–137.)

COUNTRY, Dependency Official Name (if different)	CAPITAL(S) (Island location)	PRINCIPAL LANGUAGES OFFICIAL and other languages	AREA km²	POPULATION	POPULATION DENSITY per km²	NATURAL POP. GROWTH % gain	LIFE EXPECTANCY Male	Female
AUSTRALIA *Commonwealth of Australia*	Canberra	ENGLISH	7 692 208	20 264 082	2.6	0.5	77.6	83.5
FIJI *Republic of the Fiji Islands*	Suva (on Viti Levu)	ENGLISH, Fijian, Hindi	18 272	905 949	49.6	1.7	67.3	72.5
French Polynesia (Fr.)	Papeete (on Tahiti)	FRENCH. TAHITIAN, Polynesian languages	4 000	274 578	68.6	1.2	73.7	78.6
KIRIBATI *Republic of Kiribati*	Bairiki (on Tarawa)	ENGLISH, Kiribati	811	105 432	130.0	2.2	59.1	65.2
MARSHALL ISLANDS *Republic of the Marshall Islands*	Rita (on Majuro)	MARSHALLESE, ENGLISH	181	60 422	333.8	2.9	68.3	72.4
MICRONESIA *Federated States of Micronesia*	Palikir (on Pohnpei)	Chuukese/Mortlockese, Pohnpeian	701	108 004	154.1	2.0	68.2	72.0
NAURU *Republic of Nauru*	Yaren District (unofficial)	English, Nauruan	21	13 287	626.7	1.8	59.5	66.8
New Caledonia (Fr.)	Noumea	FRENCH, Melanesian and Polynesian languages	18 575	219 246	11.8	1.3	71.3	77.4
NEW ZEALAND	Wellington (on North Island)	ENGLISH, MAORI	270 534	4 076 140	15.1	0.6	75.8	81.9
PALAU *Republic of Palau*	Melekeok (on Babelthuap)	PALAUAN, ENGLISH	488	20 579	42.2	1.2	67.3	73.8
PAPUA NEW GUINEA *Independent State of Papua New Guinea*	Port Moresby	ENGLISH, Tok Pisin (English Creole), Papuan and Melanesian languages	462 840	5 670 544	12.3	2.3	63.1	67.6
SAMOA *Independent State of Samoa*	Apia (on Upolu)	SAMOAN, ENGLISH	2 831	176 908	62.5	0.9	68.2	73.9
SOLOMON ISLANDS	Honiara (on Guadacanal)	ENGLISH, Melanesian languages	28 370	552 438	19.5	2.7	70.4	75.6
TONGA *Kingdom of Tonga*	Nuku'alofa (on Tongatapu)	TONGAN, ENGLISH	750	114 689	152.9	2.0	67.3	72.5
TUVALU	Vaiaku (on Funafuti)	Tuvaluan	26	11 810	461.3	1.5	66.1	70.7
VANUATU *Republic of Vanuatu*	Port-Vila (on Efate)	BISLAMA (English Creole), ENGLISH, FRENCH	12 190	208 869	17.1	1.5	61.3	64.4

EUROPE (For country locations, see pages 106–107.)

COUNTRY, Dependency Official Name (if different)	CAPITAL(S) (Island location)	PRINCIPAL LANGUAGES OFFICIAL and other languages	AREA km²	POPULATION	POPULATION DENSITY per km²	NATURAL POP. GROWTH % gain	LIFE EXPECTANCY Male	Female
ALBANIA *Republic of Albania*	Tirana (Tirane)	ALBANIAN	28 703	3 581 655	124.8	1.0	74.8	80.3
ANDORRA *Principality of Andorra*	Andorra la Vella	CATALAN, Spanish	464	71 201	153.5	0.3	80.6	86.6
AUSTRIA *Republic of Austria*	Vienna	GERMAN	83 871	8 192 880	97.7	-0.1	76.2	82.1
BELARUS *Republic of Belarus*	Minsk	BELARUSIAN, RUSSIAN	207 600	10 293 011	49.6	-0.3	63.5	75.0
BELGIUM *Kingdom of Belgium*	Brussels	DUTCH, FRENCH, GERMAN	30 528	10 379 067	340.0	0.0	75.6	82.1
BOSNIA AND HERZEGOVINA	Sarajevo	BOSNIAN, SERBIAN, CROATIAN	51 209	4 498 976	87.9	0.1	74.4	81.9
BULGARIA *Republic of Bulgaria*	Sofia	BULGARIAN	111 002	7 385 367	66.5	-0.5	68.7	76.1
CROATIA *Republic of Croatia*	Zagreb	SERBO-CROATIAN (Croatian)	56 594	4 494 749	79.4	-0.2	71.0	78.5
CZECH REPUBLIC	Prague	CZECH, Moravian	78 866	10 235 455	129.8	-0.1	72.9	79.7
DENMARK *Kingdom of Denmark*	Copenhagen	DANISH	43 098	5 450 661	126.5	0.1	75.5	80.2
ESTONIA *Republic of Estonia*	Tallinn	ESTONIAN, Russian	43 431	1 324 333	30.5	-0.3	66.6	77.8
FINLAND *Republic of Finland*	Helsinki	Finnish, Swedish	338 145	5 231 372	15.5	0.1	75.0	82.2
FRANCE *French Republic*	Paris	FRENCH	543 965	60 876 136	111.9	0.3	76.1	83.5
GERMANY *Federal Republic of Germany*	Berlin	GERMAN	357 023	82 422 299	230.9	-0.2	75.8	82.0
GREECE *Hellenic Republic*	Athens	GREEK	131 957	10 688 058	81.0	0.0	76.7	81.9

COUNTRY, Dependency *Official Name (if different)*	CAPITAL(S) (Island location)	PRINCIPAL LANGUAGES OFFICIAL and other languages	AREA km²	POPULATION	POPULATION DENSITY per km²	NATURAL POP. GROWTH % gain	LIFE EXPECTANCY Male	Female
HUNGARY *Republic of Hungary*	Budapest	HUNGARIAN	93 030	9 981 334	107.3	-0.3	68.5	77.1
ICELAND *Republic of Iceland*	Reykjavik	ICELANDIC	102 928	299 388	2.9	0.7	78.2	82.5
IRELAND	Dublin	ENGLISH, IRISH	70 273	4 062 235	57.8	0.7	75.1	80.5
ITALY *Italian Republic*	Rome	ITALIAN	301 277	58 133 509	193.0	-0.1	76.9	82.9
KOSOVO *Republic of Kosovo*	Pristina	ALBANIAN, SERBIAN, Bosnian, Turkish	10 887	2 126 708	195.3	no data	no data	no data
LATVIA *Republic of Latvia*	Riga	LATVIAN, Russian	64 589	2 274 735	35.2	-0.5	66.1	76.9
LIECHTENSTEIN *Principality of Liechtenstein*	Vaduz	GERMAN	160	33 987	212.4	0.3	76.1	83.3
LITHUANIA *Republic of Lithuania*	Vilnius	LITHUANIAN	65 300	3 585 906	54.9	-0.2	69.2	79.5
LUXEMBOURG *Grand Duchy of Luxembourg*	Luxembourg	Luxemburgian, Portuguese	2 586	474 413	183.5	0.4	75.6	82.4
MACEDONIA *Republic of Macedonia*	Skopje	MACEDONIAN, Albanian	25 713	2 050 554	79.7	0.3	71.5	76.6
MALTA *Republic of Malta*	Valletta	MALTESE, ENGLISH	315	400 214	1 270.5	0.2	76.8	81.3
MOLDOVA *Republic of Moldova*	Chisinau	ROMANIAN (Moldovan), Russian	33 845	4 466 706	132.0	0.2	61.6	69.9
MONACO *Principality of Monaco*	Monaco	FRENCH, Italian, Monegasque	1.95	32 543	16 688.7	-0.3	75.9	83.7
MONTENEGRO *Republic of Montenegro*	Podgorica	SERBIAN	13 812	630 548	45.7	0.3	no data	no data
NETHERLANDS *Kingdom of The Netherlands*	Amsterdam, The Hague	DUTCH	41 528	16 491 461	397.1	0.2	76.4	81.7
NORWAY *Kingdom of Norway*	Oslo	NORWEGIAN	323 758	4 610 820	14.2	0.2	76.9	82.3
POLAND *Republic of Poland*	Warsaw	POLISH	312 685	38 536 869	123.2	0.0	71.0	79.2
PORTUGAL *Portuguese Republic*	Lisbon	PORTUGUESE	92 152	10 605 870	115.1	0.0	74.4	81.2
ROMANIA	Bucharest	ROMANIAN	238 391	22 303 552	93.6	-0.1	68.1	75.3
RUSSIA *Russian Federation*	Moscow	RUSSIAN	17 075 400	142 893 540	8.4	-0.5	60.5	74.1
SAN MARINO *Most Serene Republic of San Marino*	San Marino	ITALIAN (Romagnolo)	61	29 251	479.5	0.2	78.2	85.5
SERBIA *Republic of Serbia*	Belgrade	SERBO-CROATIAN (Serbian)	77 474	8 023 557	103.6	no data	71.0	76.0
SLOVAKIA *Slovak Republic*	Bratislava	SLOVAK	49 035	5 439 448	110.9	0.1	70.8	78.9
SLOVENIA *Republic of Slovenia*	Ljubljana	SLOVENE	20 273	2 010 347	99.2	-0.1	72.6	80.3
SPAIN *Kingdom of Spain*	Madrid	CASTILIAN SPANISH, Catalan, Galician	505 988	40 397 842	79.8	0.0	76.3	83.2
SWEDEN *Kingdom of Sweden*	Stockholm	SWEDISH	450 295	9 016 596	20.0	0.0	78.3	82.9
SWITZERLAND *Swiss Confederation*	Bern, Lausanne	GERMAN, FRENCH, ITALIAN	41 284	7 523 934	182.2	0.1	77.7	83.5
UKRAINE	Kiev	UKRAINIAN, Russian	603 628	46 710 816	77.4	-0.6	64.7	75.6
UNITED KINGDOM *United Kingdom of Great Britain and Northern Ireland*	London (on Great Britain)	ENGLISH	242 910	60 609 153	249.5	0.1	76.1	81.1
VATICAN CITY *The Holy See (State of the Vatican City)*	Vatican City	Italian, Latin, French	0.44	932	2 118.2	0.0	no data	no data

NORTH AMERICA (For country locations, see page 38.)

ANTIGUA AND BARBUDA	Saint John's (on Antigua)	ENGLISH, English Creole	442	69 108	156.4	1.2	69.8	74.7
Aruba (Neth.)	Oranjestad	DUTCH, Papiamento	193	71 891	372.5	0.5	76.0	82.8
BAHAMAS *Commonwealth of the Bahamas*	Nassau (on New Providence)	ENGLISH, English Creole	13 939	303 770	21.8	0.9	62.2	69.0
BARBADOS	Bridgetown	ENGLISH, Bajan (English Creole)	430	279 912	651.0	0.4	70.8	74.8
BELIZE	Belmopan	ENGLISH, English Creole, Spanish	22 965	287 730	12.5	2.4	66.4	70.3
CANADA	Ottawa	ENGLISH, FRENCH	9 984 670	33 098 932	3.3	0.3	76.9	83.7

COUNTRY, Dependency _Official Name (if different)_	CAPITAL(S) _(Island location)_	PRINCIPAL LANGUAGES OFFICIAL and other languages	AREA km²	POPULATION	POPULATION DENSITY per km²	NATURAL POP. GROWTH % gain	LIFE EXPECTANCY Male	Female
COSTA RICA _Republic of Costa Rica_	San Jose	SPANISH	51 100	4 075 261	79.8	1.4	74.4	79.7
CUBA _Republic of Cuba_	Havana	SPANISH	110 861	11 382 820	102.7	0.5	75.1	79.9
DOMINICA _Commonwealth of Dominica_	Roseau	ENGLISH, English Creole, French Creole	739	68 910	93.2	0.9	72.0	77.9
DOMINICAN REPUBLIC	Santo Domingo	SPANISH	48 671	9 183 984	188.7	1.8	70.2	73.3
EL SALVADOR _Republic of El Salvador_	San Salvador	SPANISH	21 042	6 822 378	324.2	2.1	67.9	75.3
GRENADA	Saint George's	ENGLISH, English Creole	344	89 703	260.8	1.5	63.1	66.7
Guadeloupe (Fr.) _Department of Guadeloupe_	Basse-Terre	FRENCH, French Creole	1 705	452 776	265.6	0.9	74.9	81.4
GUATEMALA _Republic of Guatemala_	Guatemala City	SPANISH, Quiche, Cakchiquel, Kekchi, Mam	109 117	12 293 545	112.7	2.5	67.7	71.2
HAITI _Republic of Haiti_	Port-au-Prince	HAITIAN (French Creole), FRENCH	27 700	8 308 504	299.9	2.4	51.9	54.6
HONDURAS _Republic of Honduras_	Tegucigalpa	SPANISH	112 492	7 326 496	65.1	2.4	67.8	71.0
JAMAICA	Kingston	ENGLISH, English Creole	10 991	2 758 124	250.9	1.5	71.5	75.0
Kalaallit Nunaat (Greenland) (Den.)	Nuuk (Godthab)	GREENLANDIC, DANISH	2 166 086	56 361	0.0	0.8	66.4	73.6
Martinique (Fr.) _Department of Martinique_	Fort-de-France	FRENCH, French Creole	1 128	436 131	386.6	0.8	79.5	78.9
MEXICO _United Mexican States_	Mexico City	SPANISH, Aztec (Nahuatl), Yucatec (Mayan)	1 964 375	107 449 525	54.7	1.6	72.6	78.3
Netherlands Antilles (Neth.)	Willemstad (on Curacao)	DUTCH, Papiamento	800	221 736	277.2	0.9	73.8	78.4
NICARAGUA _Republic of Nicaragua_	Managua	SPANISH	130 373	5 570 129	42.7	2.0	68.6	72.8
PANAMA _Republic of Panama_	Panama City	SPANISH, English Creole	75 040	3 191 319	42.5	1.7	72.7	77.9
Puerto Rico (U.S.) _Commonwealth of Puerto Rico_	San Juan	SPANISH, ENGLISH	9 104	3 927 188	431.4	0.5	74.5	82.5
SAINT KITTS AND NEVIS _Federation of St. Kitts (Christopher) and Nevis_	Basseterre (on St. Kitts)	ENGLISH, English Creole	269	39 129	145.5	1.0	69.6	75.4
SAINT LUCIA	Castries	ENGLISH, English/French Creole	617	168 458	273.0	1.5	70.3	77.7
SAINT VINCENT AND THE GRENADINES	Kingstown (on St. Vincent)	ENGLISH, English Creole	389	117 848	303.0	1.0	72.0	75.8
TRINIDAD AND TOBAGO _Republic of Trinidad and Tobago_	Port-of-Spain (on Trinidad)	ENGLISH, Trinidad English	5 127	1 065 842	207.9	0.2	65.7	67.9
UNITED STATES _United States of America_	Washington, D.C.	English, Spanish	9 522 058	298 444 215	31.3	0.6	75.0	80.8

SOUTH AMERICA (For country locations, see page 88.)

COUNTRY, Dependency _Official Name (if different)_	CAPITAL(S) _(Island location)_	PRINCIPAL LANGUAGES OFFICIAL and other languages	AREA km²	POPULATION	POPULATION DENSITY per km²	NATURAL POP. GROWTH % gain	LIFE EXPECTANCY Male	Female
ARGENTINA _Argentine Republic_	Buenos Aires	SPANISH	2 780 092	39 921 833	14.4	0.9	72.4	80.1
BOLIVIA _Republic of Bolivia_	La Paz, Sucre	SPANISH, QUECHUA, AYMARA	1 098 581	8 989 046	8.2	1.6	63.2	68.6
BRAZIL _Federative Republic of Brazil_	Brasilia	PORTUGUESE	8 514 877	188 078 227	22.1	1.1	68.0	76.1
CHILE _Republic of Chile_	Santiago	SPANISH, Araucanian (Mapuche)	756 096	16 134 219	21.3	1.0	73.5	80.2
COLOMBIA _Republic of Colombia_	Bogota	SPANISH	1 141 568	43 593 035	38.2	1.5	68.2	76.0
ECUADOR _Republic of Ecuador_	Quito	SPANISH, Quechuan	272 045	13 547 510	49.8	1.8	73.6	79.4
French Guiana (Fr.) _Department of French Guiana_	Cayenne	FRENCH, French Creole	83 534	199 509	2.4	1.6	74.0	80.8
GUYANA _Co-operative Republic of Guyana_	Georgetown	ENGLISH, English Creole	215 083	767 245	3.6	1.0	63.2	68.7
PARAGUAY _Republic of Paraguay_	Asuncion	GUARANI, SPANISH	406 752	6 506 464	16.0	2.5	72.6	77.8
PERU _Republic of Peru_	Lima	SPANISH, QUECHUA, AYMARA	1 285 216	28 302 603	22.0	1.5	68.1	71.7
SURINAME _Republic of Suriname_	Paramaribo	DUTCH, English Creole	163 820	439 117	2.7	1.1	66.7	71.5
URUGUAY _Oriental Republic of Uruguay_	Montevideo	SPANISH	176 215	3 431 932	19.5	0.5	73.1	79.7
VENEZUELA _Bolivarian Republic of Venezuela_	Caracas	SPANISH	916 445	25 730 435	28.1	1.4	71.5	77.8

GLOSSARY

acid rain Rain or snow that carries acids formed from chemical pollutants in the atmosphere.

Antarctic Circle Line of latitude located at 66½°S, approximately 2620 kilometres from the South Pole.

Arctic Circle Line of latitude located at 66½°N, approximately 2620 kilometres from the North Pole.

ANTARCTIC CIRCLE (66½°S)   ARCTIC CIRCLE (66½°N)

atoll Low, ring-shaped island formed by coral reefs.

balance of trade Difference between the value of a country's exports and the value of its imports, commonly measured in U.S. dollars. A country that exports more than it imports has a positive balance of trade, or *trade surplus*. A country that imports more than it exports has a negative balance of trade, or *trade deficit*.

basin 1. Area drained by a river and its branches. 2. Area surrounded by higher land.

biofuel Renewable fuel that is made from recently living plant or animal material.

broadleaf forest Forest whose trees have broad leaves. In places with cold winters, broad leaves change colour and fall off each autumn.

climate Pattern of weather conditions for a place or region in a typical year. Climate is affected by latitude, elevation, topography, ocean currents, and wind.

climograph Graph showing annual patterns of temperature and precipitation for a specified place.

combustion Burning or other process that produces heat and light.

commercial farming Growing crops or raising livestock, largely for sale to others.

cropland Region used mainly to grow crops.

culture Beliefs, practices, and customs of a group of people.

deforestation Removal of all trees from a vast area of forest.

desert Dry region receiving little or no precipitation and with little or no vegetation.

ecozone A large area where climate, land features, water features, plants, and animals interact as a single ecological system.

elevation Height above sea level.

emigration Movement of people away from their native country or region to a new home elsewhere. The people moving away are called *emigrants*.

Equator Imaginary line that divides the earth into the Northern and Southern Hemispheres. All points along the Equator have a latitude of 0°.

ethnicity Group identity based on ancestral homeland, language, religion, and/or race.

European Union (EU) Group of European countries whose main goal is to establish themselves, for trading purposes, as a single market. (See map on page 113.)

export Sale of goods to a foreign country.

fault Boundary between plates of the earth's crust. An area where this boundary is indistinct is a *fault zone*.

forestry Use of forests for lumber, paper, and other products.

fossil fuels Natural fuels that were formed from the remains of plants and animals over millions of years. Principal fossil fuels are petroleum, natural gas, and coal.

free trade System of buying and selling of goods across international borders without restrictions.

glacier Large body of ice formed from a long-lasting accumulation of snow on mountains and in polar regions.

global warming Increase in worldwide air temperature, caused by pollution and the greenhouse effect.

grassland Region where grass grows, sometimes mixed with scattered trees and shrubs. Grasslands are often used for grazing.

greenhouse effect Trapping of solar radiation in the atmosphere due to high concentrations of gases that absorb heat, such as carbon dioxide, methane, and water vapour.

Greenwich Mean Time (GMT) Time of day along the Prime Meridian, also called Universal Time or Zulu Time. All other time zones are identified in hours before or after GMT.

gross domestic product (GDP) Annual value of all goods and services produced within a country's borders. GDP includes production by foreign-owned facilities.

hydroelectricity Electricity produced when falling water is passed through a turbine.

immigration Movement of people into a new country of residence. The people moving in are called *immigrants*.

import Purchase of goods produced in a foreign country.

indigenous Native to a particular region. Indigenous peoples are related to the earliest known inhabitants of a region. Also called *aboriginal*.

International Date Line Imaginary line located along and near 180° longitude that divides calendar days. Places west of the line are 24 hours ahead of places east of the line.

irrigation The importing of water to an otherwise arid region to grow crops.

land cover Vegetation, deserts, and glaciers covering the earth's surface.

land use Principal economic activity in an area. It is not the only activity, but it is the most significant or widespread.

landform Natural feature of the landscape, such as a mountain, plain, or island.

latitude Distance from the Equator measured in degrees. Lines of latitude, or *parallels*, are numbered north and south from the Equator and appear on maps as east-west lines.

life expectancy Average number of years that people born today may expect to live based on the prevailing death rates for that population. Life expectancy reflects the group's general health and welfare.

literacy Ability to both read and write. The percentage of literate people is a good indicator of a country's educational level; literacy standards vary by country.

longitude Distance from the Prime Meridian measured in degrees. Lines of longitude, or *meridians*, are numbered east and west from the Prime Meridian and appear on maps as north-south lines.

map projection Any system for drawing lines of latitude, lines of longitude, and earth features on a map. Projections are never completely accurate, distorting either sizes or shapes or both of the earth's land and water features.

metal Element that reflects light, conducts electricity and heat, and can be manipulated into new shapes. Metal and metal-bearing ores are mined at and below the earth's surface.

migration Mass movement from one region or country to another.

national poverty line Poverty as defined by a government for an entire country. National poverty lines are a measure of *relative poverty*.

natural population growth (NPG) Annual difference between the number of births and the number of deaths in a country or region; does not include change due to population movement.

needleleaf forest Forest of needleleaf trees, such as pines and other evergreens.

nomadic herding Raising herds of animals, moving them in a yearly cycle from one seasonal source of food and water to the next.

Oceania Collective name for islands of the central and southern Pacific Ocean, usually including New Zealand and sometimes also including Australia.

Organization of Petroleum Exporting Countries (OPEC) Association of 13 countries that control most of the world's known oil reserves. (See maps on page 128.)

permafrost Ground that is frozen most or all of the year.

plain Broad area of land that is gently rolling or almost flat.

plate Any of the sections of the earth's crust that float above the molten interior of the planet. Lighter and thicker areas of the plates form the continents, while denser and thinner areas form ocean floors.

plateau Elevated plain, usually with at least one steeply dropping or rising side; tableland.

population density The number of people living in a given area such as a square kilometre.

poverty Inability to acquire basic human needs, such as food and housing. In global terms, poverty is defined as living on the equivalent of less than C$ 1.15 a day.

precipitation Water from the atmosphere that accumulates on the earth's surface as rain, snow, hail, sleet, or dew.

Prime Meridian Line of longitude, the 0° meridian, which passes through Greenwich, United Kingdom.

rain forest Dense forest that receives great amounts of rain and stays green throughout the year, can be tropical or temperate.

ranching and herding Raising herds of livestock on large, open ranches. The livestock graze or feed on the natural grasses growing there.

region Large area that is different from the areas around it. A region can be defined by a single feature or by several features, either physical or cultural.

renewable energy resource Power source that can be grown, such as firewood, or that cannot be used up, such as wind.

rural Relating to the countryside, as opposed to cities.

Sahel Narrow, semi-arid region south of Africa's Sahara that extends east-west between Somalia and Senegal.

scale Relationship between an actual distance on the earth and the same distance as shown on a map.

semi-desert Region covered by scattered vegetation but too dry for crops without irrigation. Also called *semi-arid*.

subsistence farming Agriculture that produces only enough for the needs of a farmer and his or her family, with little or nothing left to sell.

surface current Continuous flow of water at or near the surface of an ocean.

territory 1. Part of a country that does not have the rights of a province or state. 2. Any large region, often with poorly defined boundaries.

thermal energy Energy derived from a heat source, usually natural, to create electricity.

time zone Region that shares the same time of day, usually one hour earlier than the zone to the west. Time zones are roughly centred on lines of longitude 15° apart.

trade organization Group established by an agreement between governments to promote trade. Examples include EU and OPEC.

Tropic of Cancer Line of latitude located at 23½°N. It marks the northern boundary of the tropics.

Tropic of Capricorn Line of latitude located at 23½°S. It marks the southern boundary of the tropics.

tropical rain forest Dense forest in or near the tropics that receives great amounts of rain and stays green year round.

tundra 1. Polar or mountainous area with no glaciers but too cold for trees to grow. 2. Small plants that grow close to the ground in places that are cool or cold most of the year.

urban Relating to cities and their surrounding suburbs, the opposite of rural.

urbanization Change at a place as it grows into a city or is absorbed by an expanding city nearby.

vertical exaggeration 1. Increase in the height of a cross section or other diagram in order to show landforms more clearly. 2. Ratio of vertical scale to horizontal scale. If vertical exaggeration is 32:1, one vertical kilometre appears 32 times larger than one horizontal kilometre.

weather Temperature, rainfall, and other conditions of the atmosphere over a short time in one place.

wetland Transition zone between land and water where the water level remains near or above the ground's surface for most of the year. Wetlands include swamps, marshes, and bogs.

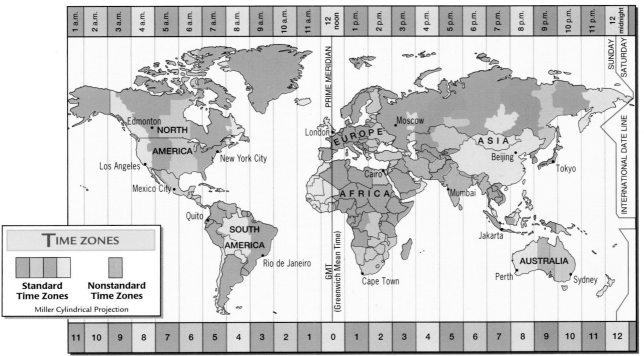

TIME ZONES

Standard Time Zones   Nonstandard Time Zones

Miller Cylindrical Projection

Subtract time zone number from GMT to obtain local time.   Add time zone number to GMT to obtain local time.

INDEX

The index lists all the place names that appear in the atlas. Entries for physical features are alphabetized by the proper part of their names, not by the descriptive part. For example, Lake Superior is listed as **Superior, L.** Entries for cities, however, are alphabetized by the first word in their names. So the city of Lake Charles is listed as **Lake Charles**. Similarly, foreign names, such as Rio Grande, are alphabetized by the first word in the name. Names beginning with St. are spelled **Saint** in the index. Abbreviations used in the index and in other parts of the atlas are listed on page 176.

Name (Pronunciation), Description (Lat., Long.) Page

100 Mile House, BC (52°N, 121°W) ... 60

A

Aachen (AH kuhn), Germany (51°N, 6°E) ... 118
Aba (ah BAH), Nigeria (5°N, 7°E) ... 102
Abbe, L., Africa (11°N, 41°E) ... 131
Abbotsford, BC (49°N, 122°W) ... 60
Abd al Kuri, island in Arabian Sea (12°N, 51°E) ... 131
Abeche, Chad (14°N, 21°E) ... 103
Abemama Atoll, Pacific O. (0°N, 174°E) ... 137
Aberdeen, Scotland (57°N, 2°W) ... 116
Aberdeen, SD (46°N, 99°W) ... 72
Aberdeen L., NU (65°N, 99°W) ... 70
Aberystwyth (ab uh RIS twith), Wales (52°N, 4°W) 116
Abidjan (ab ih JAHN), Côte d'Ivoire (5°N, 4°W) ... 102
Abilene, TX (32°N, 100°W) ... 72
Abitibi, L. (ab uh TIHB ee), Canada (49°N, 80°W) ... 64
Abitibi R., ON (51°N, 81°W) ... 64
Abkhazia, region of Georgia (43°N, 41°E) ... 119
Abu Dhabi (ahb oo DAHB ee), United Arab Emirates (24°N, 55°E) ... 131
Abuja (ah BOO juh), Nigeria (9°N, 8°E) ... 102
Abuna R. (ah boo NAH), South America (10°S, 67°W) ... 95
Acapulco (ah kah POOL koh), Mexico (17°N, 100°W) ... 86
Accra, Ghana (6°N, 0°) ... 102
Aconcagua (ah kawng KAH gwah), mt. in South America (33°S, 70°W) ... 94
Actaeon Group, Pacific O. (21°S, 137°W) ... 137
Ad Dammam, Saudi Arabia (27°N, 50°E) ... 131
Adamaoua Plateau (ah duh MAH wuh), Africa (8°N, 15°E) ... 103
Adamstown, Pitcairn Is. (25°S, 130°W) ... 137
Adana, Turkey (37°N, 35°E) ... 131
Addis Ababa (AD ihs AB uh buh), Ethiopia (9°N, 39°E) ... 104
Adelaide (AD uh layd), Australia (35°S, 138°E) ... 143
Adele I., Indian O. (15°S, 123°E) ... 143
Aden (AHD uhn), Yemen (13°N, 45°E) ... 131
Aden, Gulf of, Arabian Sea (13°N, 48°E) ... 131
Adirondack Mts., NY (44°N, 74°W) ... 75
Adlatok R., NL (55°N, 61°W) ... 68
Admiralty I., Papua New Guinea (2°S, 147°E) ... 136
Adriatic Sea, Europe (44°N, 13°E) ... 118
Aegean Sea, Mediterranean Sea (38°N, 25°E) ... 118
Afghanistan, country in Asia (34°N, 65°E) ... 132
Africa, continent ... 96–98
African (Nubian) Plate (0°, 15°E) ... 14
African (Somalian) Plate (0°, 45°E) ... 14
Agadez, Niger (17°N, 8°E) ... 102
Agadir, Morocco (31°N, 10°W) ... 100
Agalega Is., Indian Ocean (10°S, 57°E) ... 96
Agana, Guam (14°N, 143°E) ... 136
Agra, India (27°N, 78°E) ... 132
Agrihan I., Pacific O. (19°N, 146°E) ... 136
Agrinion (ah GREEN yawn), Greece (39°N, 21°E) ... 118
Aguanish, R., QC (51°N, 63°W) ... 66
Aguascalientes (ah wuh skahl YEN tuhs), Mexico (22°N, 102°W) ... 86
Aguascalientes, state in Mexico (22°N, 102°W) ... 86
Aguja, Point (ah GOO hah), Peru (6°S, 81°W) ... 94
Agulhas, Cape (uh GUHL uhs), South Africa (35°S, 20°E) ... 105
Agulhas Negras, mt. in Brazil (22°S, 46°W) ... 95
Ahaggar Mts., Africa (24°N, 6°E) ... 100
Ahmadabad, India (23°N, 73°E) ... 132
Ahvaz, Iran (31°N, 49°E) ... 131
Air Mts., Niger (18°N, 8°E) ... 102
Airdrie, AB (50°N, 114°W) ... 62
Aitutaki I. (eye too TAH kee), Pacific O. (19°S, 162°W) ... 137
Aix-en-Provence (ayk sahn pruh VAHNS), France (44°N, 5°E) ... 117
Ajaccio (ah YAHCH oh), France (42°N, 9°E) ... 118
Ajax, ON (44°N, 79°W) ... 65
Ajdabiyah, Libya (31°N, 20°E) ... 101
Akhdar Mts., Oman (24°N, 57°W) ... 131
Akimiski I., James Bay (53°N, 80°W) ... 71
Akita (ah KEET uh), Japan (40°N, 140°E) ... 135
Akosambo Dam, Africa (6°N, 0°) ... 102
Akpatok I. (AK puh tok), Hudson Str. (61°N, 67°W) ... 71
Akron, OH (41°N, 81°W) ... 73
Aksu (ahk SOO), China (41°N, 80°E) ... 134
Al Aqabah, Jordan (30°N, 35°E) ... 131
Al Aziziyah (al az ee ZEE yuh), Libya (33°N, 13°E) ... 100
Al Fashir (al FAH shuhr), Sudan (14°N, 25°E) ... 104
Al Fayyum (al fay YOOM), Egypt (29°N, 31°E) ... 101
Al Hudaydah, Yemen (15°N, 43°E) ... 131
Al Jafr, Jordan (30°N, 36°E) ... 131
Al Jawf, Libya (24°N, 23°E) ... 101
Al Kharj, Saudi Arabia (24°N, 47°E) ... 131
Al Marj, Libya (33°N, 21°E) ... 101
Al Minya, Egypt (28°N, 31°E) ... 101
Al Mubarraz, Saudi Arabia (23°N, 46°E) ... 131
Al Mukalla, Yemen (14°N, 49°E) ... 131
Al Qunaytirah, Syria (33°N, 36°E) ... 131
Alabama, state in U.S. (33°N, 87°W) ... 73
Alajuela (ah lah HWA lah), Costa Rica (10°N, 84°W) ... 87
Alamagan I., Pacific O. (18°N, 147°E) ... 136
Aland Is., Finland (60°N, 21°E) ... 107
Alaska, state of U.S. (65°N, 155°W) ... 72
Alaska, Gulf of, Pacific O. (59°N, 145°W) ... 74
Alaska Range, AK (63°N, 150°W) ... 74
Albacete, Spain (39°N, 2°W) ... 117
Albania, country in Europe (41°N, 20°E) ... 118
Albany, Australia (35°S, 118°E) ... 143
Albany, GA (32°N, 84°W) ... 73
Albany, NY (43°N, 74°W) ... 73
Albany R., ON (51°N, 85°W) ... 64
Albemarle Sound, NC (36°N, 76°W) ... 73
Albert, L., Africa (2°N, 31°E) ... 104
Alberta, prov. in Canada (57°N, 115°W) ... 62
Alborg (AWL bawrg), Denmark (57°N, 10°E) ... 118
Albuquerque (AL buh kur kee), NM (35°N, 107°W) ... 72
Albury, Australia (36°S, 147°E) ... 143
Aldabra Is., Indian O. (9°S, 46°E) ... 97
Aleppo, Syria (36°N, 37°E) ... 131
Alert Station, NU (83°N, 62°W) ... 71
Aleutian Is. (uh LOO shuhn), Bering Sea (52°N, 180°) ... 74
Aleutian Trench, Pacific O. (50°N, 165°W) ... 16
Alexander Archipelago, Gulf of Alaska (57°N, 135°W) ... 60
Alexander I., Antarctica (70°S, 70°W) ... 144
Alexandria, Egypt (31°N, 30°E) ... 101
Alexandria, LA (32°N, 93°W) ... 73
Alexandrina, L., Australia (36°S, 139°E) ... 143
Alexis R., NL (53°N, 52°W) ... 68
Algeria, country in Africa (28°N, 3°E) ... 100
Algiers (al JEERS), Algeria (37°N, 3°E) ... 100
Algonquin P.P., ON (46°N, 78°W) ... 64
Alicante, Spain (38°N, 1°W) ... 117
Alice Springs, Australia (24°S, 134°E) ... 143
Allahabad (al uh huh BAD), India (26°N, 82°E) ... 132
Allegheny Plateau, U.S. (39°N, 80°W) ... 74
Allier R. (al YAY), France (46°N, 3°E) ... 117
Alma, QC (48°N, 72°W) ... 66
Almaty, Kazakhstan (43°N, 77°E) ... 120
Almeria (ahl may RE ah), Spain (37°N, 2°W) ... 117
Alofi, Niue (20°S, 170°W) ... 137
Alofi I., Pacific O. (15°S, 178°W) ... 137
Alpena, MI (45°N, 83°W) ... 73
Alps, mt. range in Europe (45°N, 10°E) ... 118
Altai Mts. (AL ty), Asia (49°N, 90°E) ... 134
Altamaha R., GA (32°N, 82°W) ... 73
Altiplano, plateau in Bolivia (19°S, 68°W) ... 95
Altona, MB (49°N, 98°W) ... 63
Altun Mts. (ahl toon), China (40°N, 90°E) ... 134
Alvaro Obregon Res., Mexico (28°N, 110°W) ... 80
Alvorada, Brazil (12°S, 49°W) ... 95
Am Timan, Chad (11°N, 20°E) ... 96
Amadjuak L., NU (65°N, 71°W) ... 71
Amarillo, TX (35°N, 102°W) ... 72
Amazon Basin, South America (5°S, 65°W) ... 95
Amazon, Mouths of the, Brazil (0°, 50°W) ... 95
Amazon R., South America (5°S, 60°W) ... 95
Ambon, Indonesia (4°S, 128°E) ... 133
Ambovombe, Madagascar (24°S, 47°E) ... 105
Ambrym I., Pacific O. (16°S, 168°E) ... 136
American Falls Res., ID (43°N, 113°W) ... 72
American Samoa, poss. of U.S. (14°S, 170°W) ... 137
Amery Ice Shelf, Antarctica (70°S, 70°E) ... 144
Amherst, NS (46°N, 64°W) ... 68
Amiens (AM ee uhnz), France (50°N, 2°E) ... 117
Amirante Is. (AM uh rant), Indian O. (5°S, 53°E) ... 97
Amisk L., SK (55°N, 102°W) ... 62
Amman, Jordan (32°N, 36°E) ... 131
Amol, Iran (36°N, 53°E) ... 131
Amritsar (uhm RIHT suhr), India (32°N, 75°E) ... 132
Amsterdam, Netherlands (53°N, 5°E) ... 117
Amsterdam I., Indian O. (38°S, 78°E) ... 9
Amu Darya (ahm oo DAHR yuh), r. in Asia (40°N, 63°E) ... 24
Amund Ringnes I., Arctic O. (78°N, 97°W) ... 70
Amundsen Gulf, Beaufort Sea (71°N, 125°W) ... 44
Amundsen-Scott Station, Antarctica (90°S) ... 144
Amundsen Sea, Antarctica (70°S, 110°W) ... 144
Amur R. (ah MOOR), Asia (55°N, 125°E) ... 121
An Nafud (an nuh FOOD), desert in Saudi Arabia (28°N, 40°E) ... 131
Anadyr, Gulf of, Bering Sea (65°N, 178°W) ... 123
Anapolis, Brazil (16°S, 49°W) ... 95
Anatahan I., Pacific O. (16°N, 147°E) ... 136
Anatolia (an uh TOH lee uh), region of Turkey (38°N, 30°E) ... 131
Anatom I., Pacific O. (20°S, 170°E) ... 136
Anchorage, AK (61°N, 150°W) ... 72
Ancona (ang KOH nuh), Italy (44°N, 14°E) ... 118
Andaman Is., Bay of Bengal (12°N, 93°E) ... 132
Andaman Sea, Indian O. (12°N, 96°E) ... 132
Anderson R., NT (69°N, 125°W) ... 70
Andes Mts. South America (5°S, 75°W) ... 94
Andkhvoy, Afghanistan (36°N, 65°E) ... 132
Andorra, country in Europe (43°N, 2°E) ... 117
Andorra la Vella (an DAWR uh lah VEL ah), Andorra (43°N, 2°E) ... 117
Andros I., Atlantic O. (24°N, 78°W) ... 81
Anegada Passage, Caribbean Sea (18°N, 64°W) ... 87
Angel de la Guarda I., Gulf of California (29°N, 113°W) ... 86
Angel Falls, waterfall in Venezuela (6°N, 63°W) ... 94
Angers (ahn ZHAY), France (47°N, 1°W) ... 117
Angikuni L., NU (62°N, 100°W) ... 70
Angola, country in Africa (12°S, 17°E) ... 105
Angola Plain, Atlantic O. (10°S, 5°E) ... 16
Anguilla (ang GWIL uh), island in Caribbean Sea (18°N, 63°W) ... 87
Anju (AHN joo), N. Korea (40°N, 126°E) ... 135
Ankara, Turkey (40°N, 33°E) ... 131
Ann Arbor, MI (42°N, 84°W) ... 73
Annaba (an NAHB uh), Algeria (37°N, 8°E) ... 100
Annamite Mts., Asia (17°N, 106°E) ... 133
Annapolis, MD (39°N, 76°W) ... 73
Annobon, island in Atlantic O. (2°S, 6°E) ... 103
Anshan, China (41°N, 123°E) ... 134
Antalya (ant uhl YAH), Turkey (37°N, 31°E) ... 131
Antalya, Gulf of, Turkey (37°N, 31°E) ... 131
Antananarivo (ahn tuh nah nuh REE voh), Madagascar (19°S, 47°E) ... 105
Antanifotsy, Madagascar (20°S, 48°E) ... 105
Antarctic Pen., Antarctica (66°S, 60°W) ... 144
Antarctic Plate (70°S, 0°) ... 14
Antarctica, continent ... 144
Anticosti I., QC (49°N, 62°W) ... 66
Antigua and Barbuda, country in Caribbean Sea (18°N, 62°W) ... 87
Antioch, Turkey (36°N, 36°E) ... 131
Antofagasta, Chile (24°S, 70°W) ... 94
Antongila Bay, Madagascar (16°S, 50°E) ... 105
Antsirabe, Madagascar (20°S, 47°E) ... 105
Antsiranana, Madagascar (12°S, 49°E) ... 105
Antwerp, Belgium (51°N, 4°E) ... 117
Aomori (OW muh ree), Japan (41°N, 141°E) ... 135
Apalachee Bay, FL (30°N, 85°W) ... 73
Apennines, mt. range in Italy (43°N, 13°E) ... 118
Apia, Samoa (14°S, 172°W) ... 137
Appalachian Mts., U.S. (35°N, 80°W) ... 75
Aqaba, Gulf of, Red Sea (29°N, 35°E) ... 131
Aqtau, Kazakhstan (44°N, 51°E) ... 119
Aqtobe, Kazakhstan (50°N, 57°E) ... 119
Aquitaine Basin, France (44°N, 1°W) ... 117
Araar, Saudi Arabia (31°N, 42°E) ... 131
Arabian Desert, Egypt (26°N, 34°E) ... 101
Arabian Pen., Asia (20°N, 45°E) ... 131
Arabian Plate (23°N, 45°E) ... 14
Arabian Sea, Indian O. (15°N, 65°E) ... 120
Aracaju (ar uh kuh ZHOO), Brazil (11°S, 37°W) ... 95
Arad, Romania (46°N, 21°E) ... 118
Arafura Sea (ar uh FOOR uh), Indian O. (10°S, 135°E) ... 138
Araguaia R. (ah rah GWAH yah), Brazil (9°S, 50°W) ... 95
Arak, Iran (34°N, 50°E) ... 131
Aral, Kazakhstan (47°N, 62°E) ... 120
Aral Sea (AR uhl), Asia (45°N, 60°E) ... 120
Arapiraca, Brazil (9°S, 37°W) ... 95
Ararat, Mt., Turkey (40°N, 44°E) ... 131

M

ABBREVIATIONS

A

& and
AB Alberta
A.D. Anno Domini (year of the Lord)
adm. administered
AIDS Acquired Immunodeficiency Syndrome
AK Alaska
AL Alabama
Alb. Albania
a.m. ante meridiem (before noon)
Ang. Angola
AR Arkansas
Arch. archipelago
Arg. Argentina
Aus. Austria
Austr. Australia
AZ Arizona
Azer. Azerbaijan

B

BC British Columbia
Bos., Bosnia Bosnia-Herzegovina

C

C Celsius
C$ Canadian dollar
C. Afr. Rep. Central African Republic
CA California
cm centimetre
CO Colorado
Congo Rep. Congo Republic
Cro. Croatia
CT Connecticut
Cz., Cz. Rep. Czech Republic

D

D.C. District of Columbia
DE Delaware
Den. Denmark
Dom. Rep. Dominican Republic

E

E East
elev. elevation
Eq. Guinea Equatorial Guinea
Est. Estonia

F

FL Florida
Fr. France or French

G

GA Georgia (U.S. state)
GDP Gross Domestic Product
GMT Greenwich Mean Time

H

HI Hawaii
HIV Human immunodeficiency virus

I

I., Is. island, islands
IA Iowa
ID Idaho
IL Illinois
IN Indiana
Intl. International

K

km kilometre or kilometres
km² square kilometres
Kos. Kosovo
KS Kansas
KY Kentucky

L

L. lake
LA Louisiana
Lat. Latvia
Liech. Liechtenstein
Lith. Lithuania
Lux. Luxembourg

M

m metre or metres
MA Massachusetts
Mac. Macedonia
MB Manitoba
MD Maryland
ME Maine
Mex. Mexico
MI Michigan
mm millimetre or millimetres
MN Minnesota
MO Missouri
Mol. Moldova
Mon. Montenegro
MS Mississippi
MT Montana
Mt., Mts. mount, mont, mountain, or mountains

N

N North
Nat. National
NB New Brunswick
NC North Carolina
ND North Dakota
NE Nebraska
Neth. Netherlands
NH New Hampshire
NJ New Jersey
NL Newfoundland and Labrador
NM New Mexico
Nor. Norway
N.P. National Park
NS Nova Scotia
NT Northwest Territories
NU Nunavut
NV Nevada
NY New York
N.Z. New Zealand

O

O. ocean
OH Ohio
OK Oklahoma
ON Ontario
OR Oregon

P

PA Pennsylvania
PE Prince Edward Island
Pen. peninsula
p.m. post meridiem (after noon)
Pop. Population
Port. Portugal
poss. possession
P.P. Provincial Park
Prov. Province, Provincial
Pt. point
P.W.P. Provincial Wilderness Park

Q

QC Québec

R

R. river
Ra. range
Rep. republic
Res. reservoir
RI Rhode Island

S

S South
S. Afr. South Africa
San. sanctuary
SC South Carolina
SD South Dakota
Sd. sound
Serb. Serbia
SK Saskatchewan
Sl., Slovak. Slovakia
Slov. Slovenia
Sp. Spain
St., Ste. Saint, Sainte
Str. strait
Switz. Switzerland

T

Terr. territory
TN Tennessee
TX Texas

U

U.A.E. United Arab Emirates
U.K. United Kingdom
U.S. United States
US$ United States dollars
UT Utah

V

VA Virginia
Ven. Venezuela
VT Vermont

W

W West
WA Washington
WI Wisconsin
W.P.P. Wilderness Provincial Park
W.R. Wildlife Refuge
WV West Virginia
WY Wyoming

Y

YT Yukon Territory